FREUD'S TRIP TO ORVIETO

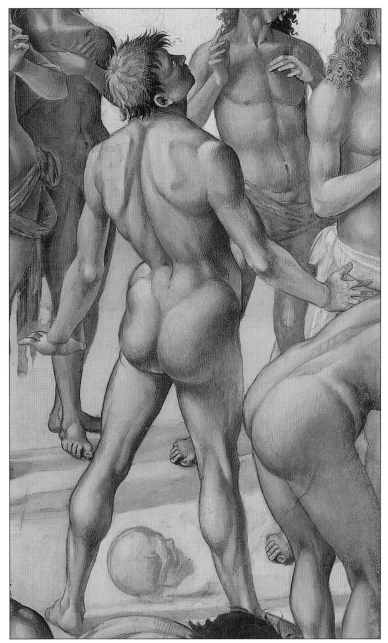

Plate 1. Detail of *The Resurrection of the Flesh*

Freud's Trip to Orvieto

The Great Doctor's Unresolved Confrontation with
Antisemitism, Death, and Homoeroticism;
His Passion for Paintings;
and the Writer in His Footsteps

Nicholas Fox Weber

Bellevue Literary Press
New York

First published in the United States in 2017 by
Bellevue Literary Press, New York

For information, contact:
Bellevue Literary Press
NYU School of Medicine
550 First Avenue
OBV A612
New York, NY 10016

Library of Congress Cataloging-in-Publication Data
is available from the publisher upon request

Bellevue Literary Press would like to thank all its generous
donors—individuals and foundations—for their support.

With thanks to the Josef and Anni Albers Foundation for their support of this book

 This publication is made possible by the New York
State Council on the Arts with the support of Governor
Andrew Cuomo and the New York State Legislature.

 This project is supported in part
by an award from the National
Endowment for the Arts.

Book design and composition by Mulberry Tree Press, Inc.

Manufactured in China.
First Edition

1 3 5 7 9 8 6 4 2

hardcover ISBN: 978-1-942658-26-9

ebook ISBN: 978-1-942658-27-6

For Lucy

Author's Note

Unless otherwise stated, all the illustrations in this book are from *The Last Judgment,* the fresco cycle painted by Luca Signorelli in the Cappella Nova of the cathedral in Orvieto between 1499 and 1504. Other works by Signorelli are identified by title only.

CONTENTS

FREUD'S TRIP TO ORVIETO

FREUD'S MEMORY LOSS

I N SEPTEMBER OF 1897, the forty-one-year-old Sigmund Freud set out
for central Italy. A high point of the trip for the Viennese neurolo-
gist, who was then fine-tuning the process he called "psychoanalysis,"
was his encounter with a fresco cycle by the Renaissance master Luca
Signorelli in the cathedral at Orvieto. This brilliantly colored group of
pictures packed into a small side chapel is a vivid depiction of muscular
nude men. Depending on the destiny meted out to them in the Last
Judgment, most of these burly specimens of raw masculine power are
consigned to forms of damnation rendered in horrific detail, while a
few ascend to a heavenly bliss. With their ripped torsos and gladiators'
limbs, they go to the limits of their physical force. Many of them are
engaged in furious battle. They inflict torture brutally or muster super-
natural strength to defend themselves against it. The selected elite have
no such struggles as they celebrate their reward for an admirable past,
but we hardly notice them in their boring calm.

A year after the visit to Orvieto, Freud started to talk to a traveling
companion about these early-sixteenth-century paintings that had
moved him deeply. Some sources—and there are numerous accounts
of the events that followed—say that the conversation occurred on a
train Freud was taking on a trip into Herzegovina, having left behind
his sick wife. But in his own version of the facts, which Freud wrote
less than a week after the journey when he enthused about the frescoes, he reports that he was on a carriage drive from Ragusa (now
Dubrovnik, on the Dalmatian coast of the Adriatic) into a nearby
village in Herzegovina for an idyllic outing during a late-summer
holiday. The person with whom he was speaking was, depending on

11

the source, either a complete stranger or a Berlin lawyer, Herr Frey-hau, whom Freud apparently already knew.

For all the discrepancies of details, the main event that concerns us is always recounted in the same way. It is that, to his immense frustration, Freud could not recall the name of the artist. Following the journey, he wrote his friend Wilhelm Fliess, "I could not find the name of the renowned painter who did the *Last Judgment* in Orvieto, the greatest I have seen so far." For at least two days (the duration varies according to the source; again we are in murky territory), Freud sustained the memory loss, and was reduced to "inner torment"—his words—as he repeatedly tried but failed to conjure the artist's name.

To his amazement, Freud could, nonetheless, see certain details of the fresco cycle perfectly in his mind's eye. Then, once he was reminded that the person who had made these powerful paintings had the last name of Signorelli, he recalled that the first name was Luca, and instantly lost his ability to envision the art.

Freud at the time was embarking on his self-analysis. Using elements of the technique that "Anna O"—the pseudonym of a patient of his colleague Josef Breuer—called the "talking cure," he was hoping to treat his own "psychosomatic disorders as well as exaggerated fears of dying and other phobias" by investigating his dreams and memories. What he could *not* remember intrigued him even more. He was startled by his inability to recall the name of an artist he felt he should have easily recalled, and considered his incapacity revelatory.

Freud became determined to understand his own mental process generated by the discussion he had been having that prompted him to envision the paintings at Orvieto and then to bury the name Signorelli. He wrote Fliess, "In the conversation, which aroused memories that evidently caused the repression, we talked about death and sexuality. . . . How can I make this credible to anyone?" It was as if he believed that the subject matter of the conversation had caused him to block out the name, and his greatest task was to have others recognize that link.

I believe that Freud, focusing only on the need to convince others of general mental processes, was managing to avoid personal truths that made him unbearably uncomfortable. The folderol about the impossibility of bringing the name Signorelli to the conscious part of his mind was like the parapraxis itself: an obfuscation. By that I do not mean a deliberate deception. I mean that Uncle Siggy, like the rest of us, just could not always cope with the complexity of being human.

Five days after describing this memory loss, Freud wrote Fliess again to say that he had completed an essay on "the phenomenon of forgetfulness," which he had sent to a medical journal. He began that early short text on the mysterious workings of the human mind almost as if he were writing a folktale: "In the middle of carrying on a conversation we find ourselves obliged to confess to the person we are talking to that we cannot hit on a name we wanted to mention at that moment, and we are forced to ask for his—usually ineffectual—help. 'What *is* his name? I know it so well. It's on the tip of my tongue. Just this minute it's escaped me.'"

Freud is describing something familiar to all of us when he then says that either we come up with a substitute name or we become convinced we know the first letter of the forgotten name. "We say, for instance: 'It begins with a "B."' If we finally succeed, in one way or another, in discovering what the name is, we find in the great majority of cases that it does not begin with a 'B' and does not in fact contain the letter 'B' at all."

Freud discounts the idea that Signorelli's paintings themselves played a role in his inability to remember the name of the person who conceived and executed them. This strikes me as a mistake, since he emphasizes the powerful impact the Orvieto frescoes had on him: "I was able to conjure up the pictures with greater sensory vividness than is usual with me." Yet rather than considering that the paintings them-selves had elements that caused the mental block, Freud maintains that it was his will to forget something he was previously considering that prompted the lapse. He says that he was deliberately trying not to bring up an indelicate subject with his traveling companion. To keep the possibly offensive topic at bay, he had, just prior to describing the Orvieto frescoes, been consciously trying not to think about the con-nection between sexuality and the end of life. He had also tried to push from his mind an anecdote related to that theme. As he explains it, his efforts brought an unexpected price. The desire he had had, a moment earlier, to force himself to forget a provocative issue had caused him to be blind to the name Signorelli. He makes the link: "The influence which had made the name *Signorelli* inaccessible to memory, or, as I am accustomed to say, had 'repressed' it, could only proceed from the story I had suppressed about the value set on death and sexual enjoyment."

THE INCIDENT OF HIS FORGETTING THE ARTIST'S NAME would preoc-cupy the father of psychoanalysis. When he wrote *The Psychopathology of Everyday Life* in 1901, he opened the book with a discussion of his inability to recall Signorelli's name and the incorrect substitutions he made for it. Again he refers to his "repressed thoughts" as the reason for the confabulation that occurred when he pictured the Orvieto frescoes and came up with various other artists' names but not the right one.

Jacques Lacan and other psychoanalysts have dug deep to try to understand what Freud was repressing. What undid Freud so that he drew a blank on the artist's name is usually interpreted pretty much in the same vein. The pundits mainly emphasize the linguistic connec-tions between the forgotten name and its incorrect substitutions and find links between the incorrect replacements for Signorelli and places important to Freud's history. The experts who have tried to unravel the psychoanalyst's own parapraxis, Freud himself among them, have mainly concentrated on dissecting the name Signorelli along with the names of the other artists that came to Freud's mind instead. These authorities on the human mind impose constraints on their investigation, focusing more on the replacements than the memory loss itself, and push their own agendas. Something essential is missing.

Until now, the parapraxis has only been considered by specialists in psychoanalysis—rather than by someone like me, for whom art is a language with greater force than words. The imagery of the frescoes has been given a secondary role at best, their aesthetics an even more minor position.

I believe that, by giving insufficient weight to what Freud actually saw in Orvieto, the mental-health experts miss the boat. In the case of the academics, it's the usual thing: They follow a footnote to an idea, and take it to the nth degree, without opening their eyes to new ways of seeing or to the importance of irrational feelings. As for Freud: I think that by minimizing the effect the painting themselves had on him, and by virtually eliminating Signorelli's art from his detailed exploration of why he could not recall the artist's name, he was either being extremely shortsighted because he unconsciously was avoiding seeing many of his own truths or else he was deliberately creating a red herring with which he appeared to be investigating his own depths but in fact was achieving a masterpiece of concealment.

I am convinced that it was the artworks themselves, which, for understandable reasons, destabilized Freud. Painted with athletic vigor in dazzling reds and yellows, they have that power. Like all researchers, I am far from objective, and I am among those people for whom the visual evokes a more direct response than does the verbal. Here I bring my own experience and feelings to bear; but in investigating this, I have discovered that on more than one occasion Freud responded to well-crafted paintings on a very personal level. He, too, was one of those people for whom good art was mind-altering. The impact of the

Orvieto frescocs on him warrants a scrutiny it has never had; it must be considered in light of his intense personal responsiveness to great paintings, not as a matter of linguistic gymnastics.

What Luca Signorelli shows in the Orvieto frescoes, consistent with a lot of other paintings he made, and the robust and convincing way in which he presents it, is, I feel, the basis—far more than any of the explanations given either by Freud himself or by others in his field—for the loss of memory that was so dramatic for a practitioner whose entire craft was based on the ability to remember and retain, and on the power of sexual feeling.

CHAPTER 1

The Reprint

M Y AWARENESS OF THIS PIVOTAL EVENT in Freud's life, known to specialists but not to most laypeople, occurred shortly after my mother died, in 1990. I was going through my parents' library following my father's sale of the house where my sister and I had grown up. I found tucked between two hardcover novels smelling of a mix of cigar and cigarette smoke, as did all their books, a scholarly reprint entitled "The Significance of Freud's Trip to Orvieto." It was written by Richard and Marietta Karpe, he a psychoanalyst, she a psychiatric social worker. My mother, as if she were declaring royal lineage, always said that these Viennese refugees, who were friends of hers and my father's, while outside their usual social orbit, had been colleagues of Anna Freud's.

I instantly grabbed the stapled twenty-page document that had faded with age. The subject sounded intriguing; beyond that, this reprint from a psychoanalytical journal conjured the richness of my childhood. The constant potential for something beyond the norm, even in the barren suburban landscape of West Hartford, Connecticut, seemed encapsulated in these crumbly pages that for years had been pressed between two of their books. My parents' many first editions—of works by Steinbeck, O'Hara, Henry Miller, Hemingway, Irwin Shaw, and the other writers whose latest work they would buy hot off the presses—also extended beyond the normal boundaries of human existence, but this document opened unexpected possibilities.

The other reason I jumped at the Karpes' names was because they were linked with an obsession of my own. Some twenty-five years prior to my standing there and emptying my parents' bookshelves, a friend of my mother's had, on a Saturday night in midwinter, appeared at the door of my bedroom shortly after midnight. I was sixteen years old at the time. I had just returned from a date with my high school girlfriend, greeted the few besotted friends of Mother and Dad's playing bridge after a dinner party, and gone upstairs. This exceptionally attractive woman managed, in the forty-five minutes in my room, to make me feel intensely alive in ways I had never before experienced.

The September following the late-night visitation—it was 1964— my parents gave a large cocktail party. As the guests began to arrive, I could think of little else but the moment when I would first spot the ravishing creature who had, ever since that Saturday night, been on my mind perpetually. For purposes of this narrative, I am calling her Susie. That name and other specifics are fictions, but her activation in me of feelings about maleness, brawn, Jewishness, and my conflicting triumph and guilt over the equivalent of Oedipal victory, the same issues Luca Signorelli's frescoes provoked in Freud, are real.

Most of my mother and father's guests that warm summer evening were packed into the living and dining rooms, where the food and bar were. The elegant few who were more in control of their hunger and thirst, and less needy of being where everyone else was, stood outside on the large wooden deck surrounded by lush plantings. I had studied the guest list and I knew that Susie and her stockbroker husband would be coming up for the party from Fairfield County, where they lived. But I had not seen her arrive and was, subtly but desperately, looking everywhere. At last I spotted her magnificent face. This was certainly not a face of straight lines, but, rather, one of curves and angles in the most perfect relationship to one another, with its distinguished features and irresistible character producing a radiant beauty, almost, but not quite, exotic, while not classical, either, enhanced by a radiance and spark that made almost everyone who saw her react as one does to a ravishing sight, even if other people did not go nuts as I did. I had found her among the independent elite in the garden.

My enchantress was talking with the Karpes. They were anomalies standing in the middle of a crowd of plucky, athletically fit, dressed-to-the-nines bourgeoisie. Both were considerably overweight, and spoke in soft voices with thick accents. Richard had the most protruding lower lip I have ever seen, and as a little boy I used to delight my parents with my juvenile imitations of the way he said *zees* for *this*. He and Marietta were dressed like correct professionals but were conspicuously lacking in vanity. She had scraggly gray hair that went to the bottom of her neck, and wore a sacklike flowered dress and sensible shoes. To the other men's madras pants and splashy summer neckties, Richard was in a loose-fitting gray suit; he may have made a pass at his wispy white hair with a comb, but he was still unkempt. The majority of couples at parties like this made a point of losing their spouses the moment they entered; these two stood side by side, inseparable. They looked like a heavy plate of goulash on a buffet where everything else is pink aspic or lime mousse.

I could not take my eyes off of their exquisite interlocutor or stop basking in the way she had recently imbued me with unprecedented confidence in myself. None of the social climbers would bother with disheveled refugees; most of them instinctively shunned anyone who was not stylish and patently prosperous. I was amused but not surprised that Susie was the only intrepid soul who had made a point of making overtures to Richard and Marietta and improving their evening. The other guests—far too many, because my former Communist mother had an inexplicable need to be friends with hundreds of golf-playing suburbanites who gave and went to a stream of vapid big parties—were busy tripping over one another, making sure they were where the action was, greeting and being greeted by the hordes. Clinging to their own kind, acting like members of fraternities and sororities, these chattering individuals were describing the putt missed on the eighteenth green, or the details of a traffic jam on the last journey to New York, a couple of hours away. The rule for these events was "conversation lite." Standing there talking with the two mental-health professionals, Susie, however, was intensely focused on whatever they were discussing, and Richard was uttering words that I am sure had rich content. Susie appeared not to notice me, but I could not stop staring at her. She wore a closely fitted navy dress with white polka dots and a large bow of the same material in her hair. Her radiant dark eyes, the self-command evident in the perfectly erect posture with which she held her small and fit body, and the playfulness of the polka dots, not to mention the sheer flirtatiousness of the wonderfully unnecessary hair bow—perhaps one should call it "a cocktail hat"—cast a spell. So did her palpable alertness. Richard Karpe, resembling an aging heavyset Germanic doctor out of central casting, looked as if he was having the time of his life; Marietta, as if she was enduring the moment.

Susie, lithe and without an ounce of fat, epitomized physical perfection. At a glance, one sensed her great skill at sports, as well as sexual aliveness in that perfectly tuned body and that fantastically pretty face, which emitted an erotic charge. She radiated a force with which she attracted others. She and the Karpes, who embodied the cerebral, were in perfect counterpoint. Everything about the Viennese husband and wife suggested observation and profound thoughtfulness, while one had the impression that they could scarcely shuffle across the floor, or that they cared about any aspect of their physical selves except their brains. But what the three of them had in common was their voracious interest in life.

A quarter of a century later, I realized that this juxtaposition of intellect (the Karpes) and sexual magnetism (Susie) pertained to what happened to Freud with the Signorelli frescoes. Visual allure and heightened activity within the human brain were conjoined.

I *had* to hear what they were saying. I soon positioned myself to stand about three people away, and foolishly gulped my gin and tonic. (Age sixteen, I had five that night, and have never had another since.) What I managed to hear was, in perfect debutante elocution, with her impeccable diction and sonorous intonations (in an accent unique to the tiny subspecies of humanity comprised of very rich Jewish women whose parents' speaking manner bore traces of Eastern Europe but who were themselves educated in WASP prep schools and Seven Sister colleges), in a voice mostly deep but with the occasional enthusiastic squeak: "Well, I have not actually *read* a lot of Sigmund Freud, but the little I know of his ideas I find *utterly* fascinating." I could not make out the rest, but I imagine it was praise heaped on the Karpes for their area of work, since Richard looked more and more enthralled and Marietta more and more impatient as the conversation continued and the crush of people obliterated the encounter from view and earshot.

WHEN I FASTENED ONTO THE REPRINT OF THE KARPES' ARTICLE among my parents' books in 1990, I was prompted in part by sheer curiosity, but I know that what excited me above all was the memory of my own intoxication with this woman who had made me feel more powerfully male than I ever had before. It was, of course, irrational that the sight of the names Richard and Marietta Karpe made me think above all, by association, of *her*—but my mind was never logical when thoughts of Susie were summoned.

Having, after many years, returned to the house where I had spent my youth—in order to cull the objects that no longer mattered to my father—I felt an overwhelming nostalgia for the time when my mother was still alive and my father supremely content. I missed my own insouciance as a teenager, my blindness to the reality of death. I also longed to have back my adolescent body, my thick head of hair, my stupid cockiness, even the acne that went with my burgeoning hormones. I dreamed of those years before I had physical ailments and muscle aches, of the feeling that everything in life was possible. To be sixteen again!

I loved remembering the time when it seemed that an infinity of years lay ahead. In the shadow of the death of my vibrant and charismatic mother, whom I missed mightily (I still do), I also kept thinking about the intense aliveness of the only other woman in my parents' circle who invested each moment with excitement and made me alert to my fingertips.

It was probably out of sheer will to manipulate others that Susie had encouraged me to such a sense of triumph, but at age sixteen I became convinced I had achieved some sort of victory by winning the regard of my mother's closest frienemy. I wanted to bring back that thrill, even if it was the by-product of Susie's manipulativness (my mother's favorite word for the friend with whom she, too, was obsessed) and of feelings I knew most people would declare unhealthy. Holding the faded pamphlet, it all felt nearer.

My assumption that my wonderful and intelligent parents had read the text on Freud and Orvieto, with pride in knowing the authors, was a further lure to take and read this document on an obscure subject.

Beyond that, I chronically long for adventure—it is a mainstay of my life—and I sensed that one lay ahead in these pages. I had no idea, however, that I would discover that the Karpes had outdone Freud himself in their fantastic insight into what Freud recognized as one of the pivotal events of his life, whereas the great psychoanalyst of others had himself either been blind to its real significance or chosen to dissemble.

Richard and Marietta Karpe, simply and eloquently, shed light on Freud's issues about maleness, and a range of other anxieties and desires and fears, that Freud appeared not to recognize when he was his own subject. The uncontrollable onslaught of emotions Freud experienced and that he then needed to cover up with the memory loss stemmed,

I would discover, at least in part from his obsession with masculine power or lack thereof, and the degree to which his father, and consequently he, were endowed with it.

A measure of strength for Freud, the Karpes would demonstrate, revolved around one's response to anti-Semitism. Freud connected the way one dealt with the realities of being Jewish with maleness. The Karpes would adumbrate the ways that Signorelli's frescoes represented Jews and their opponents, and would see this as vital to the chain of thoughts that led to Freud's parapraxis. They would present convincing evidence that Freud was unable to recall the name that began with the same three letters as his own and as the word *Signor,* the Italian title used before men's names, because of feelings derived from a certain shame at his father's inability to confront anti-Semites and Freud's own reluctance to stand up to prejudice against Jews like himself.

But Richard and Marietta fall short of exploring the impact of Freud's own ambivalence about being Jewish. It's a preoccupation I know all too well, and was one of my points of connection with Susie, which is why it was easy for me to recognize as I plunged into Freud and Signorelli. If, when the Karpes stood there talking with my parents' friend, they had diagnosed the degree to which this dark-haired beauty, whose great-grandparents had lived in shtetls, contrived every detail of her appearance and household and conduct to seem as Anglo, without the Saxon, as possible, they would perhaps have grasped a contributing factor to Freud's memory loss that eluded them. For even if Richard and Marietta understood the longing for assimilation, they were themselves too intellectually pure to comprehend that the appeal of Christmas trees and the trappings of Christian life, the taste that has in our own era made Ralph Lauren a demigod, is not simply a matter of wishing to fit in, but is an uncontrollable worship for what one is not.

Yet, even if they did not go the full distance, the Karpes would lead me to recognize that one of the contributing factors to Freud's mental block concerning a name that resembled his own stemmed not only from his notions of bravery in the face of anti-Semitism, and from his discomfort with himself as a Jew, but from his own worship of a type of man he could never be.

Josef Albers, the great Bauhaus-trained artist who established the foundation I have run for forty years, was fascinated by the mental sequence that occurs between retinal perception and emotional response. No matter what, it is a personal matter, and varies from individual to individual. I have thrilled to the pleasures of looking at art since I was a young boy, and experience such intense feelings in front of paintings and inside certain buildings that art and architecture have unparalleled force in my own life. In trying to understand what undid Freud in the Signorelli frescoes—since I am convinced it was the art itself, and not its maker's name, that upended him—it is impossible to be fully objective. Naturally, one focuses on the feelings with which one identifies, and fails to see what is entirely foreign to one's self. The Karpes may only have been able to recognize issues for Freud with which they were personally familiar. Concomitantly, I am sure I have seen in Freud's experience of the Signorellis the themes that interest me particularly. This has been easy enough, since, beyond the discomfort about being Jewish and the consequent shame or at least embarrassment over my own ambivalence, many of the other feelings the art in Orvieto enflamed in the great psychoanalyst are ones with which I closely identify: a sharp awareness of one's own future death; the thrill of eroticism, however complex or unacceptable to others, as a summit of awakeness; and the attraction to memories and the experiences of one's youth that determine so much of the rest of one's future life from then on.

The reprint I opened to help bring back my own adolescence and its passions would also lead me to discover Freud's deeply personal response to Italian Renaissance art on occasions other than his trip to Orvieto. Paintings awakened religiosity, poetry, lust, and, on occasion, contrariness in him. He probed his emotions in front of certain pictures, and experienced his vulnerability and passions. That level of gut reaction to great pictures is surprisingly rare, and to discover this intense responsiveness to the visual in a mind as great and far-reaching as Freud's is thrilling.

Given that he was someone who could be grabbed by artworks on a deeply personal level—as I will show you—his dismissal of Signorelli's frescoes, the pictures themselves, as the primary reason he needed to put a halt to his thought processes, and his focus on the structure of the artist's name instead, strikes me as a deliberate act of deception.

CHAPTER 2

FREUD'S PILGRIMAGES

ONCE I HAD READ THEIR LITTLE TREATISE—known only to readers of the March 1979 issue of *The Israel Annals of Psychiatry and Related Disciplines,* which is where it first appeared, or to the circle of friends to whom the Karpes had given the imprint—I became determined to get to Orvieto. I was eager to see the art central to this text, which is so brilliant in its questions yet seemingly self-censored in its answers. Several years after finding the document at my parents' house, I had the chance to visit the Italian hill town when I was traveling from Rome to Florence.

What had moved Freud so deeply was a shocking group of paintings. Signorelli's frescoes, which narrate the end of the world, were unlike anything I had ever seen.

The scenes depicted in the frescoes are intensely crowded, the loud colors overpowering. Yet these busy compositions are organized so masterfully that even when a devil is pushing down on the butt of a naked man who is being carried upside down over the shoulders of another horned and naked man, with similarly engaged nude brigands pressed into the mélange from all sides, we know exactly where each person is positioned; there is utter clarity about who is near and who far.

One has no doubt of the reality of it all. Every hair of the brutes' loincloths, made from the tails of wild animals, is articulated with perfect verisimilitude. Some of the naked men cascade, while others ascend; the motion is real, and the life of the bare flesh authentic. The older fellows' testicles sag in a way that is all too plausible.

Human skin is rendered in a lurid green, the purple of raw meat, or a reflective gold, as if it is being lit by bright flames. The colors terrify us. The amount of death and violence is destabilizing. This is both the end of life and the start of a miserable afterlife. One scene depicts paradise, but we don't notice it at first, and the majority of Signorelli's broad-shouldered wrestler types with sinewy muscles are either in hell or a horrific version of purgatory. Standing in the chapel, one feels the force of an earthquake. The powerful connection between sexuality, punishment, and death in this violent world of musclemen leaves the viewer whirling. [plate 2]

It was a brief visit, but the sight of the artwork alone struck me as ample reason for a memory loss. At the time, I had read only the Karpes' treatise on the subject, and had done so fairly quickly, but it was clear there was a lot in Signorelli's frescoes that would want to make one cover one's eyes or turn away.

I assumed that Freud, like me, perceived paintings as if they were life itself—which is why he subsequently had to forget something

Plate 2. Detail of *The Damned Cast into Hell*

about these wrenching paintings. I had my theory about Freud's responsiveness confirmed last spring, when, after I told my younger daughter, Charlotte, then a student of psychoanalysis in London, about the Karpes' study, she sent me copies of some unusual letters that Freud had written his fiancée, Martha, more than a decade before his visit to Orvieto. In this highly personal correspondence, Freud discusses the impact on him of several paintings in Dresden: a Raphael that disappointed him, a Holbein he preferred to it, and a Titian that overwhelmed him. What he divulged in private to the woman he was soon to marry reveals the psychoanalyst to have had a rare appreciation of art.

On the other hand, he suffered from some surprising misperceptions. In the intense emotional state with which he viewed these paintings in Dresden, he did not realize that the Holbein was a copy. That in itself would be no big deal, except that it makes some of Freud's observations about the work fallacious and discredits a text Freud later published in which he claims to be able to distinguish fake paintings from authentic ones.

What becomes apparent through the letters and the Karpes' writing, nonetheless, is that certain masterful canvases and frescoes, by using the power of form and color to enrich their subjects, and by organizing and framing phenomena with meticulous measure, allowed Sigmund Freud to apprehend truths that are more elusive in actual people. The personages in paintings also seemed to get inside him more than did his patients or even his friends and family. Seeing particular individuals rendered in paint affected him viscerally. An observer more than a connoisseur, Freud was impassioned by what he saw.

Freud was also fascinated by public taste. In Dresden, he was intrigued—as he surely would be today—by what the mobs flock to, and what they ignorantly overlook. He saw artworks as vessels of human understanding in part for what they were intrinsically, but also for the way that they evoke or don't evoke responses according to the alertness or blindness of the people looking at them.

Those reactions to art—whereby spectacular paintings excite emotions in a direct and personal way—have always been the ones that matter for me. What a pleasant surprise it was to discover that Sigmund Freud was among the rare people who have a consuming, irrational, response to visual imagery.

My first visit to Orvieto had been exploratory but short. I was intrigued by the Karpes' text and by Signorelli's chapel but had not considered them in depth. More recently, though, perhaps as a result of being in my seventh decade of life, certain subjects have seemed more important to me, others less. I had a brief but unforgettable conversation with Philip Roth one day on the rue du Bac in Paris in which he said, with a quirky smile, that the main topics of my biography of the painter Balthus—"sex, art, and being Jewish"—are "all that matters in life." I wouldn't go that far, but the older I have gotten, the more obsessed I have become with all three. I became compelled to go further in trying to understand Freud's powerful reactions to the Signorellis and a few other paintings.

Plate 3. Sigmund Freud, c. 1905

CHAPTER 3

The Text

THE KARPES START THEIR ARTICLE "The Significance of Freud's Trip to Orvieto" with the death of Jacob Freud, the psychoanalyst's father, in 1896. Sigmund Freud was then forty, his father eighty-one. Freud would later write that the event was central to "my own self-analysis, my reaction to my father's death—that is to say, to the most important event, the most poignant loss, of a man's life." During the following year, the traditional Jewish period of mourning, Freud not only began his self-analysis but also advanced his theories about the Oedipus complex and the origins of hysteria. Richard and Marietta set us up to see that, when Freud went to Orvieto, in spite of his disdain for Jewish rituals, he was keenly aware that the customary period of grieving was about to end. This concurred with his increasing preoccupation with an idea in which the relationship with the same-sex parent—and its intrinsic mix of attachment, competition, and rejection—determines so much in a person's behavior and desires.

Richard and Marietta elucidate a fundamental difference between Jacob and Sigmund Freud through confrontations each had with anti-Semitism. In 1900, near the start of his self-analysis, Freud would lament "the humiliation he felt when his father admitted that he was once forced off the sidewalk by an antisemitic bully who had tossed his father's cap into the gutter. 'What did you do?' the boy Sigmund asked. 'I picked up my cap,' his father answered calmly." Sigmund's son Martin Freud would describe a very different experience of *his* father. The Karpes report that when Sigmund and Martha Freud and their young children were on a summer holiday on the lake of Thunsee in Bavaria, some thugs, brandishing sticks and umbrellas, shouted anti-Semitic remarks at the psychoanalyst. He immediately approached the ruffians and forced them to stop taunting him and to disperse. As they went off sheepishly in different directions, he walked proudly through their midst.

BECAUSE RICHARD WAS A PSYCHOANALYST, and because Marietta, even if she had lesser credentials, seemed like one, and because I grew up in a world where mental health doctors were the closest things to gods, their authority beyond reproach, I accepted that they had good reasons for tendering this information as relevant to Freud's parapraxis. Besides, the stories fascinated me. How Jews deal with anti-Semitism in predominantly non-Jewish milieus is a subject that has always been a red flag for me. Even before the Karpes offered any explanation for discussing these incidents in relation to Freud's forgetting the name of Luca Signorelli, my mind was off and running. Did the Karpes discern that the beautiful Susie (it always struck me as significant that her first name began with the *S* of *Semite*), for all the assimilation she had achieved as if by a military campaign—she and her husband, a Joshua whose friends called him "Jinx," were the first Jewish members of Weeburn County Club, a WASP bastion in Darien—would never have picked up her cap meekly? The woman who looked like a Protestant Cleopatra would not just have scattered the crowd, but would have made her assailants cower.

Susie had attended a boarding school in the era when there was a 10 percent quota for Jewish students. She had been captain of the tennis team. The coach had told her not to play in a match at a club near Boston that "restricted" not just its membership but its guests. The alluring brunette with the Ashkenazi last name insisted on participating anyway. She was so triumphant with her cross-court forehands and steely net game that her blond and blue-eyed opponents and team-mates acquired new respects for the people they called "juze."

It was muttered that, especially since Susie's married name, Flinck, was far less of a giveaway than had been her maiden name, she was hor-rified when her daughter Barbara, on entering Wellesley College, not only changed it to Foote but had people start calling her "Babs." Susie was a snob, but she was too self-assured to dissemble.

Or did Richard and Marietta have any idea that their host that evening when they stood in the garden in 1964 had, as an army pri-vate, having just started basic training in the throes of World War II, responded to an anti-Semitic slur with a right hook and a left jab? Aside from the ID tags that gave his religion, my father's name, Saul, was like a badge; of course it made no difference that he had rejected what he considered to be the superstitious practices of his parents. Dad rarely told stories about himself. The tale of his and the offender's need-ing to be held back by other soldiers in the barracks was one of the few. My only problem with it is that his yearning to be respected for his boldness was too transparent. Martin Freud was proud over his father vanquishing the anti-Semites, because he witnessed it firsthand, not because his father had made it part of his own legacy.

The Karpes would make Sigmund Freud's feelings about his father, and the humiliation he felt over what he saw as Jacob's cowardice before the anti-Semites, the primary reason for Freud's forgetting the name of the man who painted the Orvieto frescoes.

I WENT TO ORVIETO A SECOND TIME TO STUDY the Signorellis more carefully and better understand their impact on Freud. The grueling images of man-to-man combat do indeed connect to how one stands up to aggression, or else cowers.

To me—as to most male viewers, I think—the presentation of all those naked men possessed by brute force makes one measure one's own strength. And most of us, when considering what sort of man we are—both our physiques and our toughness or lack thereof—compare ourselves to our fathers, whether we feel we resemble them or have chosen to be different from them.

These remarkable frescoes confront us by rendering manly attributes in close proximity. Both male and female viewers—each for his or her personal relationship to idealized, robust male bodies achieving physical dominance or succumbing to it—respond viscerally to them. Some of these guys have panache, while others seem cruel, but most of them are mightily strong.

Among the first to feel the impact of Signorelli was Michelangelo. He might never have made his erotically laden sculptures of male slaves with muscular torsos were it not for the liberating effect of Signorelli, who also worked on the Sistine Chapel and was a generation older. But one does not have to be Michelangelo to respond to Signorelli's work; it suffices simply to have a body of one's own. The Orvieto paintings, executed with spectacular effectiveness and illustrating provocative subject matter, have the power not only to rivet the attentive viewer but to destabilize him.

Without yet knowing the extent of the psychoanalytic literature that finds other, more obtuse reasons for Freud's parapraxis, when I faced the frescoes themselves, it seemed readily apparent that Freud, because of his issues concerning his maleness, exacerbated by his father's death, not only could have been made to forget an artist's name that should have come to him easily but was so undone by the naked men that he had to put a halt to his investigation of his response. Hats off to Richard and Marietta Karpe for acknowledging that the master of their profession was flummoxed to the extent that he could not comprehend his own mind! This is what provocative sights—a fresco cycle, a woman in a blue polka dot dress—can do.

READING THE KARPES ABOUT THE FATHERS AND SONS in the Freud family, most of us make comparisons to our own parent-child relationships. I feel somewhere in the middle between Sigmund and Martin in regard to how I see my father. While, compared to Jacob, Saul was satisfyingly assertive, compared to Sigmund, my father was, for me, not as quietly effective. He was always a little too proud of his rage and the resultant excitement when his fellow soldiers had to stop the fight by pulling him and the anti-Semite apart. It seemed like self-mythologizing on Dad's part; if I had, just once, seen my father stand up to my mother without ultimately caving in, I would have been more impressed with his account of his own forcefulness. For that matter, I always felt that I could get my way with him, something about which I have mixed feelings to this day. While I adored his kindness and rationality, I craved the crude force of Signorelli's warriors.

The Karpes, I would discover, pussyfooted on the issue of how Sigmund Freud dealt with anti-Semitism. His ambivalence about being Jewish resulted on other occasions in his being something less than the noble soul who, in front of his children on holiday at the lake of Thunsee, made the thugs disperse.

When I read their article, I immediately felt guilty over an event in my own youth when I failed to stand up as a Jew. Had I known that Freud, like me, had not always been as forthright as when he intimidated those anti-Semites, I would have been comforted. You might say it makes no difference, but I am one of those people for whom Freud and other psychoanalysts as well (Richard Karpe and my own doctor among them) are hero figures (I spent half of my own seven-year-long psychoanalysis working on this issue), and therefore their behavior becomes a standard for me. Before I learned more about him and still saw Freud only as the man depicted by the Karpes as outdistancing his father by confronting the ruffians with their sticks and umbrellas, I considered myself to have acted shabbily at a crucial moment when I was fifteen years old.

At the time, I was a day student at Loomis, a private all-boys school where some two-thirds of the pupils were boarders. I did not realize that there was an unwritten Jewish quota, based on the model of Yale and Harvard, whereby the number of Jews was confined to 10 percent—the same rule that had applied at Susie's school a generation earlier. Every day, before lunch, the headmaster would end grace by saying "in Christ's name we ask it," and I always nodded my head in agreement; in chapel, we sang Christian hymns and read from the New Testament. Now that I think back on those years in the early sixties, I am aware that I went along with this without even questioning it. But there was a lot I did not even think about—such as why there was only one black student in a population of about 450 during my freshman year (although there were a few more by the time I was a senior).

The incident about which I felt ashamed when I learned about Freud dispersing the anti-Semites occurred when I went with a Protestant schoolmate, Allen Minor, and his father, Charles, on a trip to Nassau, in the Bahamas. One day, Charles and Allen's uncle (Charles's sister's husband) and a third friend of theirs took us out on a boat to go deep-sea fishing. Toward late afternoon, at a point when the combination of intense sunshine and a choppy sea had me feeling almost hallucinatory, Allen's uncle turned to the other two men and, in a loud voice, began to describe a sailboat charter he was trying to organize. He explained that the skipper had named a price. "But then I JEWED him down," the uncle boasted.

It was not merely that he used *Jew* as a verb. He emphasized it, evincing great delight in having succeeded at the act of Jewing.

Charles Minor turned an even deeper red than he already was, and began to clear his throat conspicuously while pointing toward me in a way I was not supposed to see.

The uncle did not notice. "What a success!" he continued. "I was able to Jew him down to nearly a half of what he had initially asked." He was beaming with joy.

Now Charles Minor looked as if he were going to jump off the boat. Meanwhile, Allen and I simply smiled at each other, trying to hold back our laughter at the awkward situation.

I have always tried to think of the incident as funny. But I now wish I had said something—politely. Even if the Karpes had not yet explained what the specific element in Signorelli paintings was that made Freud consider how one reacted to anti-Semitic taunts, and even though Allen's uncle had not deliberately offended me, why had I not asked something like "And do you think, sir, that people like me are always angling for a lower price?" or "May I invite you to Rosh Hashanah, sir, so that you can celebrate the new year with others who have your skill at bargaining?"

CHAPTER 4

THE KARPES CONTINUE

RICHARD AND MARIETTA JUMP from the different ways Jacob and Sigmund Freud handled their confrontations with anti-Semites to a discussion of Sigmund's organization of his father's funeral details. (So far, they still have not discussed the actual paintings. Their readers, however, can leaf ahead in the article to some pale reproductions of the Signorellis that, depicting violent combat in the afterlife, suggest this commentary and Freud's inability to recall the artist's name will all tie in.) We learn that Sigmund rejected a lot that was traditional. He was determined not to identify himself with anything he associated with weakness, including a compliance with rote Jewish rituals.

Instead of paying what he considered an excessive amount of money for the traditional flowery death announcement in the newspaper, Sigmund opted for a smaller one, its graphic layout unusually direct, the name Jacob Freud in large bold type and the information minimal. Sigmund, who, as the eldest son from his father's second marriage, bore responsibility for all the details, also planned an atypically simple funeral ritual—in keeping with Jacob's taste. In 1900, he would write that the night before the funeral he had a dream in which "he saw a printed notice which read 'You are requested to close the eyes' and 'You are requested to close an eye.'" The Karpes go on to quote Freud analyzing his own dream. Freud interpreted the "to close an eye" as an instruction to the family members who "were not sympathetic to such puritanical simplicity and thought we should be disgraced" to go easy—by, in effect, winking, and overlooking the affront to tradition. "To close the eyes" was also a directive for the normal procedure with a dead body.

Then, with the same quiet grace I witnessed as they stood with Susie in the midst of the social swarm, the particular confidence they evinced as the only people not intimidated by the most beautiful as well as the richest person in the crowd, Richard and Marietta quote from a letter Freud wrote Fliess about that dream. (They don't explain who Fliess was, or even provide his first name, but given the journal for which their article was written, they could safely assume that their readers were specialists who already knew.) While Freud's published analysis of the "close the eyes" dream, written four years after the fact, in *The Interpretation of Dreams,* has always been taken to be the last word on the subject, definitive for biographers and other scholars, the Karpes point out a startling discrepancy. They begin by citing the letter to Fliess, written on November 2, 1896. "I must tell you about a very pretty dream I had on the night *after* (sic) the funeral," Freud reports. By doing nothing more than italicizing the word *after* and adding "(sic)," my parents' friends have made an astonishing statement. It seems that, in one of his most pivotal and influential of all his books, Freud rewrote history. He made a dream he had following his father's funeral, reflecting many of its details, appear, falsely, to have been prescient. In the book he wrote four years after the fact, he changed the order of events so that his unconscious anticipated significant events which in truth has just occurred.

Whether Freud truly misremembered the sequence, or deliberately restructured it to suit his needs, we assume that the account to Fliess, so close in time to the actual dream and funeral, was the accurate one. The difference between the private telling two weeks after the funeral and dream and the published retelling four years later is the distinction between an honest recapitulation of facts and an act of remaking one's self as a seer. I picture Richard and Marietta being quite smug about the deceptiveness and character flaws of the man who invented their profession. On the other hand, I suspect that Richard, like me, absolutely loved having Susie wrap him around her little finger, even if Marietta was wise to the goddess's machinations.

What Freud tells Fliess, in his intense emotional state following his father's death, also includes the information that "On the day of the funeral I was kept waiting, and therefore arrived at the house of mourning rather late." We do not learn why he was detained on such an important occasion, but through this and other snippets from his letter to Fliess we sense his general feeling of discomfort, since he also allows, "The dream was thus an outlet for the feeling of self-reproach which a death generally leaves among the survivors."

The Karpes leave it to the reader to make his own inferences about Freud. But we have no doubt what they saw, and what they have told us in their quiet way. Sigmund Freud confabulated; he also developed, in the four years following his father's death, a need to edit out "the feeling of self-reproach" he once acknowledged.

ESTABLISHING FREUD'S FEELINGS ABOUT his father's compliance with the anti-Semitic bully, and depicting Freud's rebelliousness and temerity concerning the details of Jacob's funeral, the Karpes have laid the groundwork for Freud's intense response, just prior to the first anniversary of his father's death, to the sight of Luca Signorelli's frescoes. Richard and Marietta again state, significantly, that the "Year of Mourning" was when "the idea of the Oedipus Complex crystallized in Freud's mind." In one succinct paragraph, they elucidate that earthshaking development. They quote from a letter Freud wrote Fliess on May 31, 1897: "Hostile impulses against parents (a wish that they should die) are also an integral part of the neuroses . . . It seems as though in sons this death wish is directed against their father and in daughters against their mother." Freud admits to Fliess: "I have found love of the mother and jealousy of the father in my own case too."

From there, the Karpes bring everything to a head about Freud's experience of the Signorellis: "These were the thoughts and emotions which were guiding Freud when, in September of 1897, eleven months after his father's death, he started out on a vacation trip to Central Italy."

DECADES AFTER STANDING THERE AS A GAPING TEENAGER, overwhelmed by the sight of my parents' beguiling friend as she charmed Richard Karpe and annoyed Marietta, I remain overwhelmed. Susie—lithe and svelte under the formfitting dress with those dancing polka dots— seemed to cast a spell on the Karpes, as she had on me. Something beyond the realm of words, beyond all attempts at rationalization and understanding, was prevailing, and having greater force than logic. Physical beauty and sheer aliveness had unequaled power.

Yet if at age sixteen I was intoxicated by *her* power, more than half a century later I was floored by *theirs*. Rereading the Karpes' amplification of Freud's complex response to those dynamic paintings, I was staggered by their intellect and depth. I also realized that, unconsciously, even as a teenager, I essentially gravitated to these qualities as much as to a pretty face. In a scholarly article that has, until now, been as much as lost to the world, the Karpes, in a few pages, depict incidents with the intricacy of a late Henry James novel. Their writing voice is as calm and as unusual as their presence was in the midst of the swarm of suburbanites at my parents' party.

While I thought back then that I was interested mainly in Susie, and saw Richard and Marietta as misfits who mattered mainly as foils to her vitality and sexiness and incredible grace, I now see that I was attracted by their wisdom, their quiet force, their comfort with being different from everyone around them. I adored their authority. Even as a teenager, some side of me admired their oddball appearance—which was such a refreshing reflection of reality, of clarity and sense of purpose and knowledge of things, extraordinary in any society, but particularly in West Hartford, Connecticut, in the early 1960s—and now I respect these people all the more. The Karpes were avuncular; they were smart; they had the capacity to be excited. Richard, facing Susie, also showed a wonderful ability to be immensely entertained and to relish the moment. When I read the Karpes' insightful biographical sketch of Freud at a pivotal, underexamined moment of his development, I recognized that the magnetic power of the scene in my parents' backyard was because of the characters I then considered the supporting cast as much as by the person I considered the star.

But the presence of the woman who gave me such a strong sense of myself as a male has played no little part in guiding me to understand the impact of those frescoes on Freud.

CHAPTER 5

FREUD'S TRIP

JUST BEFORE FREUD DESCRIBED AND ENVISIONED the Orvieto frescoes, and then found himself unable to name their artist, he and his traveling companion had been talking about the Turks who lived in Bosnia and Herzegovina. In recalling this, Freud observes "that the Turks show great confidence in their physician and great resignation to fate." Freud quotes himself saying that if a patient died, his family members would, afterward, assure the doctor: "Sir, if he could have been saved, I know you would have saved him." The Karpes also inform us that in his account of the journey and the conversation, Freud allows that not only was he thinking about death and the role of doctors in helping prevent it but was also mulling over other matters he did not discuss. Freud writes, "These Turks place a higher value on sexual enjoyment than on anything else and in the event of a sexual disorder they are plunged into a dispair [*sic*] which contrasts strangely with their resignation toward the threat of death."

The Karpes emphasize that, just before his upsetting inability to remember the name Luca Signorelli, the psychoanalyst was mulling over the Turkish view that impotence is worse than dying. They cite Freud quoting the Turkish patient of a colleague claiming "Sir, if that does not go any longer, then life has no value." In the flow of thoughts in Freud's mind while he was visualizing the paintings in Orvieto but failing to conjure the name of the man who made them, Freud went from observing the Turks' priority on sexual pleasure to the belief that if one is impotent, then one might as well be dead.

Given the provocative nature of that conversation, there is a lot in the Karpes' story that begs questions. We learn that Freud could not recall the name Signorelli "for several days until someone told him"; we are left wondering who the knowledgeable informant was. But what frustrated me even more when I read their text is that the Karpes say that the person with whom Freud discussed the Turkish attitude toward sexual potency, in the course of a train journey, was an unidentified stranger. Who could such a person have been? Did Freud often discuss issues about the power of doctors and then discuss erections with people he had never before met?

Freud, according to the Karpes, was on a trip with his wife, Martha; she had, however, become ill, and he was now on his way to Bosnia and Herzegovina on his own. Richard and Marietta fail to tell us, however, where he had left Martha, or under whose care; nor do they say why he elected to continue the journey solo. Perhaps they simply did not know. Maybe this is just another instance of what for a biographer, as well as for an analysand, is one of the most frustrating things in the world: that so much information has been lost to history and can never be recovered.

The Karpes cite Freud's *The Psychopathology of Everyday Life,* written in 1901, as the source of their information about the train, Martha's illness, and the stranger. In my naïve analysand's way, comparable to that of a devout practitioner of Catholicism accepting the priest's words as the gospel truth, it did not initially occur to me that I should consult the Karpes' source and read Freud's actual text in its entirety. It would only be very late in the game that I would read *The Psychopathology of Everyday Life.* There, Freud makes no reference to Martha's having been ill, and while he does say he was talking with a stranger en route to a station in Herzegovina, his reference to having "journeyed by carriage" suggest a horse-drawn carriage more than a train carriage. This seems likely, since in the essay Freud wrote in 1898, within a week of the event in question, and which I only discovered long after reading the Karpes' article (in which this earlier text is never mentioned), Freud says he was on "a carriage drive"—which hardly sounds as if it could have been on a train. Given, among other things, the enormous symbolism of trains in Freudian thought, the difference is significant.

Richard and Marietta next inform us that, on this same occasion when he was unable to conjure the artist's name, Freud "also suppressed another thought, a piece of tragic news which had reached him several weeks earlier in Trafoi, a village in the Tyrol. He learned that a patient of his had committed suicide. He states in his analysis of the parapraxis that the suppression of thoughts of death and sexuality was responsible for his forgetting the name Signorelli."

What? Why? How was the suicide connected with sexuality? The Karpes have allowed that erections were an issue on Freud's mind, with his reflections on Turkish attitudes toward their importance, and they have made this titillating reference to "thoughts of . . . sexuality," but then they put the brakes on. Having asked if we can go further, will they do so?

CHAPTER 6

NAMES

THE KARPES CONTINUE FROM THEIR ACCOUNT of Freud's thoughts about the Turkish attitudes toward death, medical care, and sex to disputing Freud's assertion in *The Psychopathology of Everyday Life* that "The reason why the name Signorelli was lost is not to be found in anything special about the name itself." They contend that "what he forgot was really the beginning of his own name." Because Freud usually signed letters and texts as "Sigm" or "Sigi," which have the same three first letters as Signorelli, it is, to them, as if, in being unable to recall the artist's name, he was quite simply pushing aside his very own self.

Here I cannot help pointing out what may simply be a coincidence or may be something more: that *significant* begins with the identical *sig* as the artist's and the psychoanalyst's names.

And to me there is yet another factor that Richard and Marietta fail to mention, perhaps because they were unaware of it, but which I think may be *the* reason Freud could not remember the name Signorelli—if in fact the paintings heightened his awareness of being Jewish. In 1878, Freud had gone from being Sigismund Schlomo Freud to Sigmund Freud. No wonder he blocked a name that had elements of both Sigismund and, because of the mellifluous sound and ending in a vowel, Schlomo! He did not want to be reminded.

The Karpes go on to explain that it was not only the letters *s, i,* and *g* that the two men had in common. The Karpes see the Renaissance painter and the inventor of psychoanalysis as having had essentially like interests. Here my parents' unusual friends make a fantastic leap. They state, in the placid but confident manner with which they stood in the garden while Susie interviewed them in her regal, respectful way, that Freud's "apparent identification with Signorelli was closely connected with the topics of death and sexuality which had important significance in the work of both men, the artist of the fifteenth century and the scientist of the twentieth. Both were trailblazers and pioneers in their own fields which in many respects overlapped."

How specific will they then be about the nature of Luca Signorelli's sexual concerns and what he presents? Could Freud, as the future biographer of Leonardo da Vinci, who in that tome gives such importance to Leonardo's homosexuality, not have recognized what all the naked male buttocks, the repeated instances of men wrapped around other men throughout the Orvieto frescoes, were all about? Was he not aware that, as Michelangelo's mentor, Signorelli transmitted along with a lot about artistic technique an intense engagement with the adoring, erotically charged depictions of men?

CHAPTER 7

ORVIETO

It is in going to Orvieto and seeing its art in the flesh that the excitement really begins.

The Karpes appear to have considered the Signorellis only in reproduction. This is regrettable, since the paintings themselves are the bomb that would have enabled them to understand unequivocally a lot that they tentatively suggest.

The arrival at the small room of frescoes in the medieval hill town halfway between Florence and Rome is itself a fantastic experience. Freud took the train, which deposited him at a station in the newer part of town, of little charm, since it exists mainly to service the medieval village looming above. We know from a postcard he sent his wife early in the morning of September 9, 1897, that he arrived the evening before and took the funicular, up through a dark tunnel into the old town, to find himself emerging to the sight of ancient buildings illuminated by electric lights, so that they were visible even at night. The way the structures were situated on a rocky peak reminded him of Hohensalzburg—the uppermost, older part of Salzburg.

Even before Freud saw the cathedral in daylight, he was struck by its polychrome facade, as he was by the local people, whom he described to Martha as "black like the Tsiganes of ancient Etruria," his nice clean room at the Hotel Belle Arti, and the famous local wine, which he compared to the whites of Portugal. He pretty much repeated that information later the same day, in a postcard he sent from Bolsena, again making the comparison between Orvieto and

Salzburg. He now added praise for the "marvelous panorama" and the Etruscan tombs there. To his wife, he made no mention whatsoever of the Signorellis. I consider that lack to be more than an oversight. He was avoiding telling Martha what was intimate to him and might have been unsettling to her.

We can easily imagine Freud's experience going to the famous cathedral. From where the funicular stops, one ascends to the cathedral square on foot via a network of narrow, winding streets lined by ancient houses. One could easily get lost with all the twists and turns and dead ends, except that from almost every vantage point one can see, looming above everything else, two exquisite, squared, marble-clad Gothic towers that are constantly in view, like beacons for sailors in an ocean fog. They crown a sublime example of Italian Gothic architecture.

I say this although the Orvieto cathedral had a Romanesque start, and part of its beauty is in the calm of the Romanesque forms that preceded the lightening effects of the Gothic. Its initial architect, beginning in 1290, was Arnolfo di Cambio, who also conceived, in Florence, both the fine church of Santa Croce and the great cathedral there. Di Cambio thought in the true Romanesque way—making interior and exterior layout a logical consequence of structural necessity, and giving his buildings especially harmonious proportions. With his design as its basis, the construction and detailing of the Orvieto cathedral continued until 1500. The impact of the building depends primarily on the furious tracery of its ornament and the rich pattern of decoration, as well as on the spectacular use of white and colored marble, which characterize the very special way Gothic architecture developed in Italy as in no other place, but the underlying order of the building, which dates from its earlier origins, also penetrates us.

This pinnacle of Italian Gothic style is among the finest of the type in the world. The Gothic in other countries took very different forms; in Italy, it inspired facades of a delicacy that was without precedent in anything humankind had ever built previously. When the future Le Corbusier left his native Switzerland for the first time, at age nineteen, the buildings that initially showed him what architecture could be were examples of this style; the feathery surfaces of the great churches of Milan and Pisa and Siena intoxicated him beyond his wildest imaginings. And the animation of those facades was only part of it. The vastness of the interiors, the sheer feat of their engineering, and the humility they evoked in their visitors opened a whole new world to the man who would devote his life to trying to give humanity salubrious and inspiring settings in which to live.

Italian Gothic buildings reveal an imagination, a flair for the beautiful, and the wish to make aesthetic elegance part of the everyday life of the masses, all of which were unprecedented in the development of the human race. When my wonderful friends Josef and Anni Albers, who had met at the Bauhaus in 1922, took a trip from Dessau to celebrate their wedding in 1925, they went to Florence, and it was the Gothic facades there that, more than anything else, sent them into a new orbit. They found the charged geometry, the rich interplay of parallel lines, the bold divisions of the fronts of buildings like Santa Croce and Santa Maria Novella, so moving that when they returned to the Bauhaus, both of them, she in weaving and he in glass constructions, worked in a parallel way to the designers who had preceded them by some six centuries. They recapitulated the Gothic era's vibrating stripes and interlocked rectangles in a completely modern, mechanically up-to-date style.

The cathedral in Orvieto was, as it still is, more remote than the structures in Florence, Pisa, and Siena; it is also, for a range of reasons, possibly the ultimate jewel in the crown. The Gothic master of Siena, Giovanni di Cecco, would subsequently design the glorious facade there with Orvieto in mind. While that better-known, similarly vibrant, geometric assemblage of pale, richly veined marbles of varying colors in Siena was once covered by sculptures by Giovanni Pisano and contained a stained glass window by Duccio, at which point it would possibly have been even more exquisite than Orvieto, by the time Freud made his trip to central Italy, a lot of those features had been removed, and Orvieto's facade had far more allure than Siena's—as it does today. The splendid cathedral at Orvieto still has its original sculptures in place. Not only does Orvieto brandish scenes in relief but it also has excellent freestanding figures in niches. Those of the relief sculptures that depict the end of the world and the Last Judgment must have had an impact on Signorelli when he illustrated the same biblical events inside the building they adorned, for he followed their general layout, even if he completely transformed the cast of characters.

The facade—which faces west-southwest—has elaborate round entrance architraves that are echoed upward and outward, like blossoming flowers, as well as six triangular pediments with elaborate scalloped edges and a rose window with a lovely decorative scheme. It culminates in four lithe towers with delicate finials. Beyond the relief sculpture and architectural ornament that blanket this highly charged building front, a profusion of painting covers the flat voids. While the painting is not of the greatest quality, it is remarkable that it exists on a building exterior, with its gold-leaf backgrounds and strong colors still intact; the art still looks as pristine as a well-preserved medieval manuscript page. To have decorated an exterior that could withstand the climatic conditions on a hilltop, even if requiring occasional restoration, is a remarkable feat. [plate 4]

The rest of the structure features bold horizontal striping of contrasting black and white marble. Mined from the local quarries, these splendid stones have been organized with the delicacy of a seven-layer cake. The juxtaposition of the rich facade covered in ornament and narrative with this handsome mass behind it defined by its bold Pythagorean geometry creates a confection that is both solid and frothy. Having lasted for centuries, it has enduring power.

The cathedral exemplifies the concept of "the heavenly city."

Plate 4. The cathedral in Orvieto

Walking up the few shallow steps as he approached the amazing facade and the noble cavern to which it invites entrance, Freud must have felt—I am using the precise words my psychoanalyst used at the start of the first session of a seven-year-long treatment—as if he were "starting a journey."

Entry is through one of two side doors, which open to the side aisles. Whether Freud headed straight down one of these aisles or, instead, used the nave to approach the altar is unknown; perhaps he wandered around and took his time. But even if he charged purposefully to the Cappella Nova—the side chapel where the Signorellis are, and which was, presumably, one of the main goals of his trip to Orvieto, as it is for many art lovers—he cannot help but have had his breathing altered by the graceful pacing of Romanesque arches supporting the architrave. Here human beings are meant to feel humble and awestruck, and there are few of us who don't experience the intended modesty and wonder. The wooden ceiling high above and the network of roof beams allow, for all their roughness and frank materiality, a heavenly space to exist beneath them. Making his way, Freud must have entered a quiet state of receptivity.

The Cappella Nova is the southernmost quadrant of the transept; you reach it by turning right from the nave a few meters before you would otherwise reach the high altar. The space of the chapel is surprisingly small given the size and intensity of the artworks it holds. The compression adds to their thunderous power. Turning into the room blanketed with paintings, one is overcome by a surcharge of energy.

The initial impression of the Signorelli frescoes is like a symphony by Tchaikovsky at the apogee of its force, with every instrument of the orchestra performing simultaneously. As with the Tchaikovsky, this has been preceded by an ambient loveliness (the cathedral facade), and then by quiet and serenity (the nave and side aisles). They lull you into a preparatory calm. The hustle of the journey and the cathedral square are behind you, your defenses dropped. Your tranquil state makes the bombast of the fresco cycle a shock.

You instantly feel an impact from these paintings, even before you begin to study them and try to fathom the precise imagery. You are struck first by the preponderance of bare human flesh. Most of it is ruddy and luminous, enveloping bodies at the peak of physical vitality. Some of it, however, has the pallor of death and hangs on creatures diminished to corpses. Regardless, in all the scenarios there is a sheer energy that makes artists like Willem de Kooning and Jackson Pollock seems laconic by comparison.

You are brought to total, 100 percent attention. The impact of the frescoes is that of three shots of espresso, a bar of intense dark chocolate, and a double dose of Ritalin—all consumed simultaneously. The vibrating mauve and dark green accents on the acres of human skin intensify the charge. [plate 5]

Then the imagery comes into focus. You have walked into a gay orgy.

Plate 5. *The Damned Cast into Hell*

This is a specialized form of homosexual pornography—left, right, and center. There is a preponderance of naked flesh, almost all of it male. Muscular buttocks come at you from every direction, and gigantic, Prometheus-like characters with ripped torsos hold other nude men, equally muscle-bound, in hammerlocks.

You expect to smell the odor of a crowded locker room where two competing football teams have just stripped down after a game. The occasional women who are caught between the athletic men in the mélange are discernible as females only by their breasts, since otherwise these women are manly in their physiques. Adding to the confusion, some of the men have their same long blond tresses.

As the eye focuses, and the details begin to come into place, you face dying and death everywhere. Writhing bodies are losing in the struggle to avoid being carried to hell, and ghastly skeletons lie inert. Corpses face young and healthy bodies; executioners do their work. Mortal violence occurs or is about to occur, and hideous tortures are carried out with repellant gusto. The swirl of forms and the shouting colors intensify the fury.

It is all painted with aplomb. There are incredible passages of color, and a deliberate, pulsating rhythm. The hues and shapes are organized in series of echoes and balances, with a lightness of touch and artistic finesse in spite of the weighty subject matter. The result of this supreme artistry is that what might otherwise disgust you, or cause you simply to flee from the small chapel, holds you fascinated.

You are seduced by the aesthetic charms, which are in such contrast to the subject matter. The symphonic structure of lively curvilinear forms and the rich spectrum of varying greens and reds and other tones entice you not just to stay but to soak in something of unparalleled richness. Whatever your reactions may be to the very complex scenario before you, to all the naked men engaged in violent activity, it is depicted in such a magisterial way that you linger, fascinated.

CHAPTER 8

What Richard and Marietta
Say About All This

After the scintillating start of their article, when the Karpes go on to discuss Signorelli's life and art, they suddenly write as if for a high school term paper. Mainly, they quote from the *Encyclopaedia Britannica* and an art historian named Maud Cruttwell— apparently their only sources for seeing and understanding the frescoes. But their summation in their own words clearly states the main point: "Signorelli was the first to succeed in depicting the nude human body in action. He was especially successful in depicting fiends, demons, angels and soldiers. . . . Signorelli emphasized nakedness, grouping and movement, but also an additional element: Aggression. Aggression is expressed so vividly that it arouses anxiety in the spectator."

If only they had seen the art firsthand! Surely they would have recognized that Signorelli's frescoes also have a fantastic allure because of how they are painted. Their visual attributes are in a different realm from their subject matter, even if their painterly virtuosity is responsible for the subject matter's being so moving, and I wish that Richard and Marietta could have witnessed this. When we compare the Cappella Nova frescoes to other fresco cycles to which art lovers make pilgrimages in central Italy, they stand apart.

For me, absolutely nothing is as beautiful, as serene, as elegant and seductive as Piero della Francesca's frescoes in Arezzo, not so far from Orvieto. They intoxicate the way that Beethoven's late chamber music does. Yet when you face the Signorellis, it is as if they are life and blood, while Piero's are so delicate and ethereal that they seem to have the limitations of a fantasy. The Signorellis are the embodiment of life's truths, harsh though they may be. Giotto's frescoes in Padua have phenomenal formal qualities, and a religious beauty that can convince even the most committed skeptic that the flight into Egypt and the adoration of the magi must have taken place just as they are shown here—with the mountain peaks echoing the donkey's form, and the golds and pinks and powdery blues becoming in our imagination the actual colors of the biblical events—but, yet again, when we see the Signorellis, these marvelous paintings by Giotto that are sublime as delicious diversions seem less valid as conveyors of the truth. The Giottos and Pieros have unequaled beauty, but they are not as robust or visceral.

There are many knowing art historians who would say, "But of course." Giotto, after all, falls into the category of an "Italian Primitive." Because of that same simplicity and relative lack of sophistication, Piero, until the early twentieth century, was not nearly as highly regarded as he has become now that we view art with eyes trained by Modernism. It is the painters of the High Renaissance, most particularly the ones who followed Signorelli by a few years—Michelangelo, Leonardo, and Raphael—who were, in earlier times, considered the great masters of painting, because of their advances beyond the Primitives. But today, in a world where taste has been universally re-formed because of the vision of Cézanne, followed by the impact of Matisse and Picasso, and then the elegant simplification of the Bauhaus masters and Mondrian, most art enthusiasts, myself included, know the Pieros and the Giottos far better than the work of the later Italians, especially a relatively minor one like Signorelli. This is a further reason that the impact of the Cappella Nova (which I would not have bothered to see were it not for Freud) is so surprising.

EVEN IF THE KARPES DID NOT GET TO THE ACTUAL SCENE, and do not venture into the territory of Freud's intense responsiveness to other Italian paintings—the intimate way he was moved by art and described it to Martha—when they tell us that, on September 22, 1898, Freud wrote Fliess, declaring the Signorellis "the finest I have seen," it is an extraordinary revelation. Richard and Marietta, perhaps, did not recognize just how unusual that assessment was. There may be no other art lover in history who has rated Luca Signorelli's work above all other paintings.

The vast majority of enthusiasts opt for the Michelangelos in the Sistine Chapel or the Raphaels in Florence. A smaller group shares my preference for the Piero della Francescas in Arezzo or the Giottos in Padua. Certain very knowing viewers—Balthus, for example, and his savvy, mysterious wife, Setsuko—put Mantegna's more-real-than-real frescoes in Mantua at the top of the list (although Balthus, if forced to make the choice, rated Piero even higher, preferring the ungraspable to the palpable). For Josef Albers, tellingly, the number one was Duccio—for Duccio's lively, anxious outlines, and the luminous, jewel-like coloring and knowing articulation that make the linear tension stimulating as opposed to threatening. Those who want to get to the origins of verisimilitude in art, and the ability to convey mass and weight, opt for Masaccio's Bramante Chapel, in Florence. Lovers of the picturesque go for the Carpaccios in San Giorgio degli Schiavone, in Venice. I personally am moved to ecstasy, even more than I anticipate, every time I go to see either of these two groups of paintings and the Mantegnas. Aficionados of the robust, meanwhile, would probably cite one or another group of Tintorettos.

Freud, I think, is unique in labeling the Signorellis "the finest." He does so with rare modesty. He says "I have ever seen." He is never as humble or insouciant as an analyst of human beings; I am enchanted by the freshness and modesty he evinces in response to the Italian master.

Freud, who knew his Italian art, had to have been aware of all the painting groups to which I refer—from their reproductions in books, if not from actual visits. That the man who chose his words so carefully wrote Fliess—a confessor figure, to whom there would have been no shambling about the truth—that Signorelli's paintings in Orvieto were, bar none, "the finest I have ever seen" is a fact of inestimable significance.

From that vital statement, we get to yet another nugget of information from the Karpes. They quote a footnote from *The Psychopathology of Everyday Life*. How like these scholarly Viennese friends of my parents

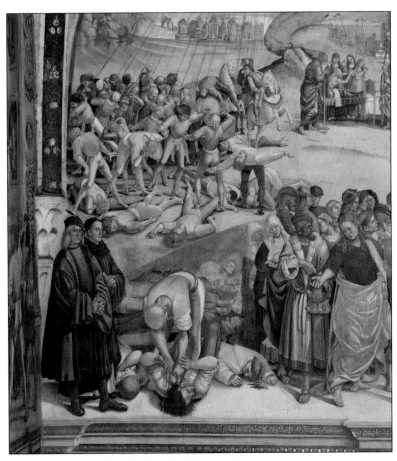

Plate 6: Detail of *Deeds of the Antichrist*

to have fastened onto a detail relegated to the footnotes, unlike the rest of Mother and Dad's chosen companions, who barely made it through articles in *Life* magazine. The Karpes' chosen detail is where Freud reveals "that during the time while he could not recall the painter's name, he saw the frescoes and Signorelli's self-portrait ultra-clearly in his mind. The visual memory faded when he was told the forgotten name."

The matter of the self-portrait is of particular interest. Sigmund Freud has revealed something extraordinary about his own mental process. He could readily envision the physical image of a fifteenth-century painter, while he was unable to conjure the name of the man whose self-portrait it was, but he could no longer see the person once he identified him with the name that began with the same first three letters of his own. The Karpes, via Maud Cruttwell, identify the Signorelli self-portrait as being one of the two figures on the left-hand side of *Deeds of the Antichrist*.

HE IS A HANDSOME BUCK WITH LONG BLOND TRESSES, a strong jaw, and prizefighter's features. This tall, beefy character stares at us with a look of certainty; he has wise eyes, and, while taciturn, betrays intense feeling. [plate 7] His face is fleshy, his skin ruddy and weathered, with the lines of someone who has lived a lot of his life outdoors. He has a classic sort of Italian nose—a mix of Robert de Niro's and Sylvester Stallone's—as if he has possibly broken it under another man's jabbing left hook. His long, thick golden hair gives him a certain wildness. But he is dressed in a proper black tunic and cloak, and, unlike his subjects, shows little of his body, except for his enormous hands, of which the long, thick fingers are interlocked with a mighty grip. His feet, in black shoes, are absolutely enormous, and even if their tremendous scale can be attributed to foreshortening because of the angle at which we see him, they are still, proportionately, like the feet of a Giacometti

Plate 7. Detail of *Deeds of The Antichrist*

sculpture of an upright man: a massive, solid base for standing tall and proud, firmly positioned on earth, as assured physically as emotionally.

Luca Signorelli had used his corporeal self to "sign" his work. Yes— "sign!"—another word or name with the letters *s, i, g,* and *n.* That is in English but the German is "die Signatur," although it is also "die Unterschrift." It is with his own face and torso that he identifies himself as the author of his artwork. For Freud, by contrast, written and verbal language, names for things and people, were the vehicles of human thought. He gave them a preeminent role. What is astonishing is that once he had Signorelli's name back in his mind, he completely eradicated from his mind the image of the man as flesh and blood. It is as if the language of identification allowed him to escape from something that troubled him so much that he could not think about it: the man as a physical being. I find that form of parapraxis even more astonishing than the blocking of the name.

The Karpes point out that "Signorelli left his signature on that painting in the form of his self-portrait. Did Freud see his own self-portrait somewhere in this painting which made such a strong impression on him? Who is Anti-Christ for Signorelli? Who is Anti-Christ for Freud?" These are interesting thoughts, but how about the idea that, for Sigmund Freud, the name for someone mattered so much more, and was so much safer, that once he again fastened his mind on it, he obliterated the man's actual physical presence?

We will need to delve further into the Karpes' questions about these relationships to the Antichrist, since they inform us that this shady character, central to one of the frescoes, was a stand-in for Jews. Shown with the devil whispering in his ear, he also represented the church hierarchy that commissioned Signorelli. Being Jewish and having the money to pay for something were, in Freud's world, connected—and like the movement of a matador's red muleta to a bull.

I HAVE TO ADMIT THAT IN MY FIRST VIEWING of the frescoes, the iconographical details explained by the Karpes were lost on me. Initially, I did not understand the symbolism of what I was looking at. It was only Richard and Marietta's explication that opened my eyes to the role of the Antichrist in the frescoes, and to the effect of his representation on various viewers. But once the Karpes caused me to consider how Freud, as a Jew, would have reacted to a portrayal of the quintessential Jew as an opponent of Christian goodness, I found these paintings even more provocative than I had to begin with. How could the painter dare to represent his patrons in the form of a traitor in concert with the devil?

The painter's self-portrait also begs another major question: What is it to see and understand a world while keeping apart from it? This is how Signorelli presents his own role. Did Freud identify with Signorelli in that capacity, and hate something about their shared role, as savvy observer of human frailties, that caused him to forget the name that resembled his own? Moreover, in spite of the one moment in front of his children when he stood up to anti-Semitism, was there not a side of him that often observed the denigration of Jews while remaining mute? Was he not also anti-Semitic, causing him to survey certain horrors, as Signorelli did, without taking action? Was he plagued by his own guilt?

CHAPTER 9

FRA ANGELICO

THE SIGNORELLI SELF-PORTRAIT AND THE FIGURE next to it are to the left of the entrance to the chapel. This is the first place to which most viewers instinctively turn upon entering the room. While everyone else in the large scene is in a sort of historical costume that suggests biblical times, these two men, in dignified black tunics and capes, with black leggings and black shoes and black headgear, seem contemporary with the making of the fresco. So they were—one precisely, the other by the relatively small gap of half a century. The more modest-seeming man behind Luca Signorelli is none other than Fra Angelico—the great early Italian Renaissance master best known for his sublime frescoes in the cells and public spaces of the monastery of San Marco in Florence. He is there, the Karpes tell us, because he started this painting and planned the others in the chapel fifty years before Signorelli was commissioned to complete them.

I imagine that most visitors to the chapel have no idea about any of this. I certainly would not have known who the two figures in modern everyday dress (for the year 1500) were had I not read the Karpes' narrative. I wonder if Signorelli gave any thought to what viewers five centuries later would think. What is certain, however, is that, once we indentify these two individuals, the way Signorelli has depicted himself dominating a recalcitrant Fra Angelico is provocative. From where they are standing on the side of the panorama of scenes of the Antichrist and his kingdom, the man whose shoes Signorelli filled appears to be looking back sideways into the tableau, while Signorelli himself is distinctly staring away from it and surveying the entire room. Angelico appears dissatisfied, as well he might be, given how little he completed of the work he set out to do in the chapel. Signorelli is the master of ceremonies.

The younger artist, nearer to us, blocks Angelico with his vast cloak and billowing sleeves. He splays his legs to make himself immobile. His thick, luminous locks under a jaunty, billowing tam have a bravura lacking in Angelico's tidy, smooth hair under a tight skull cap. Angelico is distant, in a state of reverie; Signorelli is knowing and confident.

In fact, for Luca Signorelli, Fra Angelico was a hard act to follow. To show himself dominating Angelico is true hubris. When Angelico, a Dominican monk, had been asked to work on the Cappella Nova in 1447, he was deemed "famous above all other Italian painters." The Pope had recently commissioned him to paint frescoes at the Vatican; for at least three decades, he had enjoyed immense stature for the quality of light in his work, esteemed for its visual elegance and spiritual magnitude. He skilfully utilized recent discoveries about how to represent perspective, and his figures were clearly articulated and possessed of volume.

The authorities of Orvieto, called the Opera, were proud to have landed such a master. By the time be began work on June 15, 1447, they had agreed to furnish scaffolding, supply all the colors—except for the particular blue and gold Fra Angelico liked to use, which were inordinately expensive—pay salaries to the artist's assistants as well as to Fra Angelico himself, and supply bread and wine along with a per diem. The agreement was that Fra Angelico would work for three to four months each year during the hottest summer season, which suited his goal of escaping the heat of Rome and the weather-related illnesses that went with it.

But Fra Angelico spent only one summer in Orvieto. We don't know why—whether the main factor was the demands of the Pope, or financial difficulties encountered by the Opera that prohibited their being able to cover all the high expenses—but, once he had made an overall design for the chapel, all that the Dominican executed were a Christ in judgment and some prophets.

I am sure that Fra Angelico's Christ, enclosed in a circle high above in one of the ceiling vaults of the Cappella Nova, is a beautiful painting: serene and magisterial. But while I acknowledge those qualities as facts, I cannot feel them. Even though I looked up at Fra Angelico's Christ dutifully on my two Orvieto visits, on both occasions fully aware of its importance as a work by a painter whose art normally bowls me over, it had little impact on me. One knows it is great—a triumph of competent modeling and serene vision, a perfect visual representation of equilibrium—yet, with all the drama and naughtiness below, all the titillation and provocation, it is impossible, at least for me, to respond to the quietude. To become absorbed by it would be as difficult as doing justice to the subtle flavor of a white truffle accompanied by a glass of Puligny-Montrachet when one has just been eating barbecued ribs and drinking stout; the timing makes it impossible to appreciate what would otherwise be a marvelous experience.

Like the Christ, Fra Angelico's prophets are beautiful: possessed of grace, clothed in robes of soft chalky colors. With their half-closed eyelids, their pale and luminous skin, and their look of being in receipt of a message, they seem truly holy. When we see them in reproduction, and not in the direct company of the Signorellis, they have fantastic grace and beauty. But when we are in the Cappella Nova, they don't attract us any more than the perfect child in class does when the macho, bold, bad boy is acting up.

Based on the *Last Judgment* that Fra Angelico painted elsewhere, if in fact he had been the one to complete the cycle, it might have had an aesthetic grace and refinement lacking in Signorelli's frescoes, but it would not have been nearly as exciting. There is a small *Last Judgment* by Fra Angelico on extended loan from an unspecified private collection to the Houston Museum of Fine Arts, and while it has splendid colors and consummate grace, it is absent of all drama. The damned are almost as innocent-looking as the blessed, and they are totally without corporal, let alone sexual, traits.

Normally, if I am in a museum that, like the Louvre, has work by both Fra Angelico and Luca Signorelli, I find the work of the former infinitely more moving. It is poised and serene, and it fills me with a sense of well-being. Even scenes that could be scary or threatening, a beheading or a crucifixion, have a biblical grace to them. The sheer beauty is more impressive than the terror. But in Orvieto, aside from the issue of visibility, the art of the man whose name suggest an angelic monk doesn't hold a candle to the rough, in-your-face presence of work by someone whose name signifies "light on the little man."

It took half a century before the Opera found someone to continue the chapel. Starting in about 1490, they tried to convince Perugino to take over where Fra Angelico had left off, but they failed to lure him to Orvieto. It was in 1499 that they got Signorelli. He was, at the time, painting a large cloister in the monastery of Mount Oliveto Maggiore, near Siena. With the subject matter of the life of Saint Benedict, he had already managed to put on display some swaggering lads in very tight pants. [plate 8] Seen from behind, they could be modeling for Abercrombie's; in one instance, Signorelli has torn the leggings off of a young man to expose his bare thighs and underwear. [plate 9] But he had no problem leaving it unfinished when Orvieto beckoned. Dugald McLellan—an excellent contemporary art historian whose small book on the Cappella Nova frescoes I bought from the ticket seller on my recent visit there—posits as to his reasons: "It is not clear why Signorelli abandoned that commission, but he was clearly keen to take on the Orvieto project. Perhaps it was the chance to cover such a vast, virtually uninterrupted space; perhaps it was the prospect of depicting monumental scenes of nudes in a range of different moods and states that motivated him."

Signorelli was in his fifties when he received the commission for the Cappella Nova. (By most estimates he was born circa 1441.) He was

Plate 8. *Life of St. Benedict: How Benedict Recognizes and Receives Totila,* c. 1498–1499, fresco, great cloister of the Abbey of Monte Oliveto Maggiore, Asciano, Tuscany, Italy

Plate 9. Detail of *Life of St Benedict: How Benedict Reproves the Brother of the Monk Valerian,* c. 1498–1499, fresco, great cloister of the Abbey of Monte Oliveto Maggiore, Asciano, Tuscany, Italy

from Cortona, a town in Tuscany near the Umbrian border, and he had served as an apprentice under none other than Piero della Francesca. He may have learned technique from Piero, but he acquired little of the sensibility of that most subtle and magical of painters. Once he started his own workshop, he clinched commissions for altarpieces and frescoes from towns all over central Italy, and he was employed by the Vatican—during the early 1480s in the recently built Sistine Chapel—as well as by the Medici in Florence.

By the time he was summoned to Orvieto, Signorelli had developed a specialty of the male nude, which he painted in varying poses, sometimes completely at rest, sometimes engaged "in violent action." Almost every artistic subject was an excuse for painting naked men, burly and strong. Although I have never found another writer who acknowledges it, his paintings are vividly homoerotic. This was evident as far back as one of his earliest works, an image of Pan, now in Berlin, which Bernard Berenson

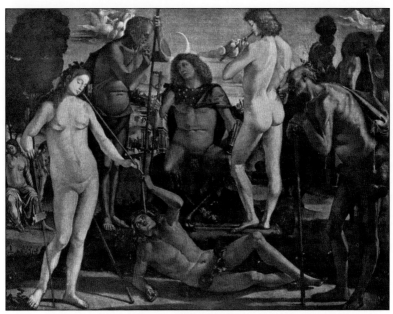

Plate 10. *Court of Pan,* c. 1484, oil on canvas, formerly in the Kaiser Friedrich Museum in Berlin; destroyed in 1945

Plate 11. *Two Nude Youths* and *Man, Woman, and Child,* c. 1488–1489,
oil on panel, from the Bichi Chapel of the Church of Sant' Agostino in Siena;
Toledo Museum of Art, Ohio

would single out as one of the painter's triumphs. [plate 10] Pan was followed by Signorelli's depiction of two lads, and its companion picture of
a man, woman, and child, both now in Toledo, Ohio, which are equally
homoerotic. [plate 11] His 1482–85 *Flagellation*, about which scholars differ on the dates, some saying c. 1475, others saying 1480–83, now at the
Brera, in Milan, shows a muscular yet rather feminine Christ looking as if
he is in a sort of reverie while being flogged by three whippers who arch
their backs to flaunt their ripped torsoes; the artist presents all these men
in the nude except for loincloths that fall well below their waists, to show,
depending on whether we are seeing the fellow from front or back, a bit of
bottom crack or pubic hair. [plates 12 and 13] In his 1498 *Martyrdom of St.
Sebastien,* painted in oil on wood, he took the well-known theme of the
saint pierced by an arrow and sexualized it, as well. Here Signorelli simply
pulled down the pants of one of the archers, while leaving his fringed

blouse on; the reproduction of this painting says more than anything I could possibly put into words. [plate 14] But in Monte Oliveto he had, for the most part, to tone things down and covered most of the men in white robes.

Orvieto would provide the chance to resume painting male nudity. While his task in the great cathedral was ostensibly to complete the decoration Fra Angelico had begun in the ceiling vaults, there is little doubt that what most attracted him was the potential to fill the bare, flat whitewashed walls below with his preferred subject matter, and take it to new extremes.

The scaffolding that had been erected for Fra Angelico half a century earlier was still in place when Signorelli began. Starting on May 25, 1499, he and his assistants used it to complete the scenes for which Fra Angelico had left drawings. Then they painted, in accord with instructions from the Opera, the four segments of the entrance-bay vault. Here they put images of virgins, patriarchs, martyrs, and the doctors of the

Plate 12. *Flagellation,* c.1475 or 1480–1483 [scholars differ on the dates], oil on canvas, Pinacoteca di Brera, Milan, Italy

Plate 13. Detail of *Flagellation,* Pinacoteca di Brera, Milan, Italy

Plate 14. Detail of *Martyrdom of St. Sebastian,* ca 1498, oil on panel,
from the San Domenico, Città di Castello; Pinacoteca Comunale,
Citta di Castello, Umbria, Italy

church. But none of this is what interests us, because all these paintings
are overhead at a great height, making them so difficult to see that they
could not have had the impact on Freud of those paintings Signorelli

painted next—pictures of the Antichrist, the damned, the elect, and other scenes of the end of the world.

Dugald McLellan does a nice job of imagining the reactions of Signorelli's patrons when he "laid before the Opera his bold and daring plan for the decoration of the walls of the Chapel. No doubt impressed with the speed of his execution, the worthy burghers were well disposed toward Signorelli. Their reaction to the plan itself can only be guessed at, however, since the prospect of acres of naked flesh must have shocked the sensibilities of many of them." In addition to the subject matter, there was the cost: They were about to spend a fortune for that rich display of male bodies.

The contract for the further work in the Cappella Nova, approved on April 27, 1500, was very precise. In the archives of the Opera del Duomo di Orvieto, it is a document that portrays the workings of the society in which it was created. With its elegant calligraphy in perfectly straight lines, it testifies to the fine machinery of the art world of Renaissance Italy. This legal agreement for the presentation of passion, of sin and the wages for it, left little to chance. It specified that Signorelli would receive 575 ducats "for his labours, paints, designs, and cartoons—as well as grain and wine. The Opera would maintain the scaffolding and supply the materials that would be used to mix and apply the plaster, and find room and board for two people. Signorelli, in return, would be obligated to follow the designs he had presented. While the contract allowed him to add to the number of characters he showed in his sketches, it prohibited his reducing the number. It also required him to paint the principle figures with his own hand, thus eliminating the diminution of quality that can occur when assistants and apprentices do too much work.

For four years, this is what he did. The result was his masterpiece; he would live some twenty years more, but never equal the frescoes in Orvieto.

CHAPTER 10

ANTICHRIST

O N MY SECOND TRIP TO ORVIETO, some fifteen years after the
first trip, I found that my focus on Freud made me think
constantly about my own psychoanalysis with a traditional Freudian. (My doctor, Albert J. Solnit, worked closely with Anna Freud,
as my mother claimed of Richard Karpe. At one time, I assumed
that the collaboration that was a certainty in Dr. Solnit's case was
my mother's mythologizing in Richard's, although I have since discovered it was true, in spades.) This is why, once I had progressed
from my initial reaction to all the naked flesh, I became transfixed
by the scene that is the focal point of the complex composition in
which Signorelli's portraits of himself and Fra Angelico occupy the
lower left-hand corner. [plate 15] What attracted my attention was
an image I took to be of Christ and the devil. It is slightly to the
right of the center, at eye level—which is to say toward the bottom—of this fresco, which occupies the large space that has the
shape of a horizontal rectangle topped by a half sphere created by
the curved vault above it. The fresco has as much going on in it as a
Cecil B. DeMille epic, with these two men as the stars of the scene.
[plate 16] The mauve and gold of the Christ character's clothing, and
the position of both figures on a pedestal and fairly near the picture
plane, contribute to the pair's preeminence, the way they attract our
attention more than any of the other well-articulated figures (I count
some 160 in all) in the fresco. But what makes us notice them above
all is the sinisterness of their encounter.

Plate 15. *Deeds of the Antichrist*

AT THIS POINT, I SHOULD EXPLAIN THE WAY I LOOK AT ART. I began loving painting at age ten, when I was at an opening of an exhibition at the Wadsworth Atheneum, the museum in downtown Hartford. My mother, who was a capable painter, had a large watercolor—of the corpse of a pheasant my father had shot—that had won an honorable mention in the show, so it was a major event for our family. But after half an hour, the crustless tea sandwiches and chattering grown-ups made me feel like an alien, and I asked permission to go up the curved staircase, which looked as if it might lead somewhere interesting.

The magical stairs led me to the museum's permanent collection. I soon happened upon a spectacular late Mondrian—his *Composition (No. IV) Blanc-Bleu*—a rhythmic interplay of horizontal and vertical black lines of differing widths and precise but offbeat spacing, with a single blue panel on its left-hand side. The painting sent me into

Plate 16. Detail of *Deeds of the Antichrist*

the stratosphere. It filled me with joy, and I ran downstairs to get my father, to whom I said I had just found something I loved the way I loved skiing and mountaintops. Dad accompanied me back to the third floor. He commended my taste, saying that he agreed that the painting was beautiful, and said, "Nicky, the artist's name is Mondrian. We have a book on him at home, if you want to see more of his work in reproductions." At the moment, life seemed perfect.

Going to see the paintings that bowled over Freud, I was still the

same person, starting with little or no knowledge of what I was looking at and simply responding with the impulses brought on by what
I was seeing.

IGNORANT OF THE ACTUAL SUBJECT MATTER OF THE SCENE before me
in the Cappella Nova, I took the central figure of the Christ-like
figure on a pedestal to be Jesus Himself. Here is the Holy Son, I
thought. His bejeweled tunic (the source of the lustrous gold), and
his billowing robe (the mauve with a hint of cassis), wrapped over
one shoulder, suggested his stature, while his sandals conferred his
essential humility. His beard and haunted look made me think the
portrait was of Jesus at the end of his earthly life, or possibly in the
next stage; his stance on a stone base conveyed the sense of arrival
one often sees in the Resurrected Jesus. I was riveted by the way this
character I assumed to be Jesus is neck-to-neck with the devil.

I know that part of what got my attention is also that, except
for his nasty red horns, the devil resembles me. Like me, he is fair-
skinned and bald, with an angular face, full lips, and popping veins
visible in his neck. [plate 17]

Even the small bit we see of the devil's torso, fairly developed
and muscular but not of the standards of the guys in some of Signorelli's other frescoes, is similar to my own. And he looks possessed
by thought, with an eagerness and intensity, and bulging eyes, that
further my notion that, without those horns, you have a pretty good
facsimile of Nick Weber here.

Writing my own name, I am feeling the way Freud did. The visual
disappears. For some reason, the confluence of letters that is a name
has an odd emotional effect. What happened just now when I put
together the letters that constitute, in language, who I am increased my
ability to fathom how Freud, after being unable to conjure the name

Plate 17. Detail of *Deeds of the Antichrist*

Signorelli for at least two days while he saw the work in his mind's eye, discovered that, once he remembered it, he could no longer mentally see the painter's self-portrait.

When the combination of letters that identifies someone is foremost in our thoughts, the particular personality of the character so identified does not easily coexist with it. I have always had this problem with the name Susie. It has something of *my* Susie's grace and femininity, but then, there are many other Susies in the world, so to identify *the* Susie with *their* name is a compromise.

Nabokov, of course, made Lolita the exception by taking Humbert Humbert's inamorata's name and the music of its sound into new territory. There is only one "Lo." Perhaps it takes another obsessive to appreciate the brilliance with which that great writer turned his irrationality into art, but I consider it sheer genius: that making of three syllables—*low-lee-tuh*—so mellifluous as to be intoxicating.

THE DEVIL IS TO OUR RIGHT OF THE FIGURE I assumed to be Christ. We see him in profile, with his lips about two inches from the left ear of Jesus, and he appears to be speaking with nonstop intensity. His proximity to his palpably troubled listener makes us imagine that he is filling Jesus' ear with hot breath. Jesus is facing us. But his eyes, while cast slightly in the direction of the devil, look off into space. He does not engage, and he appears troubled.

One has the impression that the devil's bare left arm is penetrating the slinglike fold of Jesus' mauve robe, and that it is his hand that is in front of Jesus' navel. Yet that hand is of the same construction and color as Jesus' right hand—and must surely be *His*, not the devil's. If this is so, where is the devil's left hand? Concomitantly, where is Jesus' left hand if this is the devil's? It is as if the devil and Jesus share a limb.

A young Italian man named Andrea drove me from Siena to Orvieto on this second journey to see the Signorellis. Recently married, he told me, on our ride that morning, a lot about the travails of the first year of marriage. He was bright and likable, and we quickly established a rapport. We went into the Cappella Nova together, and I asked him what he thought about the arms. I wanted a reality check from someone bright and astute but untutored in the discipline of art history. He saw the connection of the limbs exactly as I did, agreeing with me that it was impossible to determine to which of the two people the arm in question belonged.

To me, the figure I perceived as Jesus was the embodiment of a psychoanalyst, and the devil the patient. There is no doubt that the patient is confessing evil thoughts, the so-called dark side of the mind. He is desperate for the psychoanalyst to know these thoughts; he is seeking to unburden himself. He is as naked emotionally as he is physically.

The psychoanalyst figure—a stand-in for Dr. Solnit, and also for Freud himself—is taking it all in. What is unclear is whether his intense look of concern is because he disapproves, or because he is intrigued. After I had studied the pair for a few minutes, I concluded that he is tempted by some of what the devil is proffering in the way of experience.

Andrea agreed with my general take on their dialogue, although I left out the psychoanalyst bit. During our conversation in the car, he had been very open about his wife's jealousy concerning him and other women, her awareness that he apparently had had about half the women of the right age in Siena and the surrounding villages prior to meeting her. He told me repeatedly, with a commitment I found convincing, that, with his illustrious track record behind him, he was determined never to cheat on the woman who was his ultimate love.

Rather, he wanted to father children with her and be faithful and assume a traditional family role. His zeal about his domestic existence equaled the enthusiasm with which he had succumbed to every female temptation up to his engagement to his future wife.

Andrea saw Jesus as being intrigued by the realities of physical lust, listening to the devil attentively (there seemed no doubt to either of us that the devil is discussing sex), while remaining worthy of the pedestal on which he stands. How sympathetic this Jesus seemed to both of us: nonjudgmental, open to the possibilities of things, righteous but not holier-than-thou.

There the comparison between Jesus and Dr. Solnit stopped in my mind. For seven years, whatever I was discussing, I was, of course, unable to see him, since this was a traditional treatment, with me on the couch, facing away from him. In addition, I rarely had any audible response from him. If I wanted him to feel the excitement of a desire I was describing, I had no satisfaction whatsoever. Always, the ball came back to me. Only I, by being truthful to my associations, could understand the meaning of the infatuations and cravings of my youth.

Signorelli's pair seemed a wonderful fantasy—of the devilish me managing to have my arm going through Dr. Solnit's tunic. That I might connect with him, excite him with the secrets I was whispering, and bring out his humanness was a dream.

Standing before the fresco, I wondered if Freud, too, could have seen this image of Jesus and the whispering devil as a parable for the doctor-patient relationship.

ONE MIGHT HAVE THOUGHT THAT ANDREA, who served as a sort of tour guide and had grown up with Catholic imagery as part of his everyday life, would have been more accurate than I was concerning the identity of the figure we both discussed as if he were Jesus. I am relieved that an Italian educated in traditional iconography made the same mistake I did.

I have now learned, from my rereading of the Karpes' text—the precise details of which were not in my mind when I was in Orvieto—and further research, that the significance of the man in the purple robes is that he is actually the Antichrist, not the Jesus Andrea and I assumed him to be. Moreover, his features are those of Luca Signorelli himself.

Freud, the Karpes suppose, knew all of this. I am not so sure. While all the books on Orvieto, even the little flyer handed out at the entrance of the Cappella Nova, make clear that this character is the Antichrist, and, the fact declared, act as if no one could possibly have thought otherwise, I cannot believe that Andrea and I are the only two people ever to have assumed that this gripping encounter is of Jesus Christ Himself embraced by the devil.

After all, having grown up in the culture where mental-health authorities have replaced the mythological and biblical figures who were the deities of previous civilizations, naturally I saw the character I equated with Dr. Solnit, listening to the devilish me exploding about my passions, as a holy man, not a heathen.

CHAPTER 11

THE IDENTITY OF THE ANTICHRIST

IT WAS THE BOOK WRITTEN ON LUCA SIGNORELLI in 1899 by the charmingly named Maud Cruttwell that served to tell the Karpes who my Christ/Freud/Dr. Solnit figure really was.

Of course I wonder if, learned as they were, Richard and Marietta had seen the Orvieto frescoes, whether reproduced or in the flesh, without having done research, they would have made the same mistake I committed about the identity of someone who so closely resembles thousands of Jesus images.

It isn't only out of embarrassment that I maintain that Andrea and I cannot have been the only untutored people who assumed that the man cornered by the devil was Christ. Surely there are many others who enter the Cappella Nova and respond to the fantastic energy of Signorelli's figures and the powerful sensation of momentous events without knowing the precise story line.

This is not to deny how interesting the iconography is once we understand the narrative. In my swirl of reactions—to the energized and muscular men engaged in furious and often violent action all around me, to the devil whispering to the character I misconstrued as Jesus in imagery I instinctively read as caricatures of myself and my psychoanalyst—I was grateful to be corrected by the Karpes. They elucidate the facts of the scene with the same refreshing calm and clarity they had in the swirl of my parents' cocktail party. The Karpes quote their preferred source, Cruttwell, explaining that, in the scene before us, "The foreground is filled with followers of the false prophet—Anti-Christ—who, with the features of Christ, stands on a little raised dias listening with an eveil [*sic*] expression as the devil behind him, unseen by the crowd, whispers into his ear what he shall say."

My own subsequent research would inform me that, in this fresco cycle where Luca Signorelli depicts the story of the end of the world, this first scene is a foreshadowing of Armageddon that occurs when Christ is asked what will indicate that the world is going to end. He replies (in Matthew 24:4–5) "Take heed that no man deceive you. For many shall come in my name, saying, I am Christ; and shall deceive many."

So at least Andrea and I were not the only ones deceived; we were simply among the many to have been tricked, just as the Bible predicted. And since my traveling companion was Catholic, I did not have to worry that it was only Jews like me who were blind to the truth.

While I am grateful to have learned from Richard and Marietta what I was really looking at, I do not agree with Maud's judgment of the scene in their citation from her. I have no doubt that this is the Antichrist; I am not, however, convinced that his expression is "eveil." Did the Karpes make that spelling mistake because they were thinking *medieval* rather than *evil*, or because they were unconsciously acknowledging the "veil" many of us wear? The Antichrist may, according to theory, embody evil, but when you face Signorelli's version of him in Orvieto, he does not *look* evil. Rather, he appears deeply pensive, as if the devil is telling him something profoundly fascinating.

How right Maud is, though, that the crowd does not see him. Or sees neither the Antichrist nor the devil. The placement of Maud's descriptive phrase leaves her intention unclear. She may well have meant that it is only the devil who goes unobserved; on the other hand, she could have been saying that it is the Antichrist who is unseen. Or else she meant both of them. Regardless, when one considers the entire scene, part of what is utterly fascinating is the way that the dozens of characters in the foreground, busily negotiating or disputing this or that, appear totally unaware of a phenomenally interesting event taking place right in their midst. This act of having their eyes shut to the obvious would surely have fascinated Freud. "You are requested to close the eyes."

WERE THIS NOT ALL PAINTED WITH PANACHE, the depiction of this whispering of sins and of the mob's blindness to the heathens in their midst would not be nearly as effective as it is. We believe we are actually witnessing the event because the position of the figures has been articulated so surely, and the grouping of people in fantastic costumes has great verisimilitude. Moreover, our emotions are stirred by the colors, being in splendid harmony throughout the composition, with the blues and purples and golds scattered in carefully calculated proportion over the whole. The pulsating rhythm quickens our breathing. The artistic flair, whereby everyone and everything is infused by a gust of life-giving force, like a fire that has just burst into flames after a great blow from a bellows, makes the experience of seeing the fresco a confrontation after which one is no longer the same.

RICHARD AND MARIETTA DEEMED MAUD CRUTTWELL's further description of this large fresco vital to our understanding of Freud's eventual memory failure. Even if I disagree with Maud's evaluation of the expression on the Antichrist's face, I think they did well in their choice of source, for she is a superb iconographer. Maud spells out the significance of what is going on all around these two central figures. She cites the reasons for the hideous scenes of beheadings, the men stepping on other men's heads (and, in one instance, directly on a supine man's balls), the dead people on horses' backs, and the profusion of soldiers in combat. Maud explains that these scenes represent, among other things, "the false teachings and miracles of Anti-Christ and . . . the fall of the false prophet and the destruction of his followers." That information, which would elude the ordinary viewer, is essential to our understanding the anxiety the Karpes will amplify as a major cause of Freud's parapraxis.

Maud also identifies the troop of men, all hooded and dressed from head to toe in black, in the distant background. And she gives meaning to the impressive structure with its many ionic columns in front of which these Ku Klux Klan–style characters do their hideous dance. Viewers like me, while riveted to this tour de force of painting—whereby contrasting forms and colors, and heighted light effects on circular forms, bring the visual intensity to a fever pitch—and who delight in the classical architectural folly with all those columns and wings, would not have a clue as to what it is without Maud or some other savant's guidance. Fortunately, the Karpes quote her explaining that this is the Antichrist's "temple with armed men going in and out of its open portico.'" Here, too, Richard and Marietta are laying the groundwork for their explanation of Freud's trauma.

The design of the vast temple to the Antichrist has something wrong and crazy about it that encapsulates the spirit of all these horrors. The events that precede the end of life are terrifying in a way that could only have exacerbated Freud's anguish following the intensified recognition of mortality that inevitably came with the death of his father. This was especially true because, as the Karpes will explain, the Antichrist could be regarded as emblematic of Jewish belief, with his miserable followers being Freud's coreligionists.

What Maud Cruttwell, and the Karpes fail to mention, however, is that there are few women in the scene. Moreover, most of the cast of characters sport very tight pants and substantial codpieces. The Antichrist himself is oddly androgynous in an image where he has his hand out to take a bribe. Here the heathen has flowing blond tresses and wears a smart red tunic with a gold-lined blue wrap around it—he holds it up like a skirt, the way a lady might pull up her skirt to avoid tripping on it—although his large hands and feet and flat chest are male. The man from whom he is taking bribes is the quintessential olive-skinned, hooked nose Jew, who carries his money in a sack with two Stars of David embroidered on it. The knuckles of the Antichrist's left hand are practically touching one of the most globular of all of Signorelli's male butts. The price for all of these weaknesses is exemplified in the torture shown in the image on the right below [Plate 18.]

 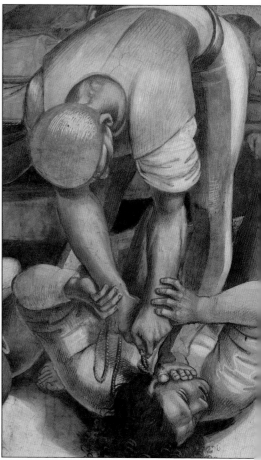

Plate 18. Detail of *Deeds of the Antichrist*

CHAPTER 12

MAUD CRUTTWELL

IT HAPPENS MORE AND MORE AS ONE GETS OLDER that one is desperate to pose a question to someone no longer alive. What I want to ask the Karpes at the moment is what they knew about Maud Cruttwell.

Did they just pick up her book on Luca Signorelli in the West Hartford Public Library, find out what they wanted to know, and then return the volume to that nightmarish, dust-smelling place on the town's main street? Or did Richard and Marietta devote months to studying the entire oeuvre of Maud Cruttwell? Now that, because of the Karpes, I have investigated this art historian, previously unknown to me, I think she is worthy of a great biography; I would like to know if the Karpes turned to her as their source because they were familiar with her in general, or because her book was all they could find.

I am fascinated, of course, that Richard and Marietta, who seem so meticulous, got the spelling of both the first and the last name of Maud Cruttwell wrong, making her Maude Crutwell in all of their many references to her. This error makes me think that, alas, they knew nothing about her. They probably just got the book in the dreaded library staffed by white-haired biddies and pale, shoulderless young men, diligently made some notes, and returned the volume before the two-week lending period was over. If the book had been in their house while they were actually writing their paper, Cruttwell's name would have been in front of them, and they would not have added an *e* to her first name and removed the second *t* from her family name.

In any case, the name Maud Cruttwell was an invention. She was really Alice Wilson—of which, one assumes, she could not stand the plainness. In 1894, Cruttwell, who was a young English art historian and had met Bernard Berenson and his future wife, Mary Costelloe, in England, became their housekeeper. Initially, she lived with them in the apartment Berenson was then renting in San Domenico, near Fiesole, on the outskirts of Florence—before they moved to the legendary I Tatti.

Cruttwell was openly lesbian. It is said, inexplicably, that she was personally responsible for Mary Berenson, who was overweight to begin with, becoming even fatter. No source gives the reason for this, although I assume the implication is that Mary—known as an advocate of free love, with Bertrand Russell among the men with whom she had had affairs, and Oscar Wilde a close friend—might have felt a need to develop a physical barrier against another object of her desires. Cruttwell left the Berenson household in 1899, when she was asked by the London publisher George Bell to write her volume on Luca Signorelli for their Great Masters series. She was, nonetheless, a witness at Bernard and Mary's wedding the following year, after the Quaker Mary's husband had died, and she was free to marry the Lithuanian Jew. (Berenson's name at birth had been Valvrojenski. Born beyond the Pale, he grew up in Boston, where he later did his best to de-Jewify himself. *De-Jewification* is my own term, derived from my adolescence, when I became a keen observer and sometimes practitioner of the process.)

The book Cruttwell wrote at age thirty-nine about Signorelli was such a success that she was commissioned to write numerous others afterward. These include well-regarded texts on Mantegna, Pollaiuolo, the della Robbias, and Madame de Maintenon. The last, one of her best-known books, was published a few years before she died in Paris, at age seventy-nine.

The Karpes probably turned to her book because it was the only monograph they could find on Signorelli. They must have been pleased to discover a text that was written only a couple of years after Freud's visit to Orvieto. That coincidence of dates means it would have reflected the theories about the frescoes prevailing at that time. But did the Karpes realize not only that their key source was far above the norm for the spirited way in which she viewed art, no doubt impacted by her connection with the Berensons, but that her choice of Signorelli, and the way she viewed his work, may have been a by-product of her own sexuality?

The information that Cruttwell supplied for the Karpes became the basis of their diagnosis of what the issues were for Freud in these paintings. Having taken us to the idea of the importance of the *sig,* and to the way that Freud could remember the imagery but not the name—yet once he knew the name could not retain his vision of the imagery—and going from there to the conclusion that Freud's unconscious identification with Signorelli will lead us to understand the nature of the underlying issues that he felt a need to repress, they next turn to focus on the meaning of the Antichrist for the Italian painter.

The Karpes now provide the fascinating information that the Pope at the time Signorelli painted the frescoes, "Alexander VI, the infamous Roderigo Borgia . . . could be considered the most perfect model for Anti-Christ. He had cast aside all show of decorum, living a secular and immoral life, indulging in indecent orgies." It was, they explain, Pope Alexander VI who brought on the "fanatical" opposition of the renowned monk Girolamo Savonarola. Eventually, the Pope excommunicated Savonarola; then, in 1498, he had the monk hung on a cross and burned to death. The papal crime wave did not stop there. Savonarola's followers were soon executed in droves. The Catholic hierarchy had different rules back then, and the Pope had a son, Cesare Borgia.

Caesare's father appointed him as "Protector of Orvieto," and this man in whose cathedral Signorelli was painting his frescoes was considered the likely suspect "of many unsolved murders whose perpetrators were never found. Countless victims of these atrocities were pulled out of the River Tiber. Signorelli might well have had the Borgia clan in mind when he painted the fresco of Anti-Christ. Freud, in his letter to Fliess, calls the frescoes 'powerful.' Their power lies mainly in an increase in anxiety in the viewer."

What, exactly, are Richard and Marietta saying here? After all, they did not, it seems, see the frescoes. Nor did they consider the way, for example, that Freud succumbed to Raphael's *Sistine Madonna* in Dresden—he suggested in a letter to his fiancée, Martha, that the young woman in the painting was so sexy and earthy that it made him long to be with her, and that for this reason the painting failed in its attempted religiosity. Freud went so far, with the Raphael, as to liken the Madonna to a "nursemaid," an interesting choice, since it is no secret that his nursemaid was a more central figure in his early life than was his mother. In these reactions to the Raphael, Freud demonstrated his highly personal reactions to paintings. I maintain that when he wrote to Fliess that Signorelli's work was "powerful," Freud may have been referring less to the anxiety the Karpes describe, which would have required a knowledge of Luca Signorelli's attitude toward the Borgias as well as of the representational meaning of the Antichrist, than to more immediate issues of his own. Receptive as Freud was to the intrinsic qualities of the particular artwork in front of him, when he was surrounded by the Signorellis, he would have felt a deep response to their forceful forms and colors, a keen awareness of the impact of looking at muscular naked men thrust against one another in various modes of action, and a wish to reevaluate, in his own way, the concept of the Last Judgment. His anxiety would have been linked less to the history of the Borgias than to his own private fears.

While the Last Judgment is a central tenet of Catholicism, it was contrary to the teachings of the Judaism with which Freud had been raised. But viewed through the lens of psychoanalysis, the underlying concepts of which were already in Freud's mind when he was in Orvieto, the Last Judgment has great relevance. Freud was fascinated by the way desire plays out in the human psyche—even if he paid relatively little attention to the Christian notion of God's determining either the punishment or rewards people merit for the way in which they responded to those desires in their actual behavior. For Freud, the great judge was the self. Torture took the form of self-imposed guilt—not of the hammerholds and neck snapping that Luca Signorelli depicts as the fate of people destined for hell. But whatever the form of the consequences, there is a price to pay for many types of lust and other incarnations of what is conceived of as "sin."

CHAPTER 13

"A GODLESS JEW"

THE KARPES INVEST CONSIDERABLE MEANING in what Signorelli's depiction of the end of the world signified to Freud as a Jew. They point out that the "Anti-Christ was supposed to have his center in Jerusalem and be mainly accepted by Jews," and they posit that "Freud, though never a religious Jew, was very much aware of his Jewish origin and the accusation against Jews as Anti-Christ might well have been on his mind." Anti-Semitism was rampant in 1897, when Freud saw the Signorellis, as it had been when this scene was painted in 1500 and the Spanish Inquisition was at its peak. As a Viennese, Freud was feeling particularly vulnerable, since, Richard and Marietta tell us, Karl Lueger, a "notorious anti-Semite," had just been elected the city's mayor for the third time. The Karpes see a lot in Freud's reactions stemming from that detail. Lueger, "a forerunner of Hitler, based his whole political philosophy on the persecution of the Jews." The Austrian emperor had refused to confirm his two previous elections, in 1895 and 1896, but had done so this third time, and on April 20, 1897, Lueger assumed his position. The effects were already apparent. Lueger was so determined "to eliminate 'destructive' Jewish influences" from the University of Vienna that he had put a halt to the appointment of Jewish scientists on its faculty; this was the reason Freud would never become a full professor there. The implication is that all these issues swirled in Freud's head as he stood looking at that Antichrist in the Cappella Nova, knowing that this character complying with the devil was considered a prototypical Jew.

This is all the more meaningful in light of what the Karpes have already told us: that Freud, in this period following his father's death, was particularly conscious of his father's timidity in the face of anti-Semitism. His residual shame and anger plagued him. Facing Signorelli's horrific depiction of the havoc wrought by the personification of Jewish beliefs in opposition to the new beatific realm offered by Christianity and evident in the lunette of *The Elect,* he felt, at the very least, out of place and intensely uncomfortable. He struggled simultaneously with his disappointment in his father's inability to be victorious over the man who attacked him as a Jew and with his own ambivalence about being Jewish. The combination was hard to bear.

In Signorelli's world, to be Jewish was to side with the devil and to be destined for hell. Yet that milieu so unsympathetic to Judaism was fertile for the nurturing of masterful art. It provided rich opportunities, such as the possibility of painting a chapel in this utterly exquisite Gothic church on a hilltop. Did Freud, who responded viscerally to such beauty, suffer not only from his feeling of displacement but also for a longing to be at home in the desirable, enviable paradise of the cathedral itself and of the frescoes that present the rewards of being a good Christian just as they illustrate the price for not being one?

WAS THIS NOT ALSO, IN A DIFFERENT WAY, the burning issue of the existence of any number of people in my childhood? The paradise in which they wanted entry had nothing to do, of course, with the Italian Renaissance or fin de siècle Vienna. But it was another milieu from which Jews were often ostracized, or at best, tolerated as outsiders.

I am referring to the America of J. P. Marquand and F. Scott Fitzgerald, of Colonial houses with Chippendale furniture and eagle finials on lamps where the Declaration of Independence decorated the shades. This was a milieu where the Yale-Harvard football game was the event of the season. In my own childhood, that sports spectacle, with its tailgate parties in the parking lot, was the equivalent, even for those who had not gone to either university, of what a ball hosted by the Habsburgs was to the Viennese. Once I reached a certain age, the feeling I had of being from a different planet and always slightly under threat was just another version of what Jews have experienced in so many places at so many times. A fair number of Jews whom I knew wanted to fit in comfortably with the wooden station wagon–driving majority. I did not care, but I certainly was aware of the cultural differences.

It had not been a big deal—this Jewish or not-Jewish issue—when I was little, in spite of my father's army incident. But when I was ten, and a girl I am renaming Augusta Parkinson and I "went steady"—a privilege I earned by helping her with her spelling homework—she told me one day that her mother had instructed her not to tell her father that we were an item, "as there is something about Nicky Weber he wouldn't like." She had no idea what it was. Nor did I.

After I got home from school that afternoon, I asked my mother if she could imagine what the "something" might be. She explained that it was the same reason for which Gussie and so many of my other friends went to Miss Mary Alice for dancing lessons at the Hartford Club, while I went to Mr. and Mrs. John Hammond Daly, at the Town and County Club. The uniforms and dancing techniques were the same at both institutions, but the constituencies were not. It was in the company of Catholics as well as fellow Jews that I sweated away in my blazer and flannels and white gloves as I learned how to fox-trot and waltz.

The "mackerel snappers" and "chosen ones"—my best friend Ricky, a Protestant of Swedish Scottish ancestry, told me his older brothers' nicknames for Catholic and Jews—were not deprived of privilege, but in the segregated social and country clubs and other local institutions, the Protestants bastions had an allure the others did not. I think what I most envied was their shabbiness. The frayed collars of Ricky's oxford-cloth shirts, and the holes in the Lacostes he had as hand-me-downs from those very sporty and cool brothers, conferred class on them. I wanted overcooked Protestant roast chicken and canned vegetables instead of my mother's Julia Child recipes, my friend Tuggy Howe's mother's white cake from a Duncan Hines mix instead of the baba au rhum I was supposed to love. And the smell of Ivory soap combined with wood smoke in houses like Chip Dewing's appealed to me. (These names are real; I have changed only that of the girl with the father who would have disapproved of my background when she and I were both ten years old.)

For a brief period at Columbia College, I masqueraded as a Gentile. The New York–style Jewishness of some of my fellow students was more than I could bear, and my taste in girls was more for blond debutantes in madras shirtwaist dresses and circle pins than either dolled-up Jewesses or bushy-haired bohemians in Indian sacks and rawhide sandals. That preference was so strong that one summer I tortured my parents by working for Nelson Rockefeller rather than Eugene McCarthy. I tried to avoid the *J* word. (I was fascinated to learn, years later, that this was at one time also the practice of *The New Yorker* magazine.)

My sophomore year, when I studied Jan van Eyck's and Rogier van der Weyden's work, I became convinced that there was no way those miraculous Annunciations could have been painted unless Jesus' conception had really occurred as they showed it. I was so moved by that faith that I felt impelled to worship my new God. One Sunday morning, when I was kneeling devoutly at Saint Thomas, an Episcopal church, I saw some friends of my parents, from Wilmington, Delaware, down the pew. The man owned a printing company, as did my father, and they met every year at a printing presidents' convention at a luxury resort, which was where I had been introduced to them. They invited me for lunch, and never asked why I was in church; I still admire their discretion.

I may never know if I believed in the divinity of Jesus during my few weeks of intense religiosity because of what I would call "pure" reasons, or if I was impelled to develop my faith by a longing to fit in with Protestant America. I cannot deny that the church I chose to go to, five Sundays running, was one of the most fashionable, and aesthetically appealing, Episcopal houses of worship in New York. I don't imagine I would have been as religious in less attractive circumstances. I am loath to admit all this, but I think Freud had some of the same hang-ups, which is why I am reconsidering my own.

Today it seems laughable. I well remember my mother's delight when, fifteen years after Mrs. Parkinson alerted her daughter about my "problem," Gussie and her cousin, Pooh Bradley (only her last name is a pseudonym), both students at Sweet Briar College, came back to West Hartford from a semester in Florence, both of them having become engaged to Italian men who spoke no English and sold postcards in front of the Uffizi. Clearly "that bastard Thorston Parkinson would have preferred Nicky Weber," Mother said, laughing, after telling me that Blissie Bradley, Pooh's mother, had complained that her new son-in-law was terribly "greasy," which she pronounced as *greezie,* with the softest of *z*'s.

But, funny or not, this factor of background mattered, in infinite ways, and was linked with ideas of who one was, and of personal power, as it was for Freud. I find it plausible that what forced him to forget the name Signorelli, which the Karpes felt had elements of forgetting his own name, Sigmund, was because, as he looked at those frescoes, he did not want to be himself, which meant being Jewish. He didn't want to stand up and confront the anti-Semites; he wanted what was easier, which is not to have been Jewish.

Or am I saying this only because it's how I imagine myself feeling had I been he? With the conflict, which I believe Freud had as well, that I was also very proud to be Jewish, and consider it a rich heritage.

I realized in the course of working on this text that I had repressed two other incidents when I stood silent while people made anti-Semitic remarks. I gnash my teeth writing this, because I know that one of the reasons I remained mute on the occasions in question was that I was pleased not to have been recognized as a Jew who would have been offended.

When I was a tennis camp counselor, I was invited on a day off to a wonderful house on a lake in southern New Hampshire. A female counselor in training, a couple of years younger than I, Trish Troupe, asked me there.

That summer, I was driving a white Ford Mustang convertible. (I had bought it in June, knowing I would need to sell it in September, since I was at college in New York and could not afford to keep a car.) Life was bliss. We headed to Trish's house with the top down on a perfect summer day in the wonderful dry air of New Hampshire. This pleasant girl next to me on the red leather upholstery of the Mustang, the freedom of a day off, the curving mountain road—everything was paradise. The Troupes' house was a Shingle Style summer "cottage"—in fact a mansion—in a colony of about a dozen similar structures, with a large screen porch overlooking the crystal clear Lake Winnipesaukee, a vast body of water framed for the most part by pine trees.

Trish's mother greeted her daughter warmly and was extremely gracious to me as we drank weak coffee and ate the local coffee shop's soggy Danish pastry as if we were having a feast, which is what it felt like compared to camp cooking. We talked about what we would do during the day, and I allowed that in spite of spending every day teaching tennis, I would love to play, since I had spotted the wonderful court next to their house. Yes? Of course I would also like to swim and fish—whatever other people wanted to do.

Trish was about to enter her senior year in high school, and so the subject of colleges was very much on her and her mother's minds. Mrs. Troupe asked where I went and looked very approving when I replied "Columbia." "You know," she said agreeably, "I hear great things about Barnard from some people, but others say it is mainly filled with Jews these days."

I let it go. But when I played tennis against a friends of theirs, purportedly a first-rate tennis player, a preppy Protestant named Ed—who could not have been nicer—I played as if my life depended on it. I won the first set, after which he challenged me to another, when he got even fewer games, and I continued to vanquish him for three more sets, until he agreed to quit. Trish and her mother watched some of the games, but no one had any idea what the key to my beating a better player was. I did what I often did to pump up my tennis. Whenever I served or rushed the net, I would tell myself I was fleeing Auschwitz and could only avoid the gas chambers if I won the point. Hitting forehands was like scaling the barbed wire, and placing backhands at a sharp angle across the court was like getting past a prison guard.

IN 1984, MY WIFE, KATHARINE, AND I WENT TO SEE the large Balthus exhibition at the Met. This was a big deal for us; we did not often get away together from our small children, and we both were fascinated by Balthus's work.

As we approached the galleries with some of the remarkable, utterly peaceful landscape paintings Balthus made in 1943 and 1944, as World War II raged, we saw Bob and Elodie Osborn. I had met them on various occasions. Robert Osborn was an illustrator/cartoonist of impeccable liberal credentials, and Elodie used to organize traveling exhibitions for the Museum of Modern Art. I had borrowed work by Alexander Calder from them for an exhibition I had organized in Litchfield, Connecticut, near where they lived, and had more than once enjoyed discussing Josef Albers with Bob, and Alfred Barr with Elodie. We had a world of interests in common.

They were a distinguished-looking couple—he very tall, with white hair; she rather diminutive, with gray hair. They were probably in their late sixties at the time.

They asked me how Anni Albers was, and somehow Bob, who had a bellowing voice, took the subject from Albers at Yale (he had been the main speaker at Josef's memorial service) to a recent communication he had had from Harvard. He said that it came from the Graduate School of Design at the Carpenter Center, and he had hoped it was about the direction they were taking educationally. "But what was it about?" Bob asked so loudly that passersby turned.

He answered his own question. "*Money,* naturally. The fellow who wrote me—an accountant, Jewish, of course—didn't care about what I thought, but only about how much I might give."

I let it go. So did Katharine.

I now know that the paintings we were admiring just before that dreadful moment were painted when Balthus avoided the issue of being half-Jewish in Paris in 1942 by moving to Switzerland. His brother, Pierre Klossowski, was, at the same time, caring for their mother in the free zone, as she was totally Jewish and therefore at risk of being deported from occupied Paris. I would spend years dealing with Balthus's obsessive need to lie about being half-Jewish, and the myths he spun so that no one would know. He had an unequaled compulsion to deny his religion. This grandson of the cantor of the main synagogue in Breslau tried to convince me on one day that his mother was a Huguenot from Alsace, on the next a Catholic from the Midi, as well as a Romanoff, a Poniatowski, and a direct descendant of Lord Byron. At least when he made anti-Semitic remarks in front of me, I had had the balls to say I was Jewish.

Of course you may think the "how to be Jewish question" is less important than I have chalked it up to be. But for Freud, at least in the eyes of the Karpes and many other people, it was the crux of the matter. The Karpes attached such significance to Signorelli's treatment of the Antichrist, as explicated by Maud Cruttwell, because they thought that concerns in a predominantly Christian, and often anti-Semitic, world were exacerbated by his recognition in the frescoes of the Antichrist's sinfulness, and of the fate of those who sinned by not adhering to New Testament teachings. He had as much discomfort about being Jewish, and deplored Jewish traditions to such an extent, that this subject matter threw him for a loop.

In 1918, Freud would write a letter to Oskar Pfister, a Swiss Protestant minister who was also a lay psychoanalyst with a particular interest in the overlaps between theology and psychology, in which he asked, "Why did none of the devout create psychoanalysis? Why did one have to wait for a completely godless Jew?"

He accepted that the term *Jew* applied to him. Neither his upbringing nor his personal beliefs, however, caused him to practice Judaism. When Jacob Freud married his third wife, Amalia Nathansohn, the woman who would be Sigmund's mother, the wedding was in a Reform synagogue, but religion played little role in their lives afterward. Sigismundo Schlomo was circumcised but not bar mitzvahed, and went to no form of religious school.

Jacob did, however, read the Bible in Hebrew, which Sigmund Freud would always refer to as "the holy language" or "the sacred language," and the family celebrated Passover. They practiced no other rituals, though, and once he was a grown man, he did not merely reject Jewish rites; he actively disdained them. When Freud married Martha Bernays, the granddaughter of Isaac Bernays, chief rabbi of Hamburg, in 1886, he banned the traditions that she would have liked to maintain. This was just after Freud had opened his own medical practice, specializing in neurology, and he refused to be overruled about an issue that contradicted what he considered the truth of science.

In 1938, shortly after the Freud family had fled Vienna following the Anschluss, a young philosopher based in Oxford came to call on them. "Martha Freud joined them and said to the visitor, 'You must know that on Friday evenings good Jewish women light candles for the approach of the Sabbath. But this monster—*Unmensch*—will not allow this, because he says that religion *is* a superstition.' Freud gravely nodded and agreed: 'Yes,' he said, 'it is a superstition.'" (I cannot help wondering if the source of this story, whom Peter Gay interviewed in 1984 but leaves unnamed, was Isaiah Berlin.)

Martin Freud would recall, however, that when he was growing up, while his father consciously eschewed anything having to do with Jewish religious rites that might be associated with superstition, Christian ones were perfectly fine with him. Sigmund Freud would write, "I adhere to the Jewish religion as little as to any other," and in *Totem and Taboo* he would declare that he was "wholly estranged from the religion of his father, as from every other," but, in contradiction to that insistence, he had his family celebrate Christmas and Easter. They had a Christmas tree with candles, and the children all painted Easter eggs. On the other hand, the children never once, on any occasion whatsoever, went into a synagogue, any more than they acknowledged the Jewish New Year, the Day of Atonement, or any other Jewish holiday.

Have I gone even further than the Karpes in assuming that the frescoes and Signorelli's name were directly connected with the issues of assimilation because it pertained to Freud, or more because I have spent a lifetime observing people for whom this was true?

Susie, I knew, furnished her house with Queen Anne furniture and upholstered chairs in flowered chintz not necessarily because that was her aesthetic choice, but because it was so Protestant. (This was before the era when Ralph Lauren made a fortune selling Jews products to make them feel like denizens of the social milieu of people who play polo, a sport associated above all with snooty English aristocrats: rarified, elitist, and restricted almost exclusively to white Protestants.) My wife's grandfather, James Warburg, was known to cut his Sunday roast beef paper-thin and to let everyone leave the table hungry because this was so distinctly non-Jewish: the same reasons for which he preferred thin madras bow ties to anything more fashionable. When he was, at the start of the twentieth century, at Middlesex, one of the few New England boarding schools that allowed Jews in, someone slipped an *E* between the *J* and the *W* of his initials when they were posted on a list that many people saw; from then on he was always JPW, using his middle name of Paul, and the race was on. He neglected to tell his children that they were Jewish, and my mother-in-law often recalled her experience of being ten years old, in the early 1930s, at the New York private girls school Brearley, and having one of her classmates, Florence Straus, tell her that they were the only two Jews in the class. She had no idea what Florence was talking about, and bemoaned the idea of anything they had in common, since she considered Florence homely and awkward. She rushed home and asked for an explanation. Her mother, whose maiden name was Katharine Faulkner Swift, explained the facts easily enough, but JPW was less comfortable with the matter. His second of three Episcopalian wives, from a patrician Yankee family and in the *Social Register,* told Katharine and me that he was so anti-Semitic that when she invited Jewish guests to dinner parties they gave, he was furious at her. Nonetheless, she got his third daughter, Kay (originally Kathleen), into her alma mater, Miss Porter's. Poor Kay was one of two freshman given a single room—she told Katharine and me that the other one so assigned was a pigmy—which, in fact, was a converted broom closet; when she asked the dorm parent why, she, like her sister, had the experience of learning for the first time that she was Jewish, unknown to her until that moment.

Part of the fascination for me of Susie was that she had assimilated totally, yet she didn't pretend. Her daughter and one other girl were the first Jewish debutantes ever to come out at a fashionable cotillion in Greenwich—not because they hid their background, as did the Greens, who had been the Greenbergs, and Bill Learsy, who had reversed the letters of his name from Israel, but because they were rich and athletic and popular, and so generous to the right charities, that they gained entry undisguised. She had a Christmas wreath and always got a bright red dress for the holidays—a new one every year—but she did not pretend.

How remarkable that it was to Richard and Marietta to whom Susie made a beeline in public. But she could afford to be in the presence of conspicuously Jewish refugees with no risk whatsoever that anyone could think they and she were cut from the same cloth. With what was a burning issue for many of us, she had emerged victorious, and with the comforting knowledge that, like the Rothschilds, she had achieved noble status without lying.

WAS SIGNORELLI'S TERRIFYING DEPICTION OF WHAT HAPPENS when you don't believe in Jesus one of the things that pushed Freud to adopt Christian traditions once he had children?

Leave it to my darling daughter Charlotte to have come up with the following story told by Lou Andreas-Salomé (to whom I practically feel related by association, since she was Rilke's lover, as was Balthus's mother).

> Listening to Anna talking about her father; picking mushrooms when they were children. When they went collecting mushrooms he always told them to go into the wood quietly and he still does this; there must be no chattering and they must roll up the bags they have brought

under their arms, so that the mushrooms shall not notice; when their father found one he would cover it quickly with his hat, as though it were a butterfly. The little children— and now his grandchildren—used to believe what he said, while the bigger ones smiled at his credulity; even Anna did this, when he told her to put fresh flowers every day at the shrine of the Virgin which was near the wood, so that it might help them in their search.

As Paul Vitz, who has written brilliantly on Freud's attraction to Christianity, points out: "This was, after all, a family in which Freud forbid even the lighting of candles to mark the Jewish Sabbath, to his wife's annoyance, because Freud said he was opposed to all religious superstition!"

MARTHA FREUD WOULD NOT HAVE BEEN SURPRISED that shrines to the Virgin impressed her husband in spite of his alleged antipathy to the trappings of what he called "superstition." In the fall of 1885, only a year before they married, he wrote her a letter saying, "You are right, my darling, in saying that I have even more to tell you than before, and usually there is something I even forget to tell you, for instance my visit to Notre Dame de Paris on Sunday. My first impression on entering was a sensation I have never had before: This is a Church. . . . I have never seen anything so movingly serious and somber, quite unadorned and very narrow."

Fifteen years later, recalling the brief time he lived in France, Freud wrote "The platform of Notre Dame was my favorite resort in Paris; every free afternoon I used to clamber about there on the towers of the church between the monsters and the devils." Of course this was the aspect of the sculptural work that attracted him—more than all the images of Christ's life and of the Evangelists that also adorn the cathedral. Demons, as they were conceived and depicted in Christian eyes, attracted Freud like magnets.

Some letters Freud wrote as a teenager, and that were unknown to everyone except for the recipient until 1969, make clear that his attitudes toward Sabbath candles and other traditions were not simply the by-product of his philosophical beliefs. He had his prejudices.

When Freud was sixteen years old, he and two friends went to spend their summer holiday in Freiberg, the town in Moravia where he had been born in 1856 but which his family left when Sigmund was three and Jacob moved to Vienna for his work. (Moravia is today in the Czech Republic; in the nineteenth century, it was part of the Austro-Hungarian Empire ruled by the Habsburgs.) The teenagers stayed with family friends of the Freuds, the Flusses, who had three sons and two daughters. That summer, Sigmund struck up a relationship with one of the daughters. He later thought of it as the first time he was enchanted by a girl, even if it fell far short of an actual romance. His son Ernst Freud, in 1969, quoted from an unpublished letter from Sigmund to Martha, written in 1883, when she was his fiancée, in which he says that one of the Fluss sisters, Gisela, "was my first love when I was but 16 years old . . . You can have a good laugh at me . . . because I never spoke a meaningful, much less an amiable word to the child. Looking back, I would say that seeing my old home-town again had made me feel sentimental."

Even if Sigmund communicated little with Gisela, following that summer holiday, he remained close with one of her brothers, Emil. To Emil, he wrote some letters in which he revealed his innermost self.

Until 1969, nearly a hundred years after he sent these missives, which are among the very few testimonies to what the teenage Freud was like, they were lost. They had had a history full of twists and turns. In the 1930s, Dorothy Burlingham had taken the letters to Vienna—we assume she had obtained them from a descendant of the Fluss family—and given them to her friend Anna Freud. After the Nazis occupied Vienna, Marie Bonaparte protected these precious documents by taking them to Paris; she subsequently gave them back to Anna once the Freud family had found refuge in London in 1938. But while Ernest Jones quotes one of these letters, which was published in 1941, in his Freud biography, Jones says that unfortunately it was the only one that remained.

The letter Jones cites, was, of the seven letters that we now know, the most readable. The other letters were faded and in handwriting that is barely legible. Yet Jones had them in his possession. In 1969, Masud Khan, who was then the archivist and librarian at the London Institute of Psychoanalysis, found an envelope with all these letters among the papers Jones had been given by the Freud family and which Jones subsequently left to the institute upon his death. We know all this from a narrative Ernst Freud wrote a few months after Khan found the letters and they were published in their entirely in the *International Journal of Psychoanalysis*.

The very first of these letters, written when Sigmund Freud was sixteen—the same impressionable age I was when I gaped at Susie and the Karpes behind my parents' house—reveals how he felt, at that time of life when one is so opinionated and uninclined to self-censorship, about being Jewish. On September 18, 1872, Freud, after addressing Emil Fluss as "Dear new Friend," reports on his trip from Freiberg back to Vienna. He allows that the memories don't come easily, even though he had taken the journey by train only the day before. It seems that the arrival back in his parents' house had the effect of forcing them from his mind: "I have lost almost all recollection of past events, submit to everything without protest as if dazed—questions, caresses, congratulations—and don't open my mouth. I'll have a hard time finding my memories of yesterday."

I think that the real reason it was such a struggle to conjure his memories was not so much the excitement of his reunion with his family as the same factor that made it impossible to come up with Signorelli's name: the nature of his thoughts. At age sixteen, Freud recognized his discomfort and possible embarrassment over them, prefacing his commentary to his new friend, "I shall confess the unvarnished truth to you—but to you alone, and I trust that no one will be allowed to see what was not meant for him to see. But should this happen nevertheless and you are unable to prevent it, then please do not tell me about it or that would be the end of the truth and all you would hear would be smooth-tongued platitudes that won't tell you anything."

From there, the sixteen-year-old proceeds to describe the train trip of the previous day. He had been seated next to a young woman whose face was "terribly disfigured by boils." Although the sight upset him greatly, he did not want to hurt her feelings by conspicuously changing seats. "But my plight became more and more unbearable," he tells Fluss. "And when to top it all she started to speak and lifted her head-scarf repulsion won out over the forbearance I owed a suffering human being." He and his traveling companions left the train compartment and moved to another.

Young Sigmund Freud next informs Fluss that, following the change of seats, "This being my unlucky day, I ended up in the company of a most venerable old Jew and his correspondingly old wife with their melancholy languorous darling daughter and cheeky young 'hopeful' son. Their company was even more unpalatable."

Freud made an innocuous remark to the Jewish family of four. Their response evoked further disdain on his part, for the way they conformed to certain Jewish stereotypes made them even more insupportable than the woman with boils. He confides to Fluss:

Now this Jew talked in the same way as I had heard thousands of others talk before, even in Freiberg. His very face seemed familiar—he was typical. So was the boy, with whom he discussed religion. He was cut from the cloth from which fate makes swindlers when the time is ripe: cunning, mendacious, kept by his adoring relatives in the belief that he is a great talent, but unprincipled and without character. . . . I have enough of this lot. In the course of the conversation I heard that Madame Jewess and family hailed from Meseritsch [another town in Moravia, between Freiberg and Vienna]: the proper compost-heap for this sort of weed.

In 2010, Michel Onfray, a well-known French populist intellectual, wrote a book called *Le Crépuscule d'une idole,* which for a while inspired a flurry of reactions and was much on people's tongues. In it, Onfray, among other things, refers constantly to Freud's anti-Semitism. He sees it manifest above all in Freud's 1939 book, *Moses and Monotheism*—in which Freud tries to discern Jewish character traits. Onfray treats Freud's book as a form of patricide, with the psychoanalyst killing off the father of the Jews. He also points out that Freud, who wrote long attacks on communism, Marxism, and bolshevism, never openly opposed Hitler or national socialism. And Onfray quotes Freud on Jewish self-esteem, suggesting that Freud disparaged a certain sense of superiority as a general Jewish attitude, clearly unattractive. It's a one-sided argument, part of an anti-Freud propaganda campaign, but I have to admit that Onfray's point about Freud's never once writing about Hitler is provocative.

KNOWING HOW FREUD FELT WHEN HE WAS SIXTEEN YEARS OLD, and seeing the merits of Onfray's theories, much as I dislike his know-it-all tone and relentless need to put down Freud, I am increasingly convinced that the Karpes were right in thinking that Freud's discomfort about being Jewish must have been central to his being so traumatized by Signorelli's frescoes that he forgot the artist's name while seeing the paintings vividly in his mind and discussing them animatedly. If Freud recognized the Antichrist as a Jew, and considered the punishments being meted out to the heathens going to hell as the fate for all Jews, and feared such suffering for himself, yet also felt guilty for his own contempt of Jews, and experienced the horrific discomfort of what was in effect self-loathing yet did not feel like self-loathing, since he had deliberately distanced himself from his identification as a Jew even though the outside world still labeled him as one, and the frescoes summoned all these thoughts, no wonder something in his mind could not cope with it all.

Moreover, the way that Signorelli's frescoes depict the afterlife would have reminded him of his early awareness of a key aspect of what it meant to be Jewish in a non-Jewish milieu. Freiberg was about 3 percent Jewish, 3 percent Protestant, and the rest Catholic. There was no synagogue there, but there were plenty of Catholic churches, and Freud, for the first two years and eight months of his life, was unusual among the Jewish children in the town for having been taken, regularly, to such a church. It was his nursemaid, whom he later said was more important in his formative years than his mother, who took him there for Christian worship.

During his self-analysis when he was in his forties, Freud wrote Fliess that this nursemaid "was an ugly, elderly but clever woman who told me a great deal about God and hell, and gave me a high opinion of my own capacities." When Freud asked his mother what she recalled of the nurse, his mother replied, "'She was always taking you to church. When you came home you used to preach, and tell us all about how God [*der liebe Gott*] conducted His affairs.'" The nursemaid made the little Sigmund believe in heaven and hell. She also offered him the greatest consolation for the death of his brother

Julius, who was born when Sigmund was a year and five months old, and died shortly before Sigmund's second birthday; it was that Julius would be resurrected, for he had an innocent soul.

The beliefs one acquires in early childhood remain part of one's psyche, even if one later disavows them. Maybe there was some side of Freud that still held out the hope, as he stood there in the Cappella Nova, that Julius would somehow come back to life. What is even more likely is that Freud thought, or at least feared, that he, Sigmund, belonged among the damned.

AGAIN, THE WRITER/RESEARCHER HAS IMPOSED HIMSELF. Half a year after writing the last sentence of the paragraph above, I reread it. How on earth could I know this to have been the case with Freud? How could I have had the temerity to declare that he considered himself sinful as well as privileged? This is, of course, a simple case of projecting.

CHAPTER 14

AM I A MENSCH OR A WUSS?

WHEN I INITIALLY WROTE MOST OF THIS TEXT, I forgot— or repressed—a major event in my own life. This may be because I did not initially stand up to an anti-Semitic slur, and felt myself to be like Jacob Freud, and could not stand the memory. More likely, though, it is because in my own way I finally resolved the matter and put it to rest.

If the incapacity to confront anti-Semitism is, for me, as it was for Freud, a sort of character flaw—although in his case it was troubling because it signified his father's cowardice, while in mine the pain came from feeling like a wuss compared to my braver, more comfortable father—I had, at last, dealt with it in a way that enabled me to check it off of a sort of ridiculous mental list I carry in my head of problems to resolve, a form of personal housecleaning.

The incident occurred at Yale Graduate School in 1971. I was in the final term of a two-year program to get my master's in art history. It was, at best, a confusing moment in life. Having been at Columbia College when the university was shut down by my classmates in 1968, I, at the end of my first year in New Haven, again witnessed a battle between academia and what seemed to most of us to be issues that mattered more than our studies. This time the occasion was the trial of Bobby Seale and other Black Panthers, all accused of murder. I was, I am now sorry to say, like Freud with regard to Karl Lueger, the anti-Semitic mayor of Vienna: an observer rather than a participant in the fight against bigotry. More enlightened members of the Yale community demonstrated in front of the New Haven courthouse on May Day 1970 to assure that Seale and others, accused of murder, get a fair trial. Ricky, with whom I had remained a close friend for all those years and who had become a specialist in French communism and the student uprisings of 1968 in Paris, and was en route to a Ph.D. in political science at Yale, and I were, however, mainly focused on how funny it was when the architecture historian Vincent Scully could be seen running around with a gas mask on—we nicknamed him "Vincent of Arabia"—in case the police attacked the demonstrators. The face covering was theatrical and unnecessary. Nonetheless, in spite of my usual finding of something to mock, and my passivity, which embarrasses me in retrospect, I was torn apart inside by the clash of life-and-death issues with the minutiae of studies, which included a course entitled "Seurat and the Iconography of Entertainment."

That seminar required my researching, for six weeks in the depths of Sterling Library, an enormous neo-Gothic edifice, the use of gas lighting in public spaces in nineteenth-century France in order, supposedly, to understand the art of a great master who died at age thirty-one. That traditional art historical emphasis on information of dubious relevance struck me as ridiculous and wasteful. But at the same time I was overwhelmed by my love of Seurat's achievement, and the extraordinary form of beauty he had contributed to civilization in the course of his short lifetime. At age twenty-two, I imagined that, were I to die nine years later, I would leave behind a legacy of no value. I was creating nothing of meaning; nor was I fighting any battles or contributing to humankind as a whole.

The Vietnam War and the presidency of Richard Nixon only made matters worse. It was nearly impossible to focus on the art and architecture that usually filled me with joy, whether Seurat's drawings with their sublime range of grays achieved by his using the side of his pencil on laid paper, Greek white-ground vase painting—another of my passions, the lightest and most elegant form of ancient art, with a Picasso-like aliveness—or German Rococo architecture, which still amazes me for its Mozartian lightness and the ways the plaster appears to sculpt light. I would have liked to learn more about these subjects, but I was essentially out of kilter throughout the two years at Yale. The same professor I had derided, Vincent Scully, did, however, improve life immeasurably for many of us when he provided a spectacular vision of clarity at the end of the semester. Vince—we have since become friends, and he put us on a first-name basis thirty-five years after the time period in question when he phoned me with great warmth and enthusiasm for my biography of Le Corbusier—began a lecture in those troubled times by discussing the current political climate. With the Seale trial then taking place within walking distance of where he was giving his class, he juxtaposed the salient issues with our study of architecture. We were at that moment in 1970 focusing on Mies van der Rohe's exquisite designs for brick and concrete country houses, which still strike me, simply in their floor plans—neither project was ever realized—as being poetic in the same way as Mondrian's splendid "pier" paintings, the rhythm of right angles and perfectly calibrated horizontal and vertical lines infused by air. Vince told the hundreds of students packed into the auditorium of the Yale Law School, the only lecture hall big enough to accommodate his very popular course, that the previous evening he had been listening to an early Beethoven string quartet while wondering if that was not an indulgence while the world seemed to be burning. Then, he explained, he realized that one thing did not rule out the other, that human beings always need art and beauty. He added that this was true in fraught moments even more than in peaceful ones. In his charismatic way, this professor who Jackie Onassis once told me was "one of the most attractive men" she had ever seen, concluding his gripping commentary with an ecstatic look on his face and calling out, in a voice like King Lear's at the end of Shakespeare's play, "Everyone needs everything!"

I have never forgotten the glow with which he stated that magnificent utterance, which remains a guidepost to me. It was what enabled me to continue at Yale for a second year, even while I was at odds with a mentality whereby people became excited over the footnotes to knowledge and appeared to be blind to what I considered the vital issues of life.

So in the final stages of my pursuit of my M.A., I participated in a seminar devoted to connoisseurship with regard to American decorative art of the seventeenth through nineteenth centuries. There were only three of us, all graduate students, in this class that met once a week for a two-hour session with one of Yale's most esteemed professors, Charles Montgomery. Mr. Montgomery (it is a Yale thing not to address faculty as "Professor," which we did at Columbia, or "Dr.," even if they have their Ph.D.s) had been for many years the private curator, and then the director, at Winterthur, a spectacular and enormous home, now a museum, in Wilmington, Delaware. Winterthur houses the collection of Henry du Pont, who had the means as well as the eye to amass an unparalleled holding of fine American furniture created by some of its greatest makers. To have the opportunity to study in such intimate conditions with the distinguished authority who had worked for Henry du Pont and who was now head of the Garvan Collection at the Yale Art Gallery—another exceptional repository of American antiques—was a sort of Rolls-Royce of educational experiences. Once I gained admission to the tiny seminar, I believed it would be the crowning glory in the program, for which I was supported by a full fellowship awarded by Yale.

For some two months, I enjoyed learning about veneers and the proportions of finials. I took great pleasure in writing a paper about Queen Anne tea tables—real ones, hand-carved in Massachusetts in the eighteenth century, not the overpolished knockoffs I associated with Jews of recent wealth trying to give the look of "old money." At their best, these tables are sublimely graceful and confer a dignity and warm elegance to everyday living. Their legs, which resemble the necks of swans, have the quality of social encounters where the acts of pouring and receiving cups of tea harmonize with patient conversational giving and taking.

There was something slightly ridiculous to me about Charles Montgomery, though. A tall and unctuous man, he seemed to live for waxed finishes on mahogany and the joy of holding ornate silver soup ladles, with no apparent interest in anything else in life. I did not like him. Yet I respected his expertise in determining authenticity and recognizing the nuances of quality, and I was determined to get along with him, in part for my own future success.

Then, at about the tenth meeting of the seminar, Charles Montgomery started to talk about Chinese Export porcelain of the type that became very popular in the United States during the nineteenth century. He may well specified Rose Medallion ware, but I was so startled by what he then said that the precise details of the china escaped me. He explained, with his slight southern drawl, in slow cadences, his voice full of pleasure, "One day, when I was working for Mr. du Pont, he had some people coming from New York for lunch. They were *Jewish* collectors"—the renowned professor emphasized the word in a way I would have expected from white-haired ladies in Birmingham, Alabama—"so they loved matched sets."

I broke out into a sweat. We were seated at a table, with our professor at the head and the two other students across from me on his left. I looked first at Andy Cabitman. I think that is how he spelled his last name, although Charles Montgomery always addressed him so that it sounded like "Mr. Cabot-Mann." Andy was a tall, powerful-looking guy with a jagged nose that looked as if it had been broken by a lacrosse stick; he could have been in Hannibal's army. I knew only that he was very pleasant, had attended Groton (the exclusive boys school, which I now realize, although I did not know it then, was where Henry du Pont had gone two generations previously), and was a nice guy to chat with going to or from class. It had never occurred to me to wonder whether or not he was Jewish, even though, the moment Charles Montgomery made his remark, I asked myself the question. The third person was a meek, pale, anemic-looking woman of the type one sees in library corners, completely unprepossessing and probably very successful in academic circles, who I instantly determined could not possibly be Jewish, given her total lack of a certain life force essential to the people I now think of as my "coreligionists." (I learned this term from Katharine, who read it in a letter her grandfather, Paul Warburg, wrote his daughter, Katharine's great-aunt Bettina, when she was at the Madeira School, in about 1912. He said that he and "Mother"—his wife, Nina Loeb Warburg, a name and personality to reckon with—had been disturbed at the opera by "some of your co-religionists who were in the next box." They were, Paul Warburg continued, unacceptably noisy, as well as gaudily dressed.)

Charles Montgomery was not the sort of person to feel my panic, although I now think I probably emitted the strong skunklike odor that escapes me when I am suddenly, unexpectedly upset. He continued, "So at lunch, knowing that these *Jewish*"—he emphasized the word the same way each time he said it—"collectors would be impressed, he began by serving them soup in perfectly matched Chinese Export bowls. These people from New York could hardly believe that he had eight identical ones, for they were of a rare and highly prized design. Mr. du Pont had given instructions in the kitchen that the soup bowls were to be washed and dried immediately and used again as side dishes for the salad served with the main course. Of course, the *Jewish* collectors were stupefied, now thinking he had sixteen of them."

Charles Montgomery then leaned his enormous body back in his wooden desk chair and smiled with delight, making it clear that there was more to come. My stomach, meanwhile, had turned into a steel knot.

Next the professor, who held a distinguished university chair, thrust himself forward with the look of a preacher about to declare the Truth. He continued the anecdote, to which he clearly attributed great importance. "Then, as instructed, as soon as they cleared the table, the staff again washed the bowls, and only moments later served them with ice cream in them. The *Jewish* collectors could hardly believe it! A full set of twenty-four bowls."

That was the end of the story. My professor went on to discuss something else. I have no memory, however, of what it was—or whatever else was said—because I sat there burning: at him, and at myself for letting this all pass.

I DISCUSSED THE INCIDENT WITH NO ONE. I had no idea how Cabitman reacted. Nor did I know what the pale woman made of our teacher's remarks, although she seemed like such an unimaginative grind that I pictured her diligently taking notes about "Jewish collecting priorities." For a week, the anecdote and Charles Montgomery's telling of it must have been present in my unconscious mind, but, if so, I did not realize it.

When the seminar next convened for its usual meeting, I arrived a few minutes early. So did Andy Cabitman. Mr. Montgomery was already there, but we needed to wait for the ectoplasm to arrive before beginning the actual class.

"I trust you had a good weekend, Mr. Weber," Charles Montogomery said with unexpected courtesy.

"Oh, very good, sir," I replied. "I visited Mr. Cabot-Mann's family north of Boston." I left nearly five seconds between the Cabot and the Mann to emphasize the pronunciation of the name, which was the way Charles Montgomery said it. Cabitman, meanwhile, looked at me in complete puzzlement; we had not laid eyes on each other since the previous meeting of the seminar, a week earlier.

"And do you know, sir, it was amazing," I continued. "Mr. Cabot–Mann's grandmother—on the Cabot side, that is—had such wonderful furniture that had been in the family for generations. You would have loved it."

The professor focused on my words with fascination. I did not dare look at Cabitman, since I imagined he was thinking I should be hospitalized instantly.

I went on. I had in no way considered in advance what I would say; this was not part of a plan. It just came out, although by then I knew where it was going. "AND, sir, she showed me the most amazing pair of pieces she wanted to give to a museum, and asked my advice. They were a highboy and lowboy, perfectly matched. Both Queen Anne, they had the same cabriolet legs, identical aprons, exquisite fluted trim, and perfectly coordinated tiger's eye–maple veneer, which made me think they might be from southern New Hampshire." (New Hampshire eighteenth-century furniture, always a bit freer and more natural-looking than pieces from New York or Philadelphia, seemingly made by autodidacts, was, as it still is, by far my favorite: to Colonial style overall as Bode Miller is to other skiers.)

"They sound remarkable," Charles Montgomery affirmed.

"And, sir, as I said, Mrs. Cabot said she was just in the process of determining what museum to give them to. She said she was deciding among three: the Met, the Boston MFA, or here, to the Yale Art Gallery."

"Well, well, well, Mr. Weber," the professor continued with a broad smile. "We certainly know what you must have said to that."

"Well, sir, I suggested that she should, in fact, give them to Brandeis."

Charles Montgomery looked at me as if I had taken out a machine gun.

"I explained to her, sir, that you, the great authority on American decorative arts, had emphasized that Jewish collectors prize matched sets. So why not honor that taste by giving her perfectly matched pieces to a Jewish institution?"

This time, I allowed myself to look at Cabitman. I was now positive he was Jewish; his face bore a look of tragic understanding. Charles Montgomery appeared as if he were ready to murder me.

"In fact, Mr. Montgomery, of course I have made up this entire story. I have not glimpsed Mr. Cabitman since our seminar met last week; I have no idea who his grandparents are. But you should know, sir, that I am Jewish, and I was deeply offended by your tale last week about Henry du Pont and the visitors from New York."

There was a heavy moment of silence. I was trembling, and I imagine my face was flushed. Then Charles Montgomery began the seminar discussion as if nothing had happened. For the rest of the semester, he was, at best, curt to me. I passed the course with the lowest-possible grade, so that, while I still was entitled to receive my master's from Yale, I did so with no distinction whatsoever.

IN 1978, SEVEN YEARS AFTER THE INCIDENT with Charles Montgomery, Anni Albers and the Josef Albers Foundation, for which I had begun working two years earlier, when Josef died, gave seventy-seven major paintings and a complete collection of graphic art by Josef to the Yale University Art Gallery. I worked closely with Alan Shestack, the very sympathetic gallery director, on the selection of the gift and then on the exhibition where it would be publicly presented for the first time. In the course of our months of collaboration, I told him the story. By then, I had met and married Katharine, who also knew about Charles Montgomery and me.

There was a gala dinner to celebrate the opening of the show. It was a marvelous occasion for me personally, with Anni Albers, her wonderful lawyer, Lee Eastman, his exquisite and kind wife, Monique, and my brilliant and beautiful wife all present and all in top form. Alan Shestack ended his speech and toasts with a public acknowledgment of me that brought me, at age thirty, unequivocal pride.

Shortly after Alan sat down, someone rushed up to him and delivered an urgent message in a way that made it clear some sort of major event had occurred. He then rose again, visibly shaken. He said he was sorry to announce it on such a celebrative occasion, but he had just been informed that Charles Montgomery had died at his desk a couple of hours earlier, completely unexpectedly, of a massive stroke.

A hush fell over the room. Slowly, people resumed conversation. Then, one of the old Yale Blues, a retired professor named Sumner Crosby, clanked on his water glass with his knife and stood up—partially. He was completely in his cups. Leaning on the table with his left hand, Mr. Crosby raised his wineglass, and bellowed out, with completely slurred diction, "I don't know about Josef Albers, and I don't know about Charles Montgomery, but let's hear it for glorious Yale. To Yale!"

Lots of people in the room cheered, and the evening resumed its course.

IN THE EARLY 1990S, I WAS PROPOSED AND ELECTED as an associate fellow of Saybrook College at Yale. Josef Albers had also been a fellow of Saybrook, and I was delighted to be so honored.

At my first fellows' meeting, however, my rebellious streak unexpectedly reared its head. There was a cocktail hour before dinner and the after-dinner presentation of the evening's speaker, and I found myself, out of the blue, telling the story of what had happened in Charles Montgomery's seminar. The person to whom I was speaking was a dean of Yale College, Prish Pierce, who had been married to a man named Cheever Tyler and was now married to a very nice fellow with whom I played squash, a psychiatrist named Marc Rubenstein. The names are telling, and I thought Prish would be fascinated by my account. She had introduced me a few minutes earlier to a woman named Ruth Lord, an elegant and willowy lady who spoke like Katharine Hepburn and who worked at the Yale Child Study Center, of which Dr. Solnit was director, and whom I instantly found immensely appealing and sympathetic, and it was to the two of them that I began to recount the story of "the *Jewish* collectors" and Henry du Pont.

I was not far into the telling when I realized that Prish looked panic-stricken, while Ruth appeared to be hanging on to every word with daunting attentiveness. I knew from Prish's face that something was very wrong, but there was no stopping now that I had started, although I kept the tale brief.

By the time I was done, Prish was pale and silent. Ruth, standing tall, then said, quite simply but very slowly and deliberately, with a lovely smile, "I have to tell you—that—Henry du Pont—was—my—dad."

I started to say I had not meant to upset her, but she immediately put me at my ease, and more than. Ruth, grinning, simply said, "My father was many things, and snobby in a lot of ways, but he was *not* anti-Semitic. But don't think for a minute that that in any way contradicts your story. I had to put up with that social-climbing Charles Montgomery for years, and while my sister and other people always acted as if he was divine, I could not *stand* the man. And until now I have stayed silent about him. My deah, that is exactly the sort of thing Charlie Montgomery would tell people—because it is how *his* mind worked. May I hug you?"

I cannot say that I have reconstituted Ruth's words perfectly, but she became, starting that evening, a wonderful friend, as she remained for the rest of her life. She asked me if I would mind if she told the story to her daughter Pauline. Since then, on numerous occasions, when we were at dinner parties together, and even at the odd event at Saybrook, she asked me to retell the story of how she instantly considered me a close friend. She always laughed with utter delight at the odd confluence of events and at my having given the one-two punch to a man who was the bane of her existence.

CHAPTER 15

THE CONQUISTADOR

BUT WAS ANTI-SEMITISM, AND THE STRENGTH or weakness of a Jew's response to it, the reason, as the Karpes claim, for Freud's inability to remember the name Signorelli?

Maybe the halt within Freud's mind occurred because of his awkward response to all those naked male bodies. Perhaps the art rekindled the love for male strength that was central to his childhood, and something about the way his father was less masterful than his ideal, combined with elements of the name Signorelli—Italian for "little man"—are what caused a steel door to shut within his brain.

When Freud was growing up, his heroes were all "mighty warriors." Alexander the Great, Oliver Cromwell, Napoléon, and Massena (one of Napoléon's marshals) were his favorites. Freud would identify his toy soldiers as these men and then have them fight imaginary wars. Later in life, Freud saw himself as belonging in their ranks, declaring that he was "not at all a man of science, not an observer, not an experimenter, not a thinker. I am by temperament nothing but a Conquistador, an adventurer."

The Karpes did well to steer us to Freud's humiliation when his father recounted his crumbling before the anti-Semitic bully, and Freud's untraditional handling of his father's death rites, as the start of their attempt to understand the impact of Signorelli's frescoes. Freud himself wrote, "The essence of success is to have got further than one's father—as though to excel one's father was still something forbidden." Looking at the mighty warriors at Orvieto—dazzling incarnations of the type of men who were his heroes from the time he played with toy soldiers—when he was still in the official year of mourning following his father's death, Freud would have had an intense emotional reaction to these strong specimens. Unlike his father, such powerhouse figures could stand up to anti-Semitism, which, the Karpes are certain, was the main subject of these frescoes for Freud. Richard and Marietta are positive that Freud knew that the figure I erroneously thought was Jesus was in fact the Antichrist, and that Freud had Maud Cruttwell's knowledge of the Antichrist as a stand-in for Jews in general.

I have a different theory. I am not so sure that Freud knew the iconography of the scenes in Orvieto. Perhaps the whole thing for Freud was simply that he had an extreme reaction to virility and brute male strength—which, not incidentally, many people, especially Jews, consider to be Gentile, rather than Jewish, attributes. The sheer amount of testosterone in these paintings could in itself have had such a profound impact on him that it caused a sort of emergency fire curtain to drop.

FREUD, IN 1901, WROTE THAT HE PARTICULARLY LOATHED the idea "of being someone's protégé. . . . I have always felt an unusually strong urge to be the strong man myself." He was determined not to be like his father, sheepishly picking up his hat, which the Jew-hating bullies had knocked off his head.

In 1883, Freud wrote Martha a letter which became known only when their son Ernst quoted it in 1975. This was after the Karpes wrote their article, and I am sorry about that, because it would have given further support to their suggestion that Sigmund's feelings, the conflict as well as the pride, about being different from Jacob were central to his experience at Orvieto. In the 1883 letter, Freud describes a train trip in which he opened his window to let in some fresh air. People shouted out that he should shut it—a strong wind was coming in—and Freud said he would do so if they opened a window on the other side, as there was no other window open in the entire car. They began to debate this, and the man who had shouted the loudest at Freud said he would open the ventilation slit but not the window. At that moment, someone else shouted out, "He's a dirty Jew." The person with whom Freud had been arguing announced, "We Christians consider other people; you'd better think less of your precious self," and the man who was supposedly going to open the ventilation slit now threatened to beat Freud up. Freud tells Martha that a year earlier he would have been unable to say anything, but that now he was "not in the least frightened" and asked the first man to stop making vicious remarks while instructing "the other to step up and take what was coming to him. I was quite prepared to kill him, but he did not step up."

Freud portrays himself to Martha as sitting tight in front of the window he had opened, and saying he would not close it. When people began to jeer at him, he again instructed the man who had been attacking him the loudest to come over and duke it out. The threat worked; everyone quieted down.

I wish not only that the Karpes had known this story about Freud's machismo in the face of Jew haters but that they had told us more about the incident Martin Freud described of his father dispersing the bigots. I learned some telling details about it from the article "Freud and the Mighty Warrior," published in 1991. The place where the Freud family was on holiday was a lake; the year was 1901. Freud had seen the Signorelli frescoes four years earlier, and this was the same year when he wrote that he "would like to be a strong man myself." Freud was forty-five. His sons Martin and Oliver were fishing when some Christians yelled at them "that they were Israelites and had no right to steal the fish from the lake." It was later the same day that Freud and his sons rowed across the lake and the same people shouted anti-Semitic slurs at them. Freud got out of the boat swinging his stick, which in turn made the crowd break up so quickly that he went right through them without faltering for a moment.

In spite of his own eschewal of Jewish tradition, Freud could also be very proud to be Jewish. In 1924, he wrote that it was not "entirely a matter of chance that the first advocate of psychoanalysis was a Jew. To profess belief in this new theory called for a certain readiness to accept a position of solitary opposition—a position with which no one is more familiar than a Jew." When being Jewish meant being courageous, he was willing to accept the identity.

CHAPTER 16

Maud's Vision

I DECIDED TO SEE WHAT ELSE I MIGHT LEARN from Richard and Marietta's chosen source and went straight to the horse's mouth. Not only did I want to see what she said about Signorelli that the Karpes left out, but I had become fascinated by Maud Cruttwell.

When I managed to locate the 1899 text by the intriguing art historian, I was enthralled. She writes with a rare aliveness, and although she does not actually refer to the eroticism of Signorelli's work, she circles around it in such a way that it pulses through her words. The energy Maud Cruttwell describes in Signorelli's art permeates her own writing style.

I particularly admire Cruttwell on the subject of Luca Signorelli's debt to Donatello. Donatello's sculpture evokes human physicality with an unparalleled feeling of aliveness, and it makes sense that Signorelli looked at it. My admiration for Donatello began when I was a Columbia College freshman in 1966, and for Art History 101 was given an assignment to write about a single artwork. In keeping with the approach enforced by Meyer Schapiro (whose dazzling lectures in medieval art I was also attending at the time, but only as an "auditor," since one had to fulfill the requirement of taking this introduction to art history before being permitted to register for more advanced courses), we were to do no research. Our task was to observe and then write about what we saw with our eyes—without historical facts, reference to art movements, or biographical information about the artist whose work was selected. I chose a *Virgin and Child* relief at the Met, which at the time was attributed to Donatello, although it is now "school of." Spending hours in front of this single artwork, I could not stop marveling at the physical and emotional intensity of its simple relief structure, in which the Virgin has her arms wrapped around the infant Jesus. The act of enclosure conveys an ineffable feeling of tenderness. Whether in fact it is a true Donatello or "school of," this sublime work conjures in my thoughts a wonderful neoclassical Picasso in Baltimore of a mother holding a baby. From there my thoughts jump to the sight of my very beautiful wife on the two occasions of her having just given birth. I can see Katharine with fifteen-minute-old Lucy on her breasts and enclosed in her arms, and then, twenty months later, at a parallel moment with Charlotte. Donatello conveys in marble the physical and emotional connection of mother and infant so successfully that his art was the first way in which I came to feel them, paving the way for the moments when, later on, I would have the good fortune to witness them even more richly in my own life.

When I was an art history student at Yale Graduate School, I went to Florence in the summer and feasted on Donatello in the Bargello. My sister Nancy had told me that Donatello's *Mary Magdalene* was the most moving sculpture she had ever seen—she always had a thing for the Magdalen—and seeing it and the other figures in the world in which Donatello had made them was one of the greatest experiences imaginable for the boy brought up in Connecticut. To this day, I consider Donatello's *David* a far greater sculpture than Michelangelo's better-known version of the same subject, because the Michelangelo is too perfect, too much the ideal, the dream god, the perfect model for hair fixative, while Donatello's, with his slightly extended belly and his wry smile, the dimples on his flesh and the appropriate flaws in his body, is the essence of humanity.

By linking Signorelli to Donatello, with enthusiasm and insight, Maud Cruttwell greatly increases our sense of the artist whose work Freud admired so deeply. Using the sculptor as her starting point,

Cruttwell makes Signorelli's subjects sound sexually potent, even if she cloaks the sentiment, as was required by the mores of the time period in which she was writing: "Forty years before the birth of Signorelli, Donatello had been able to carve the human form with absolute perfection of anatomy, and not only that, but to endow it with freedom of limb and overflowing life."

When Cruttwell refers to the perfection of anatomy, she means anatomy as it really *is,* and is presented in Donatello's work, rather than the idealized anatomy à la Michelangelo. "It is easy to suppose the impression his statues must have made on the youth, [Signorelli], whose spirit was so much akin to his own in exuberant energy, and who had the same uncompromising love of realism. The two artists had much in common in their confident self-reliance, and almost arrogant buoyancy of nature, which was the true Renaissance expression, and the outward sign of immense strength."

Bravo, Maud! And Bravo, Richard and Marietta, for having gone to the library and found her book and chosen to quote it, and hence having led me to it. I still lament their not having gone to Orvieto, but at least they found a good source.

Yet I think that the Karpes missed what is most important in Cruttwell's text, and what would have brought them closer to the real reason that Freud could not remember Signorelli's name. Richard and Marietta considered mainly what that 1899 book says about iconography. They mined Cruttwell's text for material that buttressed their argument that the big issue for Freud in Orvieto was what it meant for him to be Jewish. I think they would have done better to have focused on Cruttwell's emphasis on male strength in this art. For, in her energetic prose, my Maudila evokes the salient qualities of Signorelli's artistry, and, concomitantly, of Sigmund Freud's longings! "Confident self-reliance, and almost arrogant buoyancy of nature": This is an utterly perfect expression of everything that was lacking in Jacob Freud when he picked up the cap and scurried off the sidewalk onto the road.

Instead of picking what they did from Cruttwell's narrative, the Karpes should have focused on sentences like the following: "Signorelli caught and revived the very essence of Donatello's spirit—the love of bodily life in its most hopeful and vigorous manifestations."

Please, my readers, mull over those words as you look at the reproductions of Signorelli's figures from the chapel in Orvieto. [plate 19] That "love of bodily life" is what pervades. It matters more than all

Plate 19. *The Resurrection of the Flesh*

the notions of sin and punishment that dominate the literature on the chapel, and it is the factor that surely impressed Freud far more than any of the Last Judgment issues, or, at the very least, as part and parcel of the Last Judgment issues. "It is significant that the swaggering posture which became such a special feature of his painting, should have originated with Donatello."

Oh, Maud, how you have *looked*! How you have gone further than all the psychoanalysts who act as if they followed the instruction to close the eyes! It is only with close observation that you could have come up with that most perfect of words: *swaggering*. "Donatello was, before all things, a realist, and it was probably the habitual attitude of the cavalry soldier of the day, accustomed to straddle over the broad back of his war-horse, but there is little doubt that it was adopted by Signorelli from the 'S. George" of Or San Michele, and perhaps

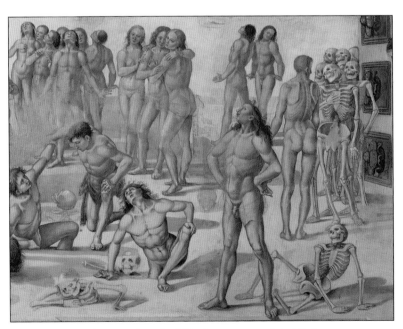

Plate 20. Detail of *The Resurrection of the Flesh*

half-unconsciously signified to him—what that statue so well embodies—the confident spirit of youth and strength."

Again, I hope the reader will consider Maud's observations while
looking at images from Orvieto. Her emphasis on dash and athlet-
icism, the bold style with which the cavalry officers straddle their
warhorses, evokes the robustness of the frescoes. Looking at this art,
Freud beheld his conquistadors. [plate 20]

This "confident spirit of youth and strength" of Signorelli's naked
men belongs to what for many people is the golden age of human
life. When I wrote the biography of Balthus, over a period of seven
years, I came to realize, but only after sorties in many other directions, that the artist's true elixir was the sheer aliveness and vitality
of youth. He considered the first years of maturity to be life's finest
moment. For Balthus, the pinnacle was late puberty, while Signorelli's powerhouses appear to be in their early twenties, but the significant thing is that age has not yet taken its toll, and that physical
abilities are at their apogee.

After the age of fourteen, Balthus spent the rest of his life enthralled
with adolescence. The power of burgeoning sexuality, the emotional
intensity, the imperviousness to the realities of money, the lack of obli-
gations to the next generation—these delights of the onset of one's
teenage years loomed for him as the essence of a freedom, and a self-
ishness, that were his ideals. Many of these same qualities would have
presented themselves to Freud, and transfixed him, in Signorelli's men
demonstrating their phenomenal physical force. In this period when
Freud was mourning his father—and, as one does at such a time, imagining his own decline—he must have felt, as Balthus did, a powerful
attraction to the feelings of power and confidence that come in those
few years when the body is at its pinnacle, which Luca Signorelli captures, as have few other artists, the age when athletes are at their best,
and when the sexual self is its most potent. [plate 21]

After the Balthus book, for nine years I wrote the biography of the

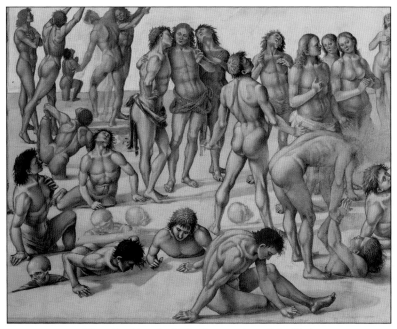

Plate 21. Detail of *The Resurrection of the Flesh*

very different Le Corbusier. To my surprise, I discovered him to have the same passions. I saw him obsessed with virile soldiers, with the ability to scale stairs two at a time (he thought the invention of the escalator part of the downfall of civilization), and with his own erections. Throughout his life, physical fitness and sexual prowess were among life's essentials. (He could have been a Turk.) He worked out almost every day with a trainer, before this was a common practice. He claimed that Switzerland, his birthplace, was a land of "dirty neuters." Like Freud, he was a man of great imagination and genius who was obsessed with masculinity and physical condition, to a degree that many other people of the same intellectual depth would find surprising.

All these thoughts are of a piece with what led me to open the Karpes' reprint to begin with. The memories of being sixteen, feelings of my own maleness, beckoned. I relished the return to that time in my life when I jauntily took in the beguiling Susie in counterpoint to the scholarly Austrians, downed my gin and tonic, and felt ridiculously full of myself.

At the end of her brilliant paragraph on Signorelli and Donatello, Maud Cruttwell outdoes herself in articulating the swagger and spectacular confidence on which one feasts in the Cappella Nova. Berenson's savvy housekeeper brings Perugino and Botticelli into her discussion for comparison. She elucidates what makes them different from Signorelli and Donatello. The male figures in the work of the first two artists "seem to spread their legs because they are too puny to bear the weight of the body in any other manner, while with Signorelli, the attitude became the keynote of his resolute indomitable nature, and so much a part of his work, that one is apt to forget it did not originate with him."

Not only does Maud Cruttwell understand Signorelli's force and impact but she gives us insight as to how he achieves them. "It is . . . by form rather than colour that Signorelli obtains his best effects. . . . His line is firm and clear, simple and structural, of unerring sweep and accuracy, as we see in his numerous *predella* paintings; but even more remarkable is the wonderful plastic quality of his modeling. By this he makes us realise better than any one before him the tenseness of sinew, the resistance of hard muscle, and the supple elasticity of flesh, giving a solidity and weight to his forms that make them impressive as grand sculptures."

What carefulness and acuity Cruttwell put into her study of the Cappella Nova. She is on the mark about the exquisite predellas with their portraits of Renaissance figures, and equally perceptive about the sinew and muscle and the modeling with which Signorelli gave sculptural presence to his Herculean characters.

Maud Cruttwell also leads us to see another part of the appeal of Signorelli to Freud, given Freud's abhorrence of humiliated or meek men. For, she astutely observes, the artist was so uninterested in weakling characters—the sort of men who might have resembled Jacob Freud cowering before the anti-Semites—that he painted his scenes so that the viewer would hardly notice such people. Cruttwell writes—how I admire her courage in revealing what many would consider a shortcoming on the part of her subject!—that Signorelli

> was essentially a religious painter, but in the widest meaning of the word, and he does not seem to have felt the dignity and significance of many of the scenes in the life of Christ. When he has to paint Him bound to the pillar or nailed to the Cross, submissive to scourging and insult, his interest seems to wander from what should be the central figure, and fixes itself on some two or three of the minor actors, to whom he gives the importance he should have concentrated on the Christ. The painter *con amore* of arrogant strength, he seems to have little in common with meekness and humility that bows the head to scourging and martyrdom. Thus in nearly all of his "Crucifixions" the central figure is ignoble in type and expression, and in the "Flagellations" of the Brera and of Morra, is entirely without dignity, even ignominious. This is curious when we consider that even more than of arrogant strength Signorelli was the painter of stately and noble beauty.

There are, in fact, no crucified figures at Orvieto. Signorelli has made it the temple of "arrogant strength."

CHAPTER 17

FREUD AND THE ETRUSCANS

WHILE OPENING THE DOOR SO THOUGHTFULLY to a major psychological event in Freud's life, the Karpes missed a lot of significant clues to its possible cause by not considering the lunettes other than the one with the Antichrist at the center. When we stand in the Cappella Nova, we see imagery far more remarkable than the single scene our good sleuths studied with the help of Maud Cruttwell's book. The fresco where the devil is in concert with the quintessential Jew certainly had its impact on the middle-aged Freud, but it is only a small part of what blew his mind away that day in Orvieto.

Consider Signorelli's painting of *The Damned* [plate 22] It is, in the words of Dugald McLellan, "a virtuosic display of human anatomy in action." The presentation of male nakedness in violent, athletic movement is unparalleled. Muscular buttocks, in particular, are seen from every possible angle. How this impacts the viewer may well depend on the viewer's own gender and sexual interests, but it is a stunning presentation of raw masculinity.

The closest thing to *The Damned* in most people's experience are billboards for Calvin Klein underwear and advertisements for Abercrombie & Fitch. But the Signorelli fresco, beyond showing well-built guys brandishing their butts, is a fantastic feat of painting that makes its subject matter far more powerful than a fashion shoot. And although the naked men in effect flaunt their buff bodies, they do so not because they are deliberately posing for their viewers, but, rather, without narcissism. They are engaged in life-and-death combat,

Plate 22. Detail of *The Damned Cast into Hell*

which endows them with the allure of vitality, in a state of action that really matters.

Rather than take into account this or any of the other frescoes in the chapel, the Karpes' next step after analyzing the discomfort they believed Freud experienced in front of Signorelli's Antichrist is to contrast those feelings to the impact on him of the Etruscan antiquities he also saw in Orvieto. "If the Signorelli murals created anxiety and uneasiness in the viewer, other art treasures found in Orvieto had the opposite effect on Freud." They provide a learned, compact history of the Etruscans as "opponents and victims of classical Rome," in whose mythology, influenced by Asian and Egyptian culture, "death and sex were intertwined." In 1874, little more than two decades before Freud went to Orvieto, a remarkable necropolis—a city to house the dead—had been discovered at the base of cliffs beneath the medieval town. "The attitude of the Etruscans toward death as expressed in their cemetary [sic] may have been a great relief to Freud from the tension stirred up by Signorelli's frescoes," Richard and Marietta contend. The Etruscans, after all, provided an image of life after death "as a joyous experience"—as opposed to the Catholic notion that the afterlife is a consequence of one's behavior on earth, depending on the evaluation of that conduct. Having grown up with his nursemaid's belief that penance in purgatory or nonstop torture in hell was the fate of anyone who did not lead his life to merit the bliss of heaven, Freud embraced the alternative offered by this earlier culture.

The Karpes emphasize that for Freud the Etruscan approach addressed the afterlife in a more palatable way than the Signorelli frescoes did, and provided comfort with regard to the disconcerting issue of human mortality that was particularly vivid to him as he mourned his father. "The atmosphere of these Etruscan tombs mitigates the fear of death, representing a special form of denial of one's own death. We can have no doubt where Freud's sympathies layed [sic]. He was deeply impressed by the Etruscan culture and he preserved a life-long interest in Etruscan art." They go on to discuss a dream Freud had in 1900. Freud says he "reached a small wooden house" where he "saw two grown-up men lying on wooden benches;" Freud explains that the house was "no doubt, a coffin, that is to say a grave." He describes his experience of being in an Etruscan grave near Orvieto "with two stone benches along its walls, on which the skeletons of two grown-up men were lying. . . . The dream seems to be saying: If you must rest in a grave, let it be an Etruscan one. And by making this replacement, it transforms the gloomiest of expectations into one that was highly desirable."

Better to know the afterlife as it existed in Etruscan imagery than in purgatory or hell as illustrated by Signorelli! One could see why Freud

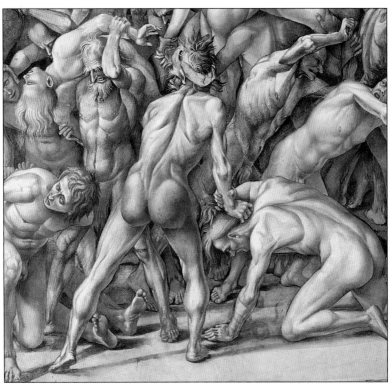

Plate 23. Detail of *The Damned Cast into Hell*

might have considered the Etruscan option more desirable. In Signorelli's *Resurrection of the Flesh* at Orvieto, the skeletons are ghastly-looking. In Signorelli's *Inferno,* which we call *The Damned,* human skin is painted a lurid green or a bloody crimson; men are having their hair pulled, their necks snapped, their wrists tied, their ears boxed [plate 23]; devils bite and strangle the few women. No wonder Freud needed to obliterate some aspect of his memory of these grizzly sights.

All well and good, but I am annoyed with my parents' friends here. They have indulged in my personal bête-noire: the failure of West Hartfordites to leave their provincial nest. How could they have merely driven up Farmington Avenue to the library, instead of taken themselves to Italy? And they have committed the crime of art historians, which is to read the literature, and to look at the reproductions someone else has chosen, rather than to go to the real thing.

I have spent my entire adult life in rebellion against those forms of inertia, to the point of frenzy, and to the dismay of some of the people I know. It is not easy to be a restless soul ever eager to burst beyond the confines, but I would rather face hell in Orvieto than purgatory in my hometown. I wish the Karpes had had some of that wanderlust. They might have concluded, as I did, that the imagery of hell in the Cappella Nova was more exciting for Freud than was the sweetness of the Etruscan necropolis.

CHAPTER 18

THE DEVIL

HAVING TAKEN FREUD TO HIS ETRUSCAN REPRIEVE, the Karpes provide the detail that after his death the great psychoanalyst's cremated remains were buried in an Etruscan urn. Unfortunately, they do not specify if this was because of his instructions, or if it was decided by others in honor of his taste.

Then the Karpes take a last look at Freud and Signorelli. Freud was, they tell us, deeply interested in demonology and associated the devil with sexuality. Earlier in the same year that he went to Orvieto, he had written Fliess, "When I am not afraid I can take on all the devils in hell." Referring to his own ideas on the origins of hysteria, he wrote that "the medieval theory of possession was identical with our theory."

Richard and Marietta quote a question Freud asked Fliess, which would make the perfect caption to some of the images by Signorelli that Freud would see a few months later: "Why were the confessions extracted under torture so very like what my patients tell me under psychological treatment?" Here one has to wonder whether Freud, when he stood in front of Signorelli's *Inferno,* with its forty or so stark naked characters falling all over one another as they are being shoved and dragged toward the flames of hell, had some image of himself and his coprofessionals as the equivalents of the devils, and of their patients as victims.

Is that healthily tanned buck of a man on the lower right Freud's worst fear of what it means to be a psychoanalytic patient? [plate 24] With his head snapped back (the neck would be broken if his chin were really at that angle) by a devil whose skin is a corpselike white tinged

Plate 24. Detail of *The Damned Cast into Hell*

by gray, he is the image of someone having his mind manipulated. This handsome lad—in today's lingo, we would say he looks like an amiable, clean-cut jock—grabs the devil's arm in a last effort to push him off, but it is too late; his life has effectively been destroyed by the horned creature who has a mass of animal fur covering his genitals. (Either that, or the fur *replaces* his genitals.)

And what about the duo just to the left of them? Here the victim, still alive, is howling in pain as the devil pulls tufts of hair with both hands. Again, the place where the devil tortures his victim is the *head,* the seat of psychoanalysis.

In this second pairing, the victim, like the first one, is a fine physical

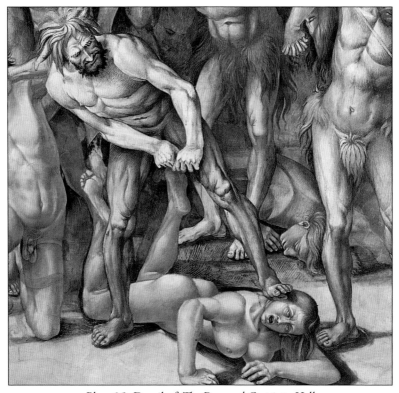

Plate 25. Detail of *The Damned Cast into Hell*

specimen with noticeably healthy skin. The devil, by contrast, not only has hair that looks like the flames of a roaring fire, and a face that personifies evil, but his body is as sinewy as the figures in medical drawings, and, while his buttocks are a truly ghastly green, his shoulders and ankles are a hideous purple.

In another pairing, a devil who is consistently a horrible grape color except for his green ankles, and who also has the telltale flaming hair, is crushing his patient's head with his left leg. The victim/patient, in this case a woman, is, as usual, a far finer physical specimen than her torturer. Her large breasts and well-rounded buttocks would give her a soft voluptuousness, the sort of womanliness we find in Aristide Maillol's sculptures celebrating female attributes otherwise absent in Signorelli's world, but her bodybuilder's arms and shoulders and football player's legs are so distinctly male, and the breasts and buttocks themselves so solidly muscular, that she loses all womanly allure. Besides, hers is hardly a pretty face, and, as my mother would have said, "her hair is a disaster." [plate 25]

To their left, as we face the painting, we have another tragic pairing. [plate 26] Here it is the devil who is in better shape than the victim. But while he is bronze-skinned, muscular, and lean, he has a grim

Plate 26. Detail of *The Damned Cast into Hell*

mauve face, and an especially volcanic head of hair. What is either a bizarre loincloth or a natural outgrowth of fur at his crotch—it looks like long, wet pubic hair—makes him all the more monstrous.

The victim could be one of the angels from Piero della Francesca's frescoes in Arezzo. He has similar features to them, their very round eyes, and the same shoulder-length blond hair. But while Piero's angels are ineffably serene, he is in agony. The devil is choking him, and his efforts to pull the devil's hands away are futile. The hair of his double in Arezzo flows with a soft curve; this angel's locks shoot from his head as if he is receiving a high-voltage electric shock. The poor fellow has a rather feminine body; his pectoral muscles are far less impressive than the devil's, his biceps are not as developed, and his belly is slightly rounded, Moreover, we cannot help noticing, because it is directly in front of us, and because his pubic hair is so scant, that he has an unfortunately small penis that falls far short of his testicles—which, in turn, sag like an old man's. His mean conqueror is more fit and more virile.

FREUD WOULD, RICHARD AND MARIETTA TELL US, write that the devil was the "personification of the unconscious instinctual life." Do these images by Signorelli suggest that to be gripped by what is unconscious and instinctual is to be strangled or crushed to death?

Given Freud's take on the devil, he could well have seen Luca Signo-relli's paintings of victorious devils and hapless victims as illustrations of the horrible consequences of our "unconscious instinctual" feelings. If Signorelli's demons represent the erotic longings that are beyond our plans or expectations, the tortures they inflict are the price one pays for being overcome by such feelings.

In the top half of the lunette, two of the damned have just been dropped by the devils above them, so that they cascade toward the mayhem below. One has his arms tied behind his back, and falls faceup and headfirst; it is as gruesome a form of descent as one could imagine. He has his right leg bent as if he will make a pathetic attempt to brace himself, but the effort is futile. The other, shooting down in a backward nosedive, has his legs splayed awkwardly and his arms spread in a last-ditch attempt to find some means to anchor himself. But clearly he doesn't have a chance.

One of the few women sinners is being flown directly toward hell on the back of a devil with fantastic pointed wings and lethal horns. He leers at her while holding her hands tight to prevent her from escaping. She is built like a man, albeit a flabby one with too much girth, but that in no way discourages the devil from looking ecstatic at the prospect of raping her. Luca Signorelli's imagination knew no limits.[plate 27]

If the artist had not presented Freud with sufficient images of torture in the contorted creatures being strangled and kicked and mutilated below, he did so in these pairings above. The consequences of sin (Sexual disinhibition? Realizing one's Oedipal fantasies and killing one's

Plate 27. Detail of *The Damned Cast into Hell*

father? Being Jewish? Freud could have picked any of these violations, or a combination, as the vice of the moment) are utterly horrid. Equally, the prospect of death, now more than ever in Freud's thoughts following his father's recent demise, is made all the more terrifying by the way that what comes after it is even worse than the event itself.

Was this nightmare the fate of human beings if they acted according to the innate instincts that were Freud's preoccupation, or simply the consequence of being Jewish, the happenstance he could do nothing about?

And why was this detail from the frescoes, of the horned devil carrying a maiden on his back, the one of which Freud bought an engraving that he kept for the rest of his life? (We know this because it remains in his personal archives, and has been published alongside the postcards from Orvieto.) He also bought a photo of the overall view of the town perched on a hilltop—a typical tourist's souvenir. But of the art, what most fascinated him was this dramatic rape.

The questions fall furiously one on top of the other, the way the naked characters do. They are as raw as all this violent action, and as relentless. Did Freud imagine Signorelli's scene as his own inferno, or at least the one he deserved, the way I do? Did he, like me, suffer from some inexplicable guilt and the burning feeling of having made dire mistakes? Can I try to understand his experience of Orvieto without imposing my own? How dare I look more at the paintings than at Freud's own persona, of which I know little more than what the Karpes have described? If Christianity says that the original sin is the reason man became mortal, and Freud singled out Oedipal and Electra attraction as the source of melancholy, was it not the confrontation with all these issues, whether their manifestation in the Cappella Nova is direct or oblique, that forced him to forget a name? As for me, I cannot help but think that one's feelings about one's father, one's mother, and one's self is why Signorelli's *Inferno* seems at times to represent not just my fate but my own mind.

CHAPTER 19

The Entrance to Hell

Ⅰ N THE QUARTER LUNETTE TO THE RIGHT OF THE ALTARPIECE of the chapel, Signorelli has painted the Antinferno, or entrance to hell.

About halfway up the scene, the artist has positioned some pathetic characters who, with their arms raised desperately, are running after a white banner flapping in the wind. They give the impression of people chasing a worthless goal. Dante, whose portrait Signorelli includes elsewhere in the chapel, describes these lost souls whom the painter shows there. They are the Neutrals, characterized in Canto II of the *Inferno* as the "worthless crew that is hateful to God and His enemies."

There is something about them, scrambling after that flag being carried by a particularly nasty devil, that reminds me, sadly, of Jacob Freud chasing after his cap. This makes sense, since the Neutrals running along the banks of the Acheron, the river that leads to Hell, were also guilty of Jacob's sin of failing to believe in the divinity of Jesus. There is no knowing how closely Sigmund Freud viewed this scenario, and whether he, too, read it as a parable to the event about which he heard as a child, causing him to feel so painfully humiliated. However, he must have felt the echoes.

A PAIR OF TERRIFYING FIGURES IN THE FOREGROUND of the Antinferno scared the daylights out of me. [plate 28] I assume that Freud had a similar reaction.

Plate 28. Detail of *The Damned Cast into Hell*

A gray-skinned Minos ("the infernal judge") looms over "the reprobate." Signorelli's Minos has to be one of the most frightening characters ever painted. His face is hideous, his color sickly. He is squashing the reprobate with his left knee while pulling his hair with one hand and getting ready to beat him with the other. The reprobate, who has flesh with a normal tint, which makes him seen especially vulnerable next to the ashen devil, cries out in pain and raises a hand to defend himself, but he doesn't have a chance. To have failed to follow the Christian God is unpardonable.

I cannot help pointing out that, again, this is the case of an unlucky character having a tiny penis. The devil, on the other hand, has either a bizarre codpiece or a long animal-like penis that seems to have a rat's tail dangling from its tip. This is not the sort of thing most art historians talk about, but it is essential to Signorelli's vision—and one of the reasons the scene makes the fate of the character with whom most of us identify so totally unbearable. So this is what happens if we fail to worship Christ, or if we commit other mortal sins!

Not only do we get squashed and punched and have our hair pulled, but we have miniaturized dicks.

In his images of the damned, the elect, and the Antinferno, Signorelli drew heavily on the representation of the *Last Judgment* on the facade of the Orvieto cathedral. Lorenzo Maitani had carved these figurees in marble between 1310 and 1330. Particularly in his fresco *The Damned,* Signorelli borrowed from his Gothic predecessor's images of kicking and grabbing and the pinching and twisting, the fever-pitch atmosphere, and the intense compression of forms. [plate 29]

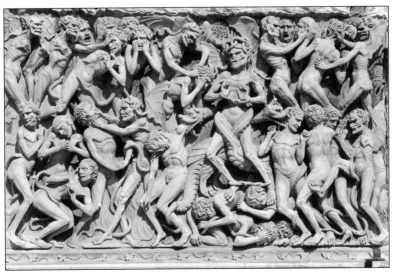

Plate 29. Lorenzo Maitani, detail of *The Last Judgment,* 1310–1330, bas-relief on the facade of the cathedral in Orvieto

Signorelli, however, brought new stylistic elements to his own version of those consigned to hell. For one thing, he was fired up by the ambient atmosphere as people focused on the meaning of the year 1500. With the world entering a new half millennium, many saw an apocalypse coming. The subject matter long familiar to Christian iconography now has a new immediacy.

More significantly, Signorelli changed the body types. He made them more robust; Maitani's figures are scrawny by comparison. And he posed them, for the most part, to flaunt their muscular behinds.

Vasari, Maud Cruttwell, Berenson—none of these art historians, brilliant as they were, discuss this, but all one has to do is look.

CHAPTER 20

MALENESS

THE KARPES LET US KNOW THAT IN *Character and Anal Eroti-cism,* which Freud wrote in 1908, he declared that "the Devil . . . psychoanalytically represents the sensual father." Tell us more! (They don't.)

What does this mean in an essay on the impact of the frescoes at Orvieto? Was Freud picturing Signorelli's devils in his mind's eye when, over a decade later, he wrote that essay? Is it possible that what really got to him in the frescoes was that all those creatures with horns—the bald one whispering in the Antichrist's ear; the ones with wild hair inflicting physical torture of such force and imagination that they could have been hired at Abu Ghraib—were associated in his thoughts with Jacob in his role as Freud's mother's lover?

Was this why the parallelism of Sig-mund and Sig-norelli, the creator of psychoanalysis and the creator of the frescoes, caused his mind to go blank? After all, both of them were obsessed with the same character. For Signorelli, it was the horned demons as the subject of his painting and the perpetrators of its action. For Freud, it was also that horned demon—as a stand-in for his recently deceased father, the same parent Oedipus kills.

I have not even mentioned the central devil-victim pairing in Signorelli's *Purgatory.* [plate 30] This may be because, when I was there and whenever I have considered it since (in reproductions), it is so frightening that I inadvertently turn my eyes from it. Part of the problem is the look on the victim's face. He is a blond lad, perhaps in his early

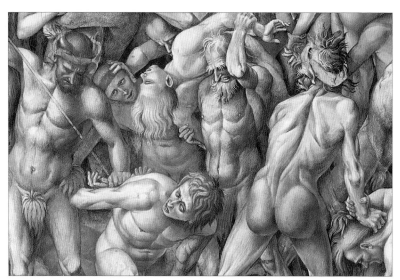

Plate 30. Detail of *The Damned Cast into Hell*

twenties. He has the hair of Michelangelo's David, is fair-skinned, and appears innocent and guileless. One of the reasons his face is difficult to look at is that it is only inches away from the firm, muscular buttocks of the devil who is pulling another victim's hair with both hands. To look at the blond guy's face requires also looking at well-formed naked male buttocks at a closer proximity than most of us are comfortable with. That isn't the only thing; between the lad's head and the muscleman's behind there is what could best be described as the long and scraggly pubic goatee of another heinous demon.

The demon in charge of the pleasant lad is one of Signorelli's worst. His skin is a sulfurous green. The expression on his face is pure evil; with his furrowed brow, big pointy nose, pencil-thin lips, and nasty glare, he is totally concentrated on the torture he is inflicting. His horns are mere embellishment; he would be just as vicious without them.

This brute is well built—like a model of manly physique. Yet the perfection of his body takes an odd twist in the way his crotch is covered. This demon with grisly features and a standout muscleman's build has, over his genitals, what looks like a wilted sunflower. Is this because he is modest or because, for whatever reason, he has something to hide?

This odious, powerful man is using his left hand to tie a rope around his victim's hands, which he has pulled behind the poor guy's back. With his right hand, he tightens the slack on the rope to strengthen the knot. He is in total command: like the anti-Semite who victimized Jacob.

On the other hand, if we follow Freud's statement from *Character and Anal Eroticism,* and the demon is associated with "the sensual father," then he is a father in the act of punishing his son. For what?

The crime committed by the blond-haired lad is visually associated with the genitals and buttocks of the two powerful devils next to him. We could imagine his open mouth or his eyes feasting on them; his interest in doing so is the offense for which he is being tortured. You may not agree with my reading of this, but I maintain that there is something about his proximity to other naked men, guys who are tougher than he is, and his intimacy with their naked "private parts," that is what makes him warrant capture and punishment.

FREUD SUMMARIZES MANY OF HIS SEMINAL IDEAS in his brief *An Autobiographical Study.* I recommend this refreshingly straightforward and succinct narrative, which he wrote in 1925 and which James Strachey subsequently translated into English, to anyone who finds the literature by and on Freud overwhelming. This late compendium helps us not just to understand the great doctor's major theories but also to appreciate that he was less didactic and absolute than he sometimes appears. Here Freud writes, "All the different variations and consequences of the Oedipus complex are important; and in particular the innately bisexual constitution of human beings makes itself felt and increases the number of simultaneously active tendencies. Children do not become clear for quite a long time upon the differences between the sexes."

Freud takes the idea further a few pages later in a short passage that reveals him to have a compassion and kindness at odds with the image of him that currently pervades:

> Looked at from the psychoanalytic viewpoint, even the most eccentric and repellent perversions are explicable as manifestations of component instincts of sexuality which have freed themselves from the primacy of the genitals and are going in pursuit of pleasure on their own account as they did in the very early days of the libido's development. The most important of these perversions, homosexuality, scarcely deserves the name. It can be traces back to the constitutional bisexuality of all human beings. . . . Psychoanalysis enables us to point to some trace or other of a homosexual object-choice in everyone.

Freud then goes on to say how the way an individual responds to these givens of his or her development is his main concern. He begins his chapter on the crux of his life's work by declaring, "The theory of resistance and of repression, of the unconscious, of the aethiological significance of sexual life and of the importance of infantile experiences—these form the principle constituents of the theoretical structure of psychoanalysis."

Here I have to admit that *aethiological* is one of those words that makes me feel squeamish. When I read it, I can feel my mind losing its grasp of meaning and wandering into a sense of vagueness and fog. (I also begin to have memories of certain fellow students at Columbia College, usually with exceptionally nasal speaking manners, who, gesticulating with their arms when they spoke in class, would, slowly and pompously, use grand words like this to show off their presumed erudition to the professor.) Looking it up in the unabridged dictionary that remains one of the essential tools of my life, I felt only more anxiety, for it was not there. But then, fortunately, I realized that the American spelling is "etiological," which enabled me to discover that the word has to do with the assignment of a cause or reason for something. All well and good. Freud certainly could have said this far more simply, but I translate the sentence to mean that in the case of his own memory loss concerning Luca Signorelli, the repression resulted from sexual feelings that went back to his own infancy.

I deliberately go no further than I can with certainty, but what is clear in our consideration of the trip to Orvieto and its aftermath is that, when confronted with a fantastic artistic representation of homoerotic subject matter, something in the experience inspired the repression of the artist's name. Maud Cruttwell and other art historians don't discuss the Signorellis the way I do; even if they acknowledge the sheer physicality of the artist's nudes, they stay away from the glaring sexuality, the way that most people writing about the *Rokeby Venus* leave out the essential point that she has been painted in part to inspire lust. (Most of the academic art historians with whom I studied, if asked to discuss Brigitte Bardot, would be more inclined to discuss "the iconography of the mammary in Mediterranean culture" or "the coincidence of like consonants in the appellations of Bernard Berenson, Bernard Baruch, and Brigitte Bardot" than simply to acknowledge how ravishing she was.) Reading between the lines of Cruttwell (and knowing she was a lesbian), we feel, however, that she is more willing to acknowledge the palpable element of sexual attraction in art. Her portrayal of Luca Signorelli suggests that the artist who presents himself to us as a man of flare and style, carefully cloaked in his dignified robes, has painted all these naked men, displaying their bodies for all they are worth, because he is excited by them.

The Karpes tell us that Freud wrote Fliess, in January 24, 1897, nine months before he went to Orvieto, about *Maleus Maleficarum*, "a very powerful and influential book by two members of the Holy Inquisition, Kramer and Sprenger, published in the fifteenth century and endorsed by the authority of Pope Innocent VIII. It described the teamwork of devils and witches as something very real, blaming all known psychopathology of those days on the devil's influence." If we apply that idea to the Signorelli frescoes, then all those people who are consorting with the devil, or have been consigned to his punishment, are there because of some form of sin or another, including the crime of unconscious thoughts that are unacceptable.

On my second visit to Orvieto, I asked Andrea—whom I considered the quintessential macho Latin man—if he didn't agree with me that part of what could make someone uncomfortable about these paintings was the sight of all the male nudity, and the unavoidability of feasting your eyes on it. He smiled and said, "Exactly. If you are afraid of that slight soft spot in you which notices other men, then you cannot look."

The experience of seeing the Signorellis is any man's encounter both with what it means to have your own particular body and to compare it. You imagine what it would be like to have the physique of one of the musclemen in these paintings, and to use it to full advantage. You also discover whether you are comfortable or not looking at particularly impressive male specimens in the buff, and to what extent you enjoy doing so. I am not sure of what the experience is like for female visitors, but, as with magazines like *Men's Health*—and for that matter, *Playboy*—the Cappella Nova seem to be intended for a male audience.

What Signorelli had already made clear in the Milan *Flagellation* is that to be physically powerful, to be a man who vanquishes weaker men, is to be endowed with erotic force. The *Martyrdom of St. Sebastian* and the pair of wooden panels now in Toledo, Ohio are, like that painting of Pan that Bernard Berenson would single out as one of the painter's masterpieces, evidence that if we did not have a current name for Luca Signorelli, he could always have been called "the Master of Naked Male Buttocks." No one I know of has dared say it, but, above all other subjects, nude male backsides are what Freud faced in Orvieto.

CHAPTER 21

The Case of Luca Signorelli

G IORGIO VASARI, THE RENAISSANCE PAINTER and architect whose *Lives of the Artists* remains, nearly five centuries later, the unique contemporary account of many of the Italian masters, provides a first-hand impression of what Luca Signorelli was like as a human being. This sixteenth-century enthusiast of everything visual—who figured in the Medici court, befriended Michelangelo, and had his finger on the pulse of artistic events in central Italy in the mid 1500s—also offers a fascinating perspective on Signorelli's art.

I'm surprised that the Karpes did not turn to Vasari, but, given that they were not art historians, they may have been unaware of him. They probably headed straight to the *S* section in the shelves of books organized by artists' names at the West Hartford Public Library, found Maud Cruttwell's opus, and decided they had what they needed. For that matter, I am sorry that Freud appears never to have discovered Vasari on Signorelli, because it would have been fascinating had he used that text as the basis for some sort of commentary on the life of the artist whose work moved him even more than did the art of Leonardo, about whose personal history he wrote so trenchantly. Vasari was related by blood to Signorelli, who, while seventy years older than he, was still alive during the first twelve years of Vasari's life. Giorgio Vasari's great-grandfather, Lazzaro Vasari, was the brother of Luca Signorelli's father, and when Signorelli was young and studying with Piero della Francesca, he had lived in Lazzaro Vasari's house. Sixty years later, he would return there briefly, when young Giorgio Vasari's parents owned the house, and by the time Signorelli died in 1523, the observant boy formed some strong impressions of this painter he greatly admired.

Vasari's short chapter on our man in *Lives of the Artists* begins with the words "The excellent painter, Luca Signorelli" and immediately provides the astounding information that "his work was more valued than that of any other master of whatever time." Vasari immediately says why. The writer's succinct assessment of Signorelli's primary achievement nails what for me is the reason that Freud both esteemed the artist among all others but then could not remember his name: "In his painting he introduced the nude and proved that it could, though not without consummate art, be made to seem as real as life."

Vasari calls "The Last Judgment" at Orvieto "a most singular and fanciful invention," and refers to the "many beautiful figures" in it. He emphasizes the influence this work had on the way Michelangelo composed some of the figures in the Sistine Chapel. But the main impact of our reading of Vasari is a highly unusual, and excruciating, detail of Signorelli's life. Vasari tells us that Signorelli's son, "a youth of singular beauty in face and person whom he tenderly loved, was killed in Cortona. In his deep grief the father had the child undressed, and with extraordinary constancy of soul, uttering no complaint and shedding no tear, painted the portrait of his dead child so that he might still be able to contemplate that which nature had given and fate taken away."

What would Freud have made of this, if only he had known? And the Karpes: Surely they would have had something to say, given their emphasis on the father/son issues invoked in Freud by Signorelli's work.

I only acquired this chilling information—one does not know which is more horrific, the death itself or the father's reaction—toward the end of my investigation of Freud's trip and Signorelli's art. It made me rethink something. If the artist's son died as a child, was his obsession with fully developed young men in part because they were what his son might have become if only he had lived? He could above all have been a bereaved father, for whom homosexuality was never an issue—in spite of what the paintings suggest. On the other hand, he could have been a necrophiliac pervert or a gay man whose love for his son had nothing to do with his own sexuality. We will never know; nor does it matter.

One thing, however, is sure. It is that Signorelli's treatment of his son's corpse was the opposite of anything Jewish. When Freud buried his father, he would have followed the tradition not just of closing the eyes but of keeping the dead body concealed from view. Embalming—which was probably necessary for Signorelli to paint his dead son—was forbidden. Tears, on the other hand, would not have been discouraged after Jacob Freud died. Stoicism has no role in traditional Jewish mourning practices.

VASARI RECOUNTS A TOUCHING STORY ABOUT SIGNORELLI from the artist's dotage. This is the time period when, "having worked for almost all of the princes of Italy and having grown old," Signorelli was back in Cortona, where he was born, and "worked for his pleasure since he could not resign himself to a life of idleness." In Cortona, Signorelli painted a *Life of the Virgin* for the nuns of Santa Margherita in Arezzo. The work was then transported to that convent. Signorelli, although eighty years old and frail, made the trip to watch the installation of the painting and to visit friends and relatives.

This was when Signorelli again stayed at the Casa Vasari, the place where he had lived some sixty years earlier while he had studied with Piero. It was now home to eight-year-old Giorgio Vasari. Vasari at the time of his writing well recalled "the good old man, who was most courteous and agreeable." On hearing that the only thing "Giorgino"—which was what everyone called the little boy—wanted to do at school was draw figures, and that he was not interested in other academic subjects, Signorelli urged the boy's father to let him learn to draw, devoting himself to other forms of learning only "afterward." Signorelli told Antonio, Giorgino's father, that "the knowledge of design, if not profitable, cannot fail to be honorable and advantageous." Vasari then describes a vivid memory from when he was eight: "Then he [eighty-year-old Signorelli] turned to me and said, 'Study well, little kinsman.' He said many other things about me which I refrain from repeating because I know I have not lived up to the expectations of the good old man."

During Signorelli's visit to Arezzo, "Giorgino" developed a "severe nosebleed." It was Signorelli who treated it: "He bound a jasper round my neck with his own hand and with infinite tenderness. This recollection of Luca I shall cherish while I live."

It is practically a form of hero worship, in which Vasari's penultimate paragraph is the coup de grace:

> Luca Signorelli was a man of the most upright life, sincere in all things, affectionate, mild, and aimiable in his dealing with all, and most especially courteous to everyone who desired his works. He was a very kind, efficient instructor to his disciples. He lived very splendidly, dressed handsomely, and was always held in the highest esteem for his many good qualities both at home and abroad.

Were it not for the way that Vasari heaps similar praise on almost every other artist about whom he writes, we might take this as the gospel. Of Giotto, he declares, "He was loved by all, most especially by eminent men of all professions." He tells us that "Andrea Mantegna was so kindly, and in every way so estimable, that his memory must ever be held in cordial respect." Of Filippino Lippi, Vasari announces, "Ever courteous, obliging, and friendly, Filippino was lamented by all, especially by the noble youth of Florence, who often availed themselves of his readiness and generosity." We learn of Pietro Perugino: "His manner pleased so in his day that artists came from France, Spain, Germany and other countries to study his methods." Leonardo da

Vinci garners such accolades that the others pale: "Nor was there ever an artist who did more to honor the art of painting. The radiance of his countenance, which was splendidly beautiful, brought cheer to the most melancholy. . . . He was physically so strong that he could bend a horseshoe as if it were lead. His generous liberality offered hospitality to rich or poor. . . . For his many admirable qualities, with which he was so richly endowed, . . . his fame can never be extinguished."

What a place the world would be if it was peopled only with artists who lived up to these descriptions!

In *The Central Painters of the Renaissance,* Bernhard (as he spelled his name for the publication of that book, although elsewhere, both before and after, he was just plain Bernard) Berenson gives his particular take on Signorelli. This was in 1899, the same year that his former house-keeper/secretary Maud Cruttwell was writing her monograph, but his main points about Signorelli's art are quite different from hers.

Berenson starts by comparing Signorelli to Piero della Francesca's other student, Melozzo da Forlì, emphasizing that for Melozzo what counted was the quintessential expression of emotions ranging from "the joy in mere living" to "solemnity and magical aloofness." Then, rising to a crescendo, he brings Signorelli into the picture: "Luca Signorelli does not glow with Melozzo's consuming fire; and yet he takes his rank beyond. His was the finer and deeper mind, his genius fetched the larger compass, his perception of value, both in life and in art, was subtler and more just. Even in feeling for the poetry in things, Luca was inferior to no man."

As if that is not enough, Berenson then credits Signorelli with having "a sense for tactile values scarcely less than Giotto's." Beyond that, he had "Masaccio's or Piero dei Franceschi's [della Francesca's] command over action."

I find this puzzling from the word go. After claiming that Signorelli lacks Melozzo's "consuming fire," Berenson then says he is unequaled in his "feeling for the poetry in things" and reached beyond Melozzo. Is that not a contradiction? The renowned art historian seems to credit Signorelli with what he has just said the painter is missing, adding confusion with that odd expression "fetched the larger compass." For me, "tactile values" are really not a big part of Giotto's work; Giotto's art is utterly heavenly, in a realm of its own, because of the distribution of color and the incredible drawing and composition, while the tactile is not particularly relevant. And "command over action" is not essential to Masaccio or Piero; the marvel of the first of these two great painters is in the solidity of the forms, their bold presence, whereas for the second it is the dreamlike, otherworldly quality that is vital. Berenson has come up with straw horses, only to knock them down.

But he is leading somewhere with all these flourishes. "Great artist he would have been with these qualities alone," writes Berenson with his odd style, "but for him they were means to an end, and that end, different from Melozzo's, was his joy in the Nude."

What I most like here is the way that Berenson has capitalized "Nude." I have never known of anyone else to do this, but he keeps it up throughout the text. Having thus elevated "the Nude" to godlike status, he explains why: "I must limit myself here to the statement that the Nude human figure is the only object which in perfection conveys to us values of touch and particularly of movement. Hence the painting of the Nude is the supreme endeavour of the very greatest artists; and, when successfully treated, the most life-communicating and life-enhancing theme is existence." While Berenson never explains his need for self-limitation, I assume he means his censoring of any specific reference to sex.

For all his circumlocution, Berenson's main point does give us insight into why Freud was overwhelmed by this art. Signorelli's achievement was to evoke human aliveness in all its magnitude.

Berenson rightly points out that the form of "life-enhancing" imagery in Signorelli's art is by and large male. Berenson makes one of his charming, slightly obtuse, sideways statements about the matter. "The female form revealed itself to him but reluctantly," the art historian points out. For this reason, while "Signorelli's Nude . . . has . . . a certain gigantic robustness and suggestions of primeval energy," it is not the equal of Michelangelo's.

Then Berenson again uses comparison to make a point. The problem, he tells us, with Signorelli is "that he was a Central Italian—which is almost as much as to say an Illustrator." From here Berenson becomes ridiculous, at least to me. He goes this way and that until he comes to the conclusion that "Michelangelo was also an Illustrator—alas!—but he, at least, where he could not perfectly weld Art and Illustration, sacrificed Illustration to Art."

Having taken himself into the ring, Berenson then calls time-out. "But a truce to his faults! . . . Luca Signorelli none the less remains one of the grandest—mark you, I do not say pleasantest—Illustrators of modern times. . . . He was the first to illustrate our own house of life." Signorelli achieves this, writes Berenson, above all in the Orvieto frescoes. "How we are made to feel the murky bewilderment of the risen dead, the glad, sweet joy of the blessed, the forces overwhelming the damned! It would not have been possible to communicate such feelings but for the Nude, which possesses to the highest degree the power to make us feel, all over our own bodies, its own state." This is another of Berenson's observations the validity of which eludes me completely. When I look at the nudes, or Nudes, in Orvieto, I don't feel, alas, that those bodies and mine have all that much in common; nor do I imagine that Freud felt he measured up to the musclemen. I wonder how Berenson evaluated his own body when he looked at Signorelli's specimens, since he certainly did not resemble them.

Yet if Berenson means that the Orvieto frescoes have an effect on our own psychological state, there he has a point. Looking around the Cappella Nova, we can feel at certain moments as if we are the ones being pulled into hell, having our heads snapped off our necks, or being trampled. Elsewhere, we identify with the characters ascending to a realm of calm and joy. This may have been the clincher for Freud. The ability of Signorelli's images to cause extreme anxiety at one moment and plentiful well-being at the next, and the reasons for which the frescoes induce such contradictory feelings, explain in part why the great investigator of the human mind was so overwhelmed that he forgot the name, so like his own, of the illustrator of these states of mind.

CHAPTER 22

HANNIBAL

After discussing Freud and demonology, the Karpes go on an interesting tangent. They report that on his trip to central Italy Freud did not get as far south as Rome—a surprising omission for a tourist who had traveled all the way from Vienna. He did, however, reach Orte, some fifty miles north of the Eternal City.

Three years later, Freud wrote about the trip and mentioned "asking the way" to Rome in a narration of one of his own dreams in the 1900 *The Interpretation of Dreams.* Freud informs us that the point closest to Rome that he reached was Lake Trasimene. This was not so; Orte was nearer. In pointing out this discrepancy, the Karpes let us know that Lake Trasimene is eighty miles north of Rome.

My parents' diligent friends attach great significance to the reason for which Freud picked Lake Trasimene and used it to replace Orte in his account. That large body of water was where "the Carthaginians under the leadership of Hannibal imposed an important defeat on the Romans." Freud, they tell us, was "an avid admirer of the Semitic hero Hannibal." In *The Interpretation of Dreams,* Freud writes, "I had actually been following in Hannibal's footsteps. Like him, I had been fated not to see Rome. Hannibal . . . had been the favorite hero of my school days." On the trail of Freud's boyhood crush on a military figure, the Karpes then produce another rich nugget. On December 3, 1897 (less than three months after looking at the Signorellis), Freud wrote Fliess, "My longing for Rome is deeply neurotic. It is connected with my school boy hero-worship of the Semitic Hannibal, and . . . I have no more reached Rome than he did from Lake Tra-misene." The Karpes elegantly present the facts without overstating Freud's manipulation. But the reader is led to see that, when writing for publication three years after the fact, Freud conveniently made the jump from knowing he had gotten thirty miles nearer to Rome than Hannibal did to declaring that he had reached the exact same place as Hannibal and stopped his journey without going farther.

The Karpes reproduce a map to show both Freud's actual travel route and the one he had intended. When we study it, we realize that, while Freud had initially planned to follow the shoreline of Lake Trasimene, he changed his program. In fact, he went from Chiusi to Orvieto, then south to Orte, and then north to Assisi via Spoleto, and from there to Arezzo, which meant that he did not even bypass the large body of water. His claim in *The Interpretation of Dreams* was a fabrication; he had not even seen the lake. (That map also serves to make it seem almost inevitable that Freud saw the Giottos in Assisi and the Pieros in Arezzo. Yet while most knowledgeable tourists visiting central Italy would have focused more on these fresco cycles than on the Signorellis, Freud did not even comment on them in any of his letters or published writing.)

Then Richard and Marietta drop another bombshell. After years of claiming he wanted to go to Rome but was unable to do so, "It was finally his courageous behavior in facing the anti-Semitic crowd at Thunsee which gave him the courage to overcome his ambivalence and to visit Rome." They quote Martin Freud saying that this trip, which Freud made with his brother, was "the fulfillment of a long and cher-ished wish and . . . a high spot in his life."

What's going on here? Hannibal was a Semite? Did Freud worship him because he proved that a Semite could be a tough guy? Why did it take his standing up to anti-Semitism to liberate him to go to the city where the Popes are resident? Was he really that sensitive to the issue of

Catholic power? Or was it the pre-Christian Romans, rather than the Catholics, who intimidated him—because of their decadence?

Why did he falsify history and invent a stop in Lake Trasimene when he had not been there? Was it really because of his craving to be like Hannibal? Is this why the Signorellis moved him so much, because they present the masculine might that was the object of what he called his "school boy hero-worship"?

I decided to pursue Freud and Hannibal a bit further in a 1938 edition of Freud's writing that belonged to Dr. Bettina Warburg. Bettina was my wife's great-aunt and, like Dr. Solnit, a psychoanalyst of the old school. Her Freud volume was translated by Dr. A. A. Brill—himself a brilliant doctor—who treated several members of the family of a rich cousin of Katharine's grandfather and Bettina's (who were brother and sister).

Freud mentions Hannibal in the same paragraph of *The Interpretation of Dreams* where he tells the story about his father and the cap. In Brill's translation, Freud's account has novelistic poignancy. The occasion of little Sigmund's learning about his father's encounter with the anti-Semite was when Sigmund was "ten or twelve years old" and on a walk with his father. Jacob's goal, Sigmund writes, was "to show me that I had been born into happier times than he." Jacob explains that he "was well-dressed, with a new fur cap on my head" when a Christian knocked the cap off his head and instructed Jacob, whom he addressed as "Jew," to get off the pavement. Sigmund asks his father how he responded. Jacob replies that he "went into the street and picked up the cap." Here Sigmund Freud continues in a way that I think has great bearing on his responses to the Signorellis:

> That did not seem heroic on the part of the big, strong man who was leading me, a little fellow, by the hand. I contrasted this situation, which did not please me, with another, more in harmony with my sentiments—the scene in which Hannibal's father, Hamilcar Barcas, made his son

swear before the household altar to take vengeance on the Romans. Ever since then Hannibal has had a place in my fantasies.

In the shadow of his father's death when he went to Orvieto, Sigmund Freud surely relived those feelings of his father's being insufficiently strong. With the memories that accompany mourning, he would have concomitantly seen himself again as "a little fellow"— yearning for a "big, strong" role model after being brought up by the opposite. What he saw in the Cappella Nova must have ignited those simmering feelings into a conflagration. The powerful men in Orvieto would have fueled his "deeply neurotic" feelings and "hero-worship"— Freud's own words—for Hannibal. He would have considered again how Hannibal gained his Herculean attributes from having a strong father. His sense of diminution and disappointment, coupled with the longing to be like Hannibal and have a father like Hamilcar, would have made him dissatisfied to be Sigmund Freud.

ONE CAN UNDERSTAND WHY FREUD MADE THE BARCA FAMILY his ideal. If the notion that they were Semitic is debatable—they were Carthaginian—at least they were safely pre-Christian, having become powerful in the third century B.C. (Hamilcar's dates are thought to be approximately 275–228 B.C.; Hannibal's are 248–182 B.C.)

What boy wouldn't want a father like Hamilcar? A general and statesman, he excelled at both. The family name meant "thunderbolt," and he lived up to it. In the First Punic War, Hamilcar succeeded in guerilla combat against Roman troops in Sicily, and he later led the Carthaginian invasion of Spain. Under his rule, Carthage expanded its territory significantly.

Halmilcar's success in Sicily came in spite of his having only a small mercenary army. When he assumed its command, he whipped it into shape in a way that conjures some of the scenes in Orvieto. To punish those who had recently mutinied because they had not yet been paid, he murdered the worse offenders at night, drowned others at sea, and shipped to Africa those guilty of only minor infractions. But Hamilcar was more brave than cruel, inspiring rare spirit and discipline in his troops of limited number. In Sicily, he wedged a position on Mount Eryx between Roman forces at both the summit and the base, and moved on from there. Even as he had vanquished those of his soldiers who actively rebelled, he had such a spirit of loyalty to the ones who were killed by the Romans, even though they had disobeyed him by plundering the local population, that he asked for a truce, during which he could give them proper burials. The Romans denied his request, instructing him that the only justification for a truce would be to save those of his soldiers who were still alive; shortly thereafter, when he was inflicting casualties on the Romans and they now begged for a truce to bury *their* dead, he granted it, claiming his only enemies were soldiers still alive. The man had style as well as compassion.

In 241 B.C., Hamilcar's army retreated from Sicily. The Romans suspended their normal practice of requiring a token of submission under such circumstances; that rare gesture toward a defeated enemy testified to their particular admiration for Hamilcar. He became a hero in Carthage, all the more so when, with Hasdrubal the Fair, who would become his son-in-law, he headed to the Strait of Gibraltar and began to move into Hispania. Here he compensated Carthage for having lost Sicily and Sardinia by conquering territory that would provide a base for future wars against the Romans. Hamilcar's military skills, diplomacy, and patriotism, as well as his will to stand up to the Roman Empire, were renowned, outdone only by his son Hannibal.

As for Freud's obsession: Besides having such a manly father, Hannibal, who was born in 248 B.C., was blessed both with his own stunning abilities as a military commander and courage as a political reformer.

On that trip when he reached Lake Trasimene—which, some twenty-one centuries later, would inspire Freud to pretend the same—he had led his army, complete with war elephants, over the Pyrenees and the Alps en route from Iberia. He and his troops occupied a considerable amount of Italian territory for fifteen years.

Even if there was no Jewish-Gentile issue in Hannibal's story, his coming from Carthage, settled by the Phoenicians on the north coast of Africa (in what is today Tunisia), made Hannibal seem like the exotic outsider in his efforts to move into the Roman Empire. Freud latched onto a hero whose hallmark was that he had led an affront to the establishment. Besides the aspects of Hannibal with which he identified, there were those he envied. For me, one aspect of maleness that Hannibal had and that I still wish I had—and I have to believe this was true for Freud, as well—is the alliance of powerful, supportive brothers. His brother Hasdrubal (not to be confused with his brother-in-law Hasdrubal the Fair) held Carthaginian ground in Spain when Hannibal led the forces to Italy, and his two other brothers would also help him command.

Sigmund Freud's own siblings offered no such alliance or support. As the firstborn child of Jacob and Amalia, he grew up aware of two half brothers who were about his mother's age, some twenty years more than his own. Minor merchants, they were a world apart from him. As a child, he was often reminded that the brother who would have been closest to him in age, a full brother, Julius, died as a baby, just weeks before Sigmund turned two; even if he had no direct memory of the event, the loss burned. He had one other younger brother and five younger sisters, but they played no major role in his life.

Hannibal was deemed "the father of strategy"; many historians consider him unequaled as a military strategist and technician. He was known to have said, "I will either find a way or make one"; I picture Freud's glee at the words. The story to which Freud often referred, that Hannibal swore to his father he would always oppose

Rome, comes from Livy. Hannibal was a boy at the time, and made the agreement after begging Hamilcar to let him join him in the Punic War. In one version of the tale, Hamilcar was holding young Hannibal over a roaring fire in a sacrificial chamber when the boy cried out, "I swear as soon as age will permit . . . I will use fire and steel to arrest the destiny of Rome."

What a way to become manly! What a perfect image for Freud to have had in mind as he looked at Signorelli's frescoes! Whatever allure there is to sadistic hazing as a way of imbuing male strength on the boy who can stand up to it and emerge triumphant had had its impact on Freud. To have had a commanding, effective father instead of the meek, unsuccessful Jacob was central to the fantasy.

Livy makes clear the qualities that Hannibal had acquired from his male parent and role model. Following Hamilcar's death in battle, Hannibal's brother-in-law (Hasdrubal the Fair) took command of the Carthaginian army, but then Hasdrubal the Fair was assassinated—in 221 B.C.—and twenty-seven-year old Hannibal was appointed commander in chief. Livy tells us that as soon as he appeared before the troops, "The old soldiers fancied they saw Hamilcar in his youth given back to them: the same bright look, the same fire in his eye, the same trick of countenance and features. Never was one and the same spirit more skillful to meet opposition, to obey, or to command." Reading these words, which were presumably the same ones Freud read in German, I, too, would like to have been Hannibal—and to have had a father like Hamilcar. The things he did! Crossing the Alps, when confronting a rockfall, he broke through it with a mixture of vinegar and fire. In Trebia, to vanquish the Roman infantry, he managed an ambush on the flank that cut them to pieces. In Etruria, in the spring of 217 B.C. (one pictures a balmy day on the Italian plains), he calculated that in order to lure Rome's main army, commandeered by Flaminius, into battle, he needed to devastate the territory Flaminius was protecting; the tactic worked, and Hannibal managed to cut Flaminius off from Rome in what military historians consider the first moment in all of time when a mass of soldiers were forced to reverse direction. It was after this that Hannibal reached Lake Trasimene, where he destroyed many of Flaminius's retreating troops in the water and killed Flaminius himself.

Freud must have loved this stuff. And he must also have thrilled to the way that Hannibal, joined by Spanish and Gallic heavy cavalry, led by his brother Hanno (yet another brave man in the Barca family), managed to hem in the much larger Roman army in Apulia. Not all went Hannibal's way—his brother Hasdrubal eventually had his head cut off by the Romans, and his brother Mago Barca was defeated in Liguria—but by the time Hannibal sailed back to Africa from Italy in 203 B.C., he was, at age forty-five, an esteemed statesman. Even though Carthage lost the Second Punic War and had its empire reduced, he became a chief magistrate on his return to his homeland.

Hannibal had the proper amount of difficulty, and wit, to make him more suitable as a Freudian hero than would have been a leader who never experienced defeat and just kept acquiring medals. As Carthage became more prosperous, the Romans grew alarmed, and he was forced into exile. It was then that, according to Cicero, he responded to a lecture given by the philosopher Phormio by publicly announcing that he had witnessed many old fools in his life but that Phormio beat them all. He spoke out similarly against Roman greed. By the time he died (either in 183 or 182 B.C.), he had made his mark not just for his physical courage but for his outspokenness.

So Freud had latched onto someone known both for the originality of his words as well as the cleverness of his battle tactics. Moreover, Hannibal was famous for his personal bravery. He was said to ask nothing of his soldiers he would not do himself. Standing in the Cappella Nova, Sigmund Freud surely felt some of that same intoxication with sheer strength and effectiveness that thoughts of Hannibal inspired in him.

Brill, who translated the revised *Interpretation of Dreams* rather than the original, includes a footnote Freud added after the sentence with the name Hamilcar and ending in "vengeance on the Romans." Freud writes, "In the first edition of this book I gave here the name 'Hasdrubal,' an amazing error, which I explain in my *Psychopathology of Everyday Life*." There was something about the name Hamilcar that was like the name Signorelli. Both evoked issues that made Sigmund Freud go haywire.

CHAPTER 23

JACKIE

NO MATTER WHAT ELSE WE WANT TO BE, most boys have a Hannibal/conquistador fantasy.

In June of 1978, Jacqueline Onassis invited Katharine and me for dinner at her New York apartment. The other people present were going to be her daughter, Caroline, and John Russell and Rosamond Bernier. It was a very hot summer evening, but, since we were going to the ballet at Lincoln Center afterward—to see *Swan Lake*—I was wearing a suit.

When we arrived, Jackie immediately told me to take off my jacket. In her unusual whispering voice, unlike the speaking manner of anyone else I have ever encountered, a softly hoarse mix conveying shyness and intelligent confidence and true politeness, she explained, "We have no air conditioning in the apartment, and it is so hot tonight."

I followed her instructions happily. In some sophomoric way, I relished the act of removing an article of clothing in front of her. Then I began to look at her pictures—for the most part, minor eighteenth-century watercolors of equestrian scenes—and make small talk about them.

After a couple of minutes, Jackie said, "I tried to open one of the living room windows, and so did my butler, but you know these old Fifth Avenue buildings. I think they are all painted shut."

"Well, I'll give it a try," I offered.

"Oh, *would you?* But don't feel bad if you can't; no one else could, and Virgil [in fact, the name of Balthus's butler, because I cannot remember the name of Jackie's] is *very* strong."

I walked over to the large sash window facing Central Park. Jackie stood right next to me as I grabbed the top of the bottom panel and tried to get it to budge. I could not even wiggle it.

"Don't worry, Nick. They're impossible. I will have to get the super or a repairman to come in tomorrow."

Of course I could not stop. I tried with every bit of might I had to force the damn thing open. I huffed and puffed and groaned, not caring if I pulled my back out forever. I was keenly aware of who was standing on my left, while Katharine looked with amusement from behind us. My mind was racing. Come on, Weber, I thought. This is the woman who was married to your hero. This is the woman you picture sitting next to de Gaulle, to Kruschev, to Pablo Casals. The least you could do is open a fucking window.

Adrenaline is miraculous. After about a minute of flat-out exertion, I felt the sealed paint crack along the sides. At last, the bottom broke free, and, haltingly at first, it budged a couple of short notches. I inhaled, made one more big push, and in an easy glide, the window went up.

The beautiful woman next to me just said, "Oh, oh, oh, oh . . . You are *so* strong. Oh thank you so much. Amazing."

It mattered more to me than any aspect of our conversation that evening.

Meanwhile, my personal obsession reappeared surprisingly in my thoughts. During dinner and the ballet, I periodically pictured Susie seeing me open the window. Here I was with the most sought-after woman in the world, accompanied by the wife whom I love profoundly and with whom I was relishing the evening with our particularly conjoined spirit. Yet my private goddess—the one who had made me first feel powerful, even electric, at the age when I was becoming a man—was my imagined witness. Hannibal's admirer, the Freud who faltered on the name "Signorelli," well knew that drive. We guys need to prove ourselves. Nothing else matches the physical.

CHAPTER 24

OUR BODIES, OUR DEATHS

GIVEN THE IMPORTANCE THE KARPES ASSIGN to the younger
Freud's attitude both toward his father and toward Jewish traditions concerning death rites as essential elements to his forgetting of
Signorelli's name, it is surprising that these scrupulous scholars left out
certain details of this missive Freud sent William Fliess from Berggasse
19, his office in Vienna, on November 2, 1896, shortly after Jacob Freud
died. Reading that letter in a different English version from the one
they used (they probably translated it from the German themselves), I
found aditional elements of great note. Freud writes:

Dear Wilhelm,

By one of those dark pathways behind the official consciousness the old man's death has affected me deeply. I
valued him highly, understood him very well, and with
his peculiar mixture of deep wisdom and fantastic lightheartedness he had a significant effect on my life. By the
time he died, his life had long been over, but in [my] inner
self the whole past has been reawakened by this event.

I now feel quite uprooted.

. . . I must tell you about a nice dream I had the night
after the funeral. I was in a place where I read a sign:

"You are requested to close the eyes."

I immediately recognized the location as the barbershop I visit every day. On the day of the funeral I was kept

waiting and therefore arrived a little late at the house of mourning. At that time my family was displeased with me because I had arranged for the funeral to be quiet and simple, which they later agreed was quite justified. They were also somewhat offended by my lateness. The sentence on the sign has a double meaning: one should do one's duty to the dead (an apology as though I had not done it and were in need of leniency), and the actual duty itself. The dream thus stems from the inclination to self-reproach that regularly sets in among the survivors.

Some of what Freud was feeling—the vital factor of "self-reproach," for example—we already know from Richard and Marietta. But their main goal, I believe, based on what they chose to quote, and then their use of italics for "after"and their addition of "sic," was to discredit Freud for having made the dream occur *before* the funeral in *Interpretation of Dreams,* just as they cast doubt on his veracity with the Lake Trasimene issue. I find this odd.

In many ways, Richard and Marietta subscribe respectfully to the Freudian canon. Why, then, in addition to having us see their master's refabrication of the sequence of events, do they simultaneously sell him short by leaving certain things out?

Is this not because they are like the son who on the one hand worships his father and on the other hand needs to outdo him?

I, for similar reasons, initially imposed a limitation on my own thinking by treating the Karpes' article as the gospel, and looking no further.

They were unimpeachable. And how easy it was to feel I had read the last word on a subject and could call it quits with impunity. The conclusiveness was irresistibly satisfying.

Then, in the same pattern as the Karpes, I increasingly saw my seers' errors. I found their mistakes, and various shortcomings, not because I wanted or needed to debunk Richard and Marietta—I would have loved to continue finding them perfect—but because the faults were real, and to be blind to them would have been stupid.

I keep thinking of Anni Albers's statement that "Kandinsky often said, 'There is always an *and*.'" How true, but at times it is against human nature to seek it out. Resolution has its lure. Fortunately, there are other occasions when the "and" is rich—as with the additional material in Freud's letter to Fliess.

It was the next generation who forced me to look further. This has often been the case for me. My elder daughter, Lucy, has often insisted that I see certain truths I would otherwise have managed to avoid; her success is in part because of the polite, even charming, way she has led me to do so—far more effective than the screaming that occurs with most firstborn children. It was her sister, Charlotte, who provided me with the entire letter to Fliess, taking me beyond the Karpes' chosen excerpts, and leading me to the additional detail of the barbershop, which strengthens the evidence that Freud offended his family. My two daughters, in different ways, one general and one quite specific, had opened me up to a whole new territory concerning Freud and his father. Moreover, inspired by both of these young women, so bright in very different ways, so reassuring in their acceptance of uncomfortable truths I instinctively would, as a child, have avoided, I felt pushed to reconsider myself, my own father, and *his* father.

CHAPTER 25

GRANDPA'S FUNERAL

THE ISSUES SURROUNDING JEWISH FUNERARY TRADITIONS, a son's sadness and conflict when burying his father, and the ways we both identify with and distinguish ourselves from our fathers at such moments, can be overwhelming.

I had, when I was twenty-two, an experience that makes me think that Sigmund Freud took a certain delight—alongside the "self-reproach"—by bucking the expected protocol on the day of his father's funeral. It occurred the day after my paternal grandfather died, when I accompanied my father to pick out his father's casket.

I was astonished by the large display room at the Jewish mortuary, with rows of one garish silk-lined coffin after another. The details and price information were on tented signboards in front of each of the fifty or so "deluxe" caskets on view. Aghast when Mr. Weinstein (whose brother, if you can believe it, named his son, the future director of their family's eponymous mortuary, Morton) tried to convince Dad "to spring"—a term I detest—for a bronze-plated nickel coffin lined with crimson silk, I remarked, "I thought that Orthodox Jews were buried in plain pine boxes."

Mr. Weinstein turned to me with visible hostility and, staring at my camel hair topcoat, simply said, "Young man, how much did that coat on your back cost?"

Dad, seeing how stunned I was, simply said, in his usual quiet and gentle voice, "Nick wasn't talking about the cost, Herman. He was talking about good taste."

That, in a nutshell, was our relationship. My father always defended me.

He did so with such calm, such resolute loyalty, such understated tenderness that my eyes are welling with tears as I remember him.

After my father stood up for me so exquisitely in response to Mr. Weinstein's high-pressure salesmanship, the indefatigable mortician just kept going. "You want good taste?" he asked excitedly. "Let me show you our Architectural Line."

In his shiny dark suit, the enthusiastic funeral home impresario strutted over to the next row and pointed out a very ornate white marble coffin, exploding, "Voilà!"

I had had it. "Mr. Weinstein," I began, in a haughty voice and tone that were far more my mother's than my father's. "That motif of the demilunettes over fluted pilasters comes directly from the style commissioned by the Medici, and therefore to me it smarts of anti-Semitism." I had absolutely no idea what I was talking about, but at least it made the midget version of Uriah Heep take two steps backward. Dad now went from being my defender to being my most enthusiastic audience. While other fathers would have been disapproving, he was totally amused whenever I behaved like this.

We settled on the simplest oak casket available; while it had some molding and was not as plain as we would have liked, at least it was dignified. Then, on the way home, Dad told me that when he was a teenager he had dated the woman now married to Mr. Weinstein, and that she had had fantastic breasts. His face assumed a look of sheer ecstasy as he remembered them. My father, who was normally not given to self-disclosure, then abruptly shifted the conversation to talking about his fear of having some of his father's weaker sides.

These were some of the issues Freud faced with those paintings at Orvieto: strength versus weakness, his sense of himself in relation to his father and the connection between death and sexuality, the ultimate aliveness. (I trust that my wife, mainly a novelist but also an essayist of unflinching candor, will forgive me for a revelation of our private life. I often think of the way we made love the night my mother died. A couple of hours after the phone call when we had the information that the end, blessedly, had finally come, Katharine and I fell into each other's arms passionately and silently, joined in a need to affirm our vitality as well as our feelings for each other.)

MASCULINITY AND JUDAISM, THE TWO SUBJECTS that obsessed Freud, continued to be on my mind a lot during the week following Grandpa's funeral. My father, my cousin Richard, my uncle Mel, and I paid daily visits to my grandmother's house while she sat shiva, and it was our role to help form a minyan. Nana had been a ballbuster for as long as anyone could remember, and my father was clearly troubled by his memory of his father's compliance with her perpetual demands and by his own fear of being a similarly docile husband.

It had amazed me when my father had acknowledged, driving home from the mortuary, that he worried that he perpetuated his father's legacy of complying with a strong-willed wife. I had often been troubled by the ways he let my mother call the shots about so many things, but I had never thought Dad was that self-conscious.

Dad was, regardless, someone with the exceedingly rare quality of strength in tandem with supreme kindness. He had gone beyond his parents in countless ways. I often think of this.

Recently, I came across a journal entry I wrote in 2009, and I was struck by the way that what I was feeling then I feel still. It was a beautiful sunny late-September afternoon in Paris. In my journal I set the date as "some six years after his death," which is odd, because it was really eight. Yet when it comes to feelings about my father, although they can vary greatly, time itself makes no difference; he could easily still be alive, robust and energetic, no matter how many years he has been dead. I miss him unbearably, and always have.

The day I wrote that journal entry, I had just returned from the Louvre. The tenderness and humanity of the Donatello relief there, unquestionably authentic, even if the one at the Met is now in doubt, made me feel overwhelmed by the connection that exists between a parent and a child. I then went to see the Louvre's single Signorelli. It is in the same room as the Piero della Francesca portrait of Sigismundo Malatesta, a painting of such quiet strength—similar to my father's—that, looking at it, I found it simply unacceptable that Dad was dead. And then I jumped to a destabilizing anguish at the notion of my own death—in part because to be dead will mean that I can no longer look at art.

There are times when I accept the idea of death with the rationality of Le Corbusier, who called it the horizontal requisite to the vertical of life. There have also been occasions when the consuming misery of clinical depression has made a side of me think that the end of life would be the only relief (although inner voices enabled me to know better and to endure the hellfire pain until the miraculous medicine kicked in). But at those moments when life is unbearably rich, human achievement staggering, the givens of the universe and of our bodies of unfathomable splendor, the idea of the end is so untenable that the only thing to do is to shut my eyes to it.

Whenever I am in the latter state, terribly excited by the beauty and wonder of things, the person to whom I want to communicate this, still, is often my father, to whom I wrote ecstatic letters from London and Paris when I made my first trip to Europe as a college student. He encouraged celebration. When my sister was about eleven, and I about five, he began taking us to a large public reservoir surrounded by woods not far from our home, and he would simply hold our hands and talk about the miracles of existence; we took these outings for years. That quality of appreciation—whether of nature or art or trapshooting or the splendor of a Brahms symphony—is what marked him as a parent.

Where did he come from? How did he emerge so unlike his parents, who were perpetually tortured by their lack of money and by my grandfather's being low man on the totem pole in the family business? What made him decide that the changing of the dinnerware for Passover was a waste of time, the wearing of a yarmulke even in a synagogue an invalid symbol, the adherence to certain but not other kosher laws a travesty when one should worry more about what one could do for humanity? Where did he get the wish for human equality that made him join the American Communist Party as a young man? And how did he find the life companion who was probably the main reason he joined the Party, and then how did he manage to marry my tall, Germanic, blue-eyed, fair-skinned mother, take over her family's business, and, by the early 1950s, fit in so perfectly as a first-class passenger on the *Queen Mary*? He was at home in the most elegant milieus not because he was a pretender (he was not), but because he had the true manners that are possible only when one is essentially kind, when one is determined to make life better for almost everyone whom one encounters (another thing that distinguished him from his parents, especially his contentious mother).

This is what sons do; we reflect on our paternal lineage. And as was true for Sigmund Freud in the Cappella Nova eleven months after Jacob's death, sometimes it is more than we can fathom or bear.

CHAPTER 26

FATHERS AND SONS

I REALIZED WHEN READING THE KARPES' ESSAY THAT, as with my own psychoanalyst, I craved their approval. And I also wanted them to know my father better than I suspected they did, since in social situations he invariably played second fiddle to my dynamic, sometimes outrageous mother.

The way that the Karpes fasten onto concerns about male strength as a major part of what flummoxed Freud at Orvieto, and Freud's disappointment that his father lacked the force of Hannibal and of Hannibal's *father* (as if a father's fortitude bestows the same on his son), with the emphasis on Jacob's cowering before the anti-Semites, makes me wish—in the irrational way that one wants psychoanalysts to know everything, to assume the God-like power in which many of us atheists put them—that they knew a specific story about my father that I learned only when my mother was dying, in 1990. (Either the Karpes had died or moved away from West Hartford by then, because otherwise they would have been in evidence in those months preceding my mother's death, and would have been at her funeral or written my father a condolence letter.)

I had decided that now was the time to ask Mom questions which otherwise would go unanswered forever. My mother had not actually acknowledged that her days were numbered, and was maintaining the charade that she was merely very tired and would eventually recover from whatever was depleting her energy, which she treated as if it were merely a virus, but there was a tacit understanding that her life was nearly over. (This powerful woman was finally succumbing to a breast cancer that had already metastasized to her liver when the illness was discovered seven years earlier. She had valiantly struggled to live as long as she did, astonishing the doctors while keeping up her life as a painter and sportswoman almost as intensely as before, in spite of the severe toll of chemotherapy; my *mother's* strength, and her expectations of me, while not part of the Freudian/Karpian canon, were central to my own formation.)

It was in about 1970, when I was in my early twenties, that I had learned that both my parents had been members of the American Communist Party in the late 1930s. My sister, Nancy, had found in the basement a packet of love letters written in 1939, the year they married—my mother was nineteen, my father twenty-three—in which they addressed one another as "Dear Comrade." There was also a newspaper published by the local cell, with articles by my mother. At the time of the discovery, Nancy and I asked our parents about their politics during that time period. My mother was hesitant to answer—my feeling was that she was dramatizing her discomfort—while my father was more forthcoming. He calmly explained that he and Mom believed in the tenets of communism and thought at the time that the policies being put into effect in the Soviet Union offered the greatest chance for well-being to the greatest number of people.

In the ensuing two decades, we would, on rare occasions, return to this subject. My mother admitted that her previous political affiliation was the reason for her having once made a remark that I had been unable to understand but which now made sense to me. I was in fourth grade at the local elementary school, and came home with a report card that was generally outstanding except for a B in science as opposed to A's in all the other subjects. "That's just as well, Nicky," Mom said at the time, "You could never get a job doing research for the government anyway."

Since she had a flare for being tantalizing, and I was so used to her deliberately baiting me but then leaving me puzzled, or trying to do so,

I had developed a technique of tuning out her provocations. When she then refused to tell me why she had made this odd statement, beyond saying, "Oh, you wouldn't pass all the background tests," I let it go; I disliked the feeling of being baited, and was determined to appear uninterested. But I never forgot Mom's odd comment, and sensed that she had a serious reason for leaving me quizzical. Now that I knew she and Dad had been Communists, and I understood what that meant, I grasped her ambivalence between being proud of that affiliation and being terrified because of the possible repercussions.

The time of the quip about my inferior science abilities was during the Eisenhower years, and my parents had both been ardent Stevenson supporters. Since most of the students at my elementary school came from Republican households, I was used to ours being different. Besides, there had been the moment when my sister, six years older than I, had, in the fourth grade at the same school, been assigned to memorize a poem by Edgar Guest. The story was often told of what happened next. Nancy had been working on her rendition of the famous line that ends "It takes a heap of livin' in a house t' make it home" when our mother announced, "That's the last straw. I've had it with that woman."

"That woman" was a teacher named Miss Ladd. Mom donned one of her Bonwit Teller suits (she favored the designer B. H. Wragge, whose clothes suited tall and thin women who preferred to look crisply intelligent than coquettish or frilly in the manner of many of their contemporaries), grabbed her Mark Cross alligator handbag, and told Nancy she would drive her back to school after lunch (we usually rode our bikes or walked). Off they went in the turquoise-blue Chevrolet convertible, a deliberate contrast to the other mothers' wooden station wagons. At school, Mom stormed into the classroom, went up to Miss Ladd (whose insistence on the singing of patriotic songs already irked her), and, in her usual bold voice, asked, "Miss Ladd, do you know what Dorothy Parker said about Edgar Guest?"

I have no idea how the woman responded before Mom continued: "'I would rather flunk a Wasserman test than read the poems of Edgar Guest.'"

Nor do I know where the conversation went from there, but since this was the sort of thing my mother did, and her account of the story included her explaining to me that a Wassermann test was for diagnosing syphilis, and then her telling me what syphilis was and making it sound like part of the exciting life of artists and writers in Paris. I was not surprised that I would not pass a background check initiated by the government. As a kid, I simply assumed it was because our family was so unlike other people.

Once I knew about my parents' communism, however, some other remarks and strange events also began to make sense to me. Mom allowed that in the fifties she had been too terrified by McCarthyism to discuss her and Dad's politics of the thirties. I now learned that their engagement party had been a fund raiser for the Abraham Lincoln Brigade. My mother never discussed ideology—but she relished certain details of the past. She often voiced her profound admiration for Lillian Hellman for having, on the day she was testifying before the House Committee on Un-American Activities, gone to purchase a new hat for the event at I. Magnin; this, Nancy and I were instructed, was true style, and what it meant to have a sense of self-worth.

On the other hand, not everything evoked that triumphant glow on Mom's face the way that her reverence for Hellman's flare did. The summer my mother read *The Book of Daniel,* E. L. Doctorow's gripping fictionalized version of the trial and execution of Julius and Ethel Rosenberg—who shared a wedding date with my parents (June 18, 1939)—she was so devastated by the book that she could hardly focus on anything else.

It was my father who explained, with Hamilcar's sense of conviction, what they believed in. He was completely at ease telling me why he had been attracted to communism—why he found it so refreshing in contrast to his parents' Orthodox Judaism, which he felt did nothing for humanity and created rules that served no purpose—while always adding that Stalin's abuse of power, and the Russian pact with Hitler, had changed everything, causing my parents to leave the Party.

In those moments at the end of my mother's life, the issue so vital to Freud—one's father's response to bigotry, his style of confrontation—really came into focus for me. Reclining on the chintz-covered chaise in her bedroom—that single piece of furniture so oddly traditional for this person who rarely followed the norm—my mother told me about the arrival of the FBI at our house in 1956. Her face yellowed with jaundice, her once-thick and naturally blond hair having come back fine and white after the complete baldness resulting from chemotherapy, she looked like a version of herself in the afterlife, but she sounded entirely present.

My mother set the scene of that event in the early stages of McCarthyism. I was eight years old, and tucked into my bed for the night. Two FBI agents came to the door. They informed my father, "Mr. Weber, you own a successful printing company. But it could be far *more* successful. As you know, United Aircraft has its main headquarters in East Hartford. They require a lot of high-security printing, and you have an opportunity to do it, all of it, without competitive bidding."

My father, who was soft-spoken but neither meek nor naïve, simply looked at his two visitors in their navy blue suits. He anticipated what was coming.

My dying mother next explained that "those goverment thugs in their badly-fitting dark suits" told Dad all he had to do was "give the names of your old associates."

My mother smiled with the love and pride she had for the man to whom she had been married for fifty years. "And so, Nicky, your father simply said, 'Good night, gentlemen,' and led the men to the door without a further word."

I am as proud writing this as Sigmund Freud was humiliated when thinking about Jacob's picking up his hat and scurrying off of the sidewalk.

Mom's story instantly brought to mind a moment when she and Dad had been visiting me at Camp Killooleet in Vermont, a place where I spent five mostly wonderful summers from 1956 to 1960 when I was aged eight to twelve. This great progressive summer camp, run by Pete Seeger's brother John and John's wife, Ellie, was, I learned well after the fact, said to be for "red-diaper babies." When I was ten, and my parents were there for visiting weekend, everything was going perfectly—they watched me play softball and do archery, and we had had a great picnic lunch together on the advanced swimmers' deck, which was off-limits without a lifeguard—when, suddenly, once we were back where the camp buildings were, I saw my mother's face turn ashen. I knew something was terribly wrong, but I had no idea what it was.

Having been totally attentive to me, Mom now seemed completely unaware that I was even there. She simply looked at Dad and said, "Saul, do you see who that is?" My father turned toward the Main House—we were standing outside Bunk VI (I can smell the wooden siding as I write this)—which was the direction my mother was glaring in. His face immediately assumed a look one very rarely saw: that of utter consternation.

"Hey, what's going on?" I asked.

Still neither of my parents appeared to notice that I was standing there, let alone that I expected them to focus only on me. Mom simply looked at Dad and confirmed what they both knew. "Yes, it's Elia Kazan."

"You mean Judy Kazan's father?" I asked, trying to get included in the conversation. Judy was a camp counselor.

My father, recognizing that I was feeling like an outsider, asked in a distracted way if I knew Judy, but I could see that he was completely in another world. I asked my parents what the big deal was. Mother, provocative as ever, simply said, "He gave names." At the time, she refused to tell me anything more, even though this time I begged for an explanation.

A FEW YEARS AGO, I WROTE A COVER STORY FOR *The New York Times Book Review* about a biography of Jerome Robbins. After I handed it in, my editor called me and said he knew I was interested in dance but that he'd had no idea I was obsessed with American communism. What most fascinated me in this excellent biography was the history of Robbins's giving names to the House Committee on Un-American Activities, and his tortured guilt ever since. I wrote about it with the confidence of someone proud of his father.

In that respect, and still thinking of Sigmund and Jacob, I remember a breakfast in my parents' dining room when I was about ten years old. It was the same routine as every other morning. My father and I were eating our bacon and sunny-side up eggs; he read the sports pages of the morning paper, while I looked at the comics. Mom, as usual, would not be seen until well after the live-in housekeeper had served her black coffee and a boiled egg and toast, and she had had her first cigarette of the morning.

Our housekeeper, a young black woman named Lucy, came in to the dining room and charged up to my father, as she had never done before, with a broad smile. She shook his hand and said, "Mrs. Weber told me what happened last night. I'm proud of you, Mr. Weber!"

I asked Dad what had happened, but he just shrugged off my question and kept checking the basketball scores. I realized I would have to ask my mother, whom I generally avoided until she had makeup on, what this was all about.

Mom, for once, was completely animated first thing in the morning. Alternating between a proud smile and a look of horror, she described the events of the previous evening. It had been the Fox Press Christmas party. This was the printing company my parents owned and my father ran. The forty-five employees had assembled at a local hotel ballroom for dinner and dancing. Mom explained that the five black employees and their spouses had been sitting at their own table. (The year was 1957, and this was their choice, an act of segregation my parents lamented.) The shop foreman, Lou Garigola, who had drunk too much, had gone up to them and started imitating their dialect.

My father jumped up and charged over to Lou, asking him what the hell he was doing. Lou turned and said, "How would you understand, you dirty Jew?" Dad simply went after him with a right hook; Lou started to fight back; other men pulled them apart.

After I heard the story, I charged back downstairs. "Will you fire him, Dad?"

"Yes, Nicky. I can't work with someone like that."

My father made life rather simple.

PART OF WHAT WAS SO REMARKABLE, I NOW REALIZE, is that he never overexplained. About a year after the Christmas party incident, the doorbell rang one morning and I opened it, to see Lucy's husband, Kenny, a smiling, rather rotund black man in his early thirties. Lucy had left my parents' house to marry him the previous spring. We had gone to the wedding, which had been a small event, our family the only white people there; it was a great occasion, with my father instantly befriending the Baptist minister who performed the ceremony.

Kenny asked for my father, and I explained he was not home. "Then give him this, please," Kenny said, handing me fifty dollars in tens.

"Sure, Kenny. Is there any message with it?"

"Not necessary," Kenny replied, with a warm expression on his face. "Your father's a wonderful man, Nicky."

When I gave Dad the money after he came home from work that day, I naturally asked to know the whole story. "It's nothing, Nicky."

I could not drop it, and Dad finally consented to give me one of his short answers. "He needed some money and I lent it to him. It was no big deal. This was the final payment. Kenny is a person of his word; he's a wonderful man, Nicky."

CHAPTER 27

ENTER JEAN-PAUL SARTRE

I N 1958, JEAN-PAUL SARTRE, AT THE REQUEST OF the film director
John Huston, wrote a screenplay about Sigmund Freud's life.

The fifty-three year old Existentialist philosopher agreed to the idea
in spite of having, when younger, been famously anti-Freudian. As he
told his frequent interviewer John Gerassi three years later, "When I was
twenty, I refused to believe that infancy or childhood predetermined
the behavior of adults. Remember, I substituted Freud's notion of the
'unconscious' with my notion of the 'lived,' meaning the constant anxiety of choosing. But over the years I moderated that point of view."

In his movie script, intended to show what counted most in Freud's
biography, Sartre dwelled on some of the same incidents in the psychoanalyst's past that the Karpes considered central to the forgetting
of Signorelli's name. That backward glance—in which, by focusing on
events in Freud's childhood, Sartre adapted Freud's approach to Freud
himself—was a surprising concession on the Frenchman's part. When
asked if certain events in his own childhood had predetermined his
later behavior, Sartre was adamant about the power of each individual's
actions in the present, regardless of so-called formative experiences.
While acknowledging that, when he once shared a bedroom with his
mother, the sight of her underarm hair had made a strong impression on him, he minimized the impact of such occurrences. Allow-
ing that, as a child, he felt a deep sense of security in the presence of
his "bearded, tall, majestic grandfather" (the words are Sartre's) "until
his double cross" (in this case, Gerassi's words), he denied that the

betrayal (which is never explained to us) violated his "sense of belonging" to such an extent that it had an impact on him subsequently. Sartre explained, "That's exactly where existential psychoanalysis tells you no, not necessarily. A choice is involved. And every choice is in the lived, in the context of everything that is happening in the world. The harder the choice, the more the anxiety. But that does not mean that the chooser is not free to make the choice."

Yet whether Sartre was inclined to follow the Freudian approach or challenge it, it's no surprise that he accepted Huston's request, for Freud was often his frame of reference. At age sixty-seven, elaborating on his own ongoing wish to fight injustice and spearhead revolution, he characterized himself as being "like Freud wanting to believe in God for just a moment to tell him off."

Sartre would eventually maintain that the reason he agreed to write the screenplay was because he was broke and Huston offered him 26 millions francs (the equivalent of half a million dollars, significant money in 1958). He ended up denouncing the result. When the film was in production, Sartre insisted that his name be removed from the credits. He complained that the movie was focusing more on Freud as a man than on "his supposed discovery of the unconscious"—which was, Sartre declared, what really mattered. Yet, for all of his announced skepticism about the importance of childhood events, and his ambivalence about considering Freud's life experiences, in his screenplay, Sartre makes the incident with Freud's father's cap pivotal. He also assigns Hannibal and Hamilcar significant roles.

The cap scene is a flashback. Jakob (Sartre's spelling for the senior Freud) is described as having a "jet black" beard. In Signorelli's frescoes, one of the few figures with a dark beard, if not a truly black one, is the Antichrist—that is, the Jew. The detail of the dark beard in Sartre's Jakob Freud confers his Semitic origins on him. "His clothes are clean but poor," Sartre wrote as advice to the costume designer. That sad fact makes Freud's father all the more pathetic. If he wore the deliberately rough garb of a Bohemian, it would be by choice, while this shabby attire with its attempted respectability suggests failure. It makes Jakob into an unsuccessful little merchant, trying to be presentable and live up to other people's standards, but lacking the means. (It is also a deliberate contradiction to Jacob's depiction of himself in fine clothing—in Sigmund's account of the incident.)

And then we get Sigmund: "a little boy of six or seven who trots along beside him, proud as Punch, and looks at him admiringly from time to time." Father and son are holding hands. Reading this, imagining it as a scene in a film, one prepares one's self for the child's devastation. The anticipation of the way the boy's high spirits will plunge becomes even more torturous when, in this flashback orchestrated by Sartre, Sigmund recalls his father saying, "You were proud! A little prince!"

Next, a man "of Herculean build" enters the scene. Could there be any more apt description for the physiques of Signorelli's powerhouses at Orvieto? Then, when the Herculean man sees the father and son, he "bears down on them with a quite threatening air." Here, too, Sartre's imagery conjures Signorelli's devils, swooping weaker beings off to hell. The assailant shouts at Jakob to get off the sidewalk—while, "with the back of his hand, he knocks his cap into the gutter."

"Pick up your cap and stay in the roadway," the brute instructs the Jew.

Sartre takes the moment and runs with it. He has the little boy attempt "to hurl himself" at the Herculean imposter. Jakob restrains the boy, so that little Sigmund is forced to try to kick, but "the stranger is already out of reach. He goes off without even turning around." Sartre could be describing precise events in Signorelli's scene of *The Damned*.

Finally, Jakob picks up his cap and puts it on his head, "without letting go of his son."

It is unbearable.

Our great Existentialist has used a brilliant device to magnify the impact of the event that was humiliating enough to Sigmund Freud when he simply heard about it from his father and experienced it secondhand. By giving the child an active, and devastatingly futile, role in the confrontation, Sartre makes the child's impotence far more palpable.

Things only get worse in the finale of Sartre's version of the episode. Jakob instructs little Sigmund to come with him onto the road. Father and son heed the instructions of the assailant together. And once they are there, "[a] carriage passes and spatters them with mud. The young Freud assumes a somber, stubborn expression (the very one we have so often seen on Freud's face)." By linking Freud's boyhood experience with his bearing forever after, Sartre makes this a defining moment in the development of Freud's persona.

In Sartre's next scene, Sigmund hands Jakob an engraving. The caption, which Jakob has to put on his spectacles to read, describes what it illustrates: "Hamilcar makes his son Hannibal swear to avenge the Carthaginians." Sigmund says to Jakob, "You're Hamilcar." Jakob says he is not; Sigmund insists. And then, "with savage fervor," the child cries out, "'I swear to avenge my father, the hero Hamilcar, and all the humiliated Jews. I shall be the best of all, I shall beat everybody and I shall never retreat.' The harshness of his intonation, so rare in a child, makes Jakob jump."

The scene continues with Jakob telling Sigmund he has never been the same since the moment of their being forced off the sidewalk, and explaining that "it was the time of the pogroms. They were just waiting for a pretext to set fire to the whole neighborhood." That pivotal bit of information is intended to assure Sigmund that his father had no choice, but we have no reason to believe it makes any difference to the boy.

And then Jakob calls him "My little Hannibal!"

Sigmund Freud's determination to be the mighty warrior even if his father was the opposite is underscored as the scene ends with an anti-Semite telling Jakob to pick up his cap, to which Jakob, offstage, answers "I'm not Hamilcar." "Little Sigmund," also offstage, is then heard to shout, "I shall avenge all the Jews. I shall never retreat. I shall never go down into the roadway. Never! Never! Never! Never!"

CHAPTER 28

WANTING TO BE HANNIBAL

ONE OF THE FUNDAMENTAL TOOLS OF PSYCHOANALYSIS is free association, which requires the patient to tell the doctor whatever has just come into his head, however illogical.

For my first year with Dr. Solnit, whom I met for four sessions a week when we were both in Connecticut (we had agreed to an unusual treatment plan that allowed for the extensive amount of traveling we both did), I screened out my associations. They would have interrupted my narrative.

Once I understood the need to tell him what my mind was seeing at all times, to reveal the odd jumps of thoughts and images, everything changed. Of course in real life one needs to limit the associations most of the time, but there are moments when they are instructive. It took me nearly three years to accept Dr. Solnit's counsel that repetition is an essential tool of the process, that psychoanalysis is the opposite of deliberate storytelling, where one edits out the things one has already said. I finally came to grasp that the spontaneous reemergence of certain themes, whatever they are, whether or not they seem noteworthy, is a means toward understanding.

This tool helped me, similarly, to understand what happened to Freud at Orvieto—or at least what I *think* happened. Just now, envisioning the scenes of Jakob and Sigmund Freud as narrated by Jean-Paul Sartre, I see about three things at once.

For one, I keep picturing Signorelli's imagery, in particular the powerful Herculean men.

At the same time, my mind presents images of my own father. I am remembering, yet again, those events when I was twenty-two and he was fifty-four and we picked out his father's casket with me being so opinionated, and then, in the car driving home, Dad allowed how troubled he was by his father's essential weakness. My father had amplified that he struggled with Grandpa's being physically the smallest of four brothers, as well as the poorest, and the way that tyrannical Nana never let him forget either deficiency.

The third group of associations is embarrassing. While thinking about the ride home from the mortuary, I pictured myself as a non-Jew. Indeed, I inherited my mother's blue eyes and fair skin. When I was little, I had her naturally blond hair. My father, on the other hand, had black hair, olive skin, and hazel eyes.

To be named Nicholas—with the middle name of Fox, to boot—is entirely different from being named Saul. Dad went to high school in the poor Jewish neighborhood in Hartford; I went to an Episcopal prep school. Moreover, to most, but not all, people—how some readers will hate this!—for many years I simply did not "seem Jewish." That has changed in recent years, and I have become more relaxed about the whole thing and accept and enjoy it as part of my identity, but then I felt differently.

SHORTLY AFTER KATHARINE AND I SENT OUT our wedding invitations in the summer of 1976, my future mother-in-law, Andrea, received a phone call from an aunt of Sidney Kaufman's, my future father-in-law. "So I see that Katharine is marrying someone who isn't Jewish," Esther Auerbach said, offering sympathy to the mother of the bride.

"What makes you know that, Esther?" Andrea asked.

"Nicholas Fox Weber: how goyish can you get?" Esther asked.

"I'll have you know his father's name is Saul," Andrea said, proud to be able to one-up the woman who criticized her for turning on lights on the Sabbath.

Esther apparently was not completely convinced. At our wedding, she handed me an envelope with a check in it. When Katharine and I opened it afterward, we saw that it was made out to "Christopher Weber."

The check was for one hundred dollars, which to us was a fortune in those days. As soon as we returned to Connecticut, I went to deposit it, having to explain to the teller at Hartford National Bank that to my new bride's great-aunt, if you were named Nicholas you might as well be Christopher. Fortunately, my family was well known at the bank and the teller allowed me to deposit it.

What strikes me is that now, as then, I loved this event. I relished it the way I did when a woman I played tennis with explained to me that she was preparing for something called "a Seder, a ritual dinner associated with an upcoming holiday we celebrate," and when I told her that my family had had Seders my whole life, she practically fell over. "Nicholas and Katharine: I assumed you were both related to the Czar!" she exclaimed. There were a number of moments like this, and I thrived on them.

I understand all too well why Freud would have wanted to close his mind to the idea of having the same faith as Signorelli's Antichrist. I am aware that, just now, writing about my wife's family, I tried to avoid using my father-in-law's name, which I have always found distasteful. No wonder Sigismundo Schlomo became Sigmund (and then forgot Signorelli, so undesirably close to the whole mess).

When I was at Columbia, I had to study German, a requirement for art historians. Although it was my maternal grandmother's first language, I did not take to it; I was uncomfortable with its guttural sounds and complex structure, and associated it with barbarians in war movies. I struggled with the introductory course.

During about the sixth week of the first term, the teacher, the very

Teutonic Herr Gutmann—out of central casting as a fair-haired SS officer—was going around the classroom, having everyone read aloud from the textbook. When the guy next to me was done, Herr Gutmann grimaced and said, "Herr Shapiro, your accent is too YIDDISH!" After I took my turn, he said, "Weber"—pronounced *Vay-burh*—and commented, *"Ya, sehr gut. Die name ist Lutheran?"* I shrugged my shoulders but said nothing.

How foolish being Jewish makes some of us! But then again, wasn't it Herr Gutmann's fault, just as it was the Viennese who were to blame for Freud's being such a schmegeggy?

DAD AND I HAD VIRTUALLY IDENTICAL FEATURES, and I speak with his voice and accent. But I have that farmer's nose and full lips in a totally different tonality, and a leaner frame, and I use that speaking manner in a life that is a radical jump from my father's. As I write this, how I love him and miss him, while feeling that I *am* him but, contradictorily, belong to a different species.

I see myself in a photo where I am wearing tennis whites as a camp counselor in New Hampshire, while I see Dad with Mother on the *Queen Mary* in 1952. In that marvelous picture of my parents, Dad looks like the Latin lover (in a white dinner jacket) of my mother, who might have been played by Lauren Bacall. In the one of me, I look as if I am the same American white bread as the rest of the staff. I even have the right sort of chipped front tooth.

Of course I am projecting; I am seeing my issues as the concerns that caused Sigmund Freud to be so disturbed, and stimulated, by elements of Luca Signorelli's frescoes that he drew a blank on the artist's name. You might accuse me of trying to psychoanalyze an experience in the life of the inventor of psychoanalysis: the height of presumption, especially for someone with no expertise whatsoever in the field. But isn't this what all human minds do? Don't we always mix up a lot that is coming from within us, feeling we do and do not understand, with our observations of other people? I by no means claim that there is a "truth." The older I get, the more elusive I find the idea of certainty. I prefer love, the sheer pleasures of good art, the thrill of sexual desire, the acceptance of complexity and the impossibility of resolution, to the idea of "a sure verdict." I am also intrigued by what one feels, as opposed to what one knows with certainty. I grew up in the tradition of what was considered rationalism, where we try to "solve" problems and assume we can pin down mysteries through research and detective work, but I am coming more and more to value gut feeling. Writing the biography of Piet Mondrian, I was astonished when I discovered that in 1941, the year after he moved to New York at age sixty-eight following two bombings of his London studio during the Blitz—having moved to London only two years earlier because he felt that Paris, which had been his home for twenty years, had become too dangerous—Mondrian had said to the artist Carl Holty that he "hated discipline." The remark was a provocation from a highly disciplined person. What Mondrian preferred was "intuition." This is what he observed and felt when Hazel Scott played Boogie-Woogie on the piano and he danced with Lee Krasner at the Café Society Uptown. I am convinced that the place to which Richard and Marietta led me with their brilliant exegesis inspiring my own associations and instinctive responses has guided me to understand why Sigmund Freud could not recall that name. The Karpes orchestrated the route, and my unplanned side trips in other directions were telling not just about me, but also about Freud.

Pivotally, the connection with Susie, which prompted the journey to begin with, resulted not only in my suspending logic, but also in my savoring the wonder of irrational attraction and the power of aesthetic beauty. I don't think I would have opened that reprint if it were not for the memory of my intoxicant, with her navy blue-and-white polka-dot hair bow, charming the bejesus out of Richard Karpe. Susie caused something like nuclear fusion within me. Jewishness and the meaning of masculinity are interwoven issues for some of us, and, for me, all that arose with Susie became the catalyst for recognizing the particular dance they also provoked within Freud. Then came the way that art can be the stimulus to beat all others. The feelings of sons toward our fathers, what today is called our sense of gender, affect us immeasurably too. You may say these are *my* issues. But I am convinced they are the same that caused Freud's much-analyzed, but never fully understood, fundamental parapraxis.

Sigmund Freud had reactions to Jacob that were amazingly parallel to my father's reactions to *his* father. Comparing the Webers to the Freuds, I belong more to Martin's generation, with Dad and Sigmund Freud aligned as the sons of Grandpa Dave and Jacob. My grandfather was always working for other men—his brothers and brother-in-law—just as Jacob Freud was never in charge in the garment business. Both men were quite unsuccessful. My father was not like my grandfather—he ran his own business, and he made a fair bit of money—yet I also identify to some degree with Sigmund, as regards the way he saw Jacob. Like Freud's father, my own depended on his wife's family (Dad took over Mother's family's printing business). To me, he was, quite simply, not a tough guy. Yet I feel guilty that I think that. And he had quiet strength, even if he never would have held me over a fire until I vowed to avenge our family's enemies.

None of it is black and white; there is no single truth. Our fathers are many things seemingly opposite, simultaneously. But what is certain is that Freud, when looking at the Signorellis, would have been measuring himself and his father against Hannibal and Hamilcar. The allure of sheer masculine strength would have been fundamental to his experience of the frescoes. The discomfort and, yes, some form of sexual charge in the face of his dream male role models were so unbearable that he obliterated the artist's name, beginning with the very same first three letters, from his mind.

CHAPTER 29

RICHARD AND MARIETTA'S CONCLUSION

HAVING IN THEIR QUIET WAY SUGGESTED so much about Freud— the sides he hid from others, feelings he may have concealed even from himself, his subtle dissembling when it suited him—the Karpes, with the trip to Orvieto as their starting point, have painted an intriguing picture by the time their article is moving toward its conclusion. Even if they have eschewed absolute declarations—with that distance and reserve that is intrinsic to the way psychoanalysts communicate with outsiders—they have entered provocative territory. And while it had prompted me to go off on personal tangents, turn to further sources, and visit Orvieto, and to develop plenty of my own theories about the impact of the name Signorelli on Freud, I remained avid to know where their musing was going to end up.

The termination of their treatise maintains the same quiet tone, scholarly yet ingratiating, with which they conversed with Susie. It takes discretion to an extreme. Fortunately, though, for all its good manners, it does not flinch in the face of the dramatic content of the frescoes and Freud's reaction to them. It is as if, for all their rationalism, the Karpes readily accepted the forces that are beyond control in our lives. I could fantasize that Richard, especially, would easily empathize with the way that the very sight of Susie, and the sound of her voice, could make my heart race.

The Karpes begin with marvelous understatement: "In summary we can say that the forgetting of Signorelli's name was highly overdetermined and that at least three points of identification would be possible

between Freud and Signorelli." From there, they proceed to the quaint-
est of adverbs—"Firstly"—which strikes me as being Marietta's. (It is
a social worker's word, not a psychoanalyst's.) What "firstly" precedes
is "Signorelli, who populated the walls of a church with nudes, evil
passions and many heathen figures was a worldly painter in spite of his
membership in a religious brotherhood. He is a pioneer depicting the
actions of the nude body. His approach could be compared to Freud's
pioneering in the investigation and honest description of instinctual
passions."

From "evil passions" to "worldly" to "nude" and then back to "passions," this time "instinctual." So they understood that what drives us
in life—to forget a name, to pull a reprinted journal article off the
bookshelf with zeal—can be forces that know no logic, that derive
from romantic lust, however unacceptable its form!

But what, specifically, do the Karpes mean by those "evil passions"?
Are Richard and Marietta referring to forms of love that are taboo? Do
they have something specific in mind? Signorelli shows both the punishments for "evil passions," and the whispering of them into the ear of
the Antichrist, but what are they?

If there is any so-called evil passion on display in these sixteenth-
century frescoes, it is the attraction to strong naked men—mainly seen
from behind—on the part of men. Signorelli does not actually show
acts in which homosexual feeling is manifest, but he reveals his own
excitement over the fantasy of lots of nude muscular males, and presents his personal erotica so vividly that few viewers, male or female,
can fail to respond to it. Whether or not those physiques turn you on,
you cannot help noticing them and the way these proud specimens
flaunt them. But the Karpes stay clear, at least for now, of linking Freud
directly with any of these "evil passions," which they consign to Signorelli's side of the equation.

"Instinctual passions"? Now those are easier.

The suggestion is that these feelings of which Freud provides an "honest description" should inspire no guilt, for they are innate. How wonderful to be let off the hook with that kind and knowing "instinctual."

The Karpes' "Secondly" is simply a reiteration of the coincidence of names, the first three letters of Sigmund being the same as those of Signorelli. Here they fail to say precisely *why* that would induce memory loss. My theory is that in their polite way they are suggesting that he could not bear his own likeness to someone with such obvious homo-erotic enthusiasm (which, depending on your school of thought, is either an "evil passion" or an "instinctual passion"). It seems to me that Richard and Marietta are implying that Freud sought a complete separation from the self that was intrigued by all those rippling male torsos twisted around one another; he needed to forget the name Signorelli in order to forget the Sigmund who liked those things. But I suspect that if I'd asked them if that was what they had in mind, they would just have smiled at me benevolently, the way they did at Susie when she expressed her schoolgirl admiration for Freud, their guiding light.

"Thirdly" falls apart. The Karpes point out that "Signorelli experienced the rule of the Anti-Christ in the person of Roderigo Borgia as Pope Alexander VI but by placing himself outside the picture he declared his non-participation. Freud suffered from Lueger's rule but avoided any public expression of his stand." We are told that Freud wrote Fliess that he "overindulged (in smoking)" when Lueger was not confirmed in office—suggesting that he did nothing productive about the matter, pleased though he was that the emperor rejected the electorate's decision. In fact, this has nothing to do with what Signorelli did. Yes, he painted himself as peripheral to the world of the Antichrist, standing as if offstage in that large scene in which this heathen and his followers carry on in their false worship, but he also painted the frescoes, and the frescoes suggest that those who follow the devil deserve to go to hell. If Signorelli indeed was representing Borgia in the form of that devil, then he was blatantly declaring and broadcasting the Pope's corruption and sinfulness; he has by no means "avoided any public expression of his stand." The scenes in the Cappella Nova are as brave in their way as Picasso's *Guernica* was in light of Franco's evils. Signorelli, in openly illustrating violence as an allegory to contemporary events, hardly shies away from participation—even if he painted himself on the sidelines.

Fortunately, in their concluding three paragraphs, Richard and Marietta get back on track. The next-to-penultimate one contains the clincher. They again quote from a footnote (like most smart people, they realize that footnotes often contain the most interesting information) on page 13 of Freud's 1901 *The Psychopathology of Everyday Life,* and they follow it with their own trenchant observation. These two sentences— one Freud's, one their own—are the most telling, and at the same time provocative, of the entire article, and it is here that my parents' friends implicitly link Freud's obsession with Hannibal and Hamilcar, and his despair over the weakness of his recently dead father, with Signorelli's presentation of masculine force. "'After all, if the repressed thoughts on the topic of death and sexual life are carefully followed up, one will be brought face to face with an idea that is by no means remote from the topic of the frescoes at Orvieto.' He [Freud] did not explain what that idea was and he left it to the reader to fill in the gap."

However the Karpes' "the reader" might "fill in the gap," there is no question of how the visitor to the scene of Freud's apocalyptic moment will fill it in. It is necessary to repeat, because it is the simple fact that most people persist in avoiding, that what you are "brought face to face with"—to use Freud's words—at Orvieto are men's buttocks. Most of them are naked, but even the clothed ones are on display for delectation. Consider the fellow who is at the very foreground of the lunette with the Antichrist, to one side of the pedestal where Jesus' shady double stands with the devil. With his right foot practically at the bottom of the scene, this character occupies the same spatial plane as Signorelli and Fra Angelico, who are far to his left; he is halfway between the picture space and our—the viewers'—space. He looks remarkably like one of the flirtatious sailors painted by Paul Cadmus or Charles Demuth, two gay American artists of the twentieth century. Cadmus and Demuth, who delighted in showing male hustlers parading and flaunting the goods, surely knew this painting.

Wearing skintight striped trousers, tied with strings just below the knee to assure that they say stretched, the fellow puts his bubble butt and its crack on conspicuous display. Broad-shouldered and burly, he has the sleeves of his sporty pleated white top pushed up so that we can admire his biceps as well as his well-developed forearms. Looking away from us, he has the stance almost of someone in the chorus line of a campy musical comedy.

In combination with all the male nudity of *Purgatory,* this is the essence of Signorelli's frescoes, and the well-behaved Karpes have, in their low-key way, implied the nature of Freud's "repressed thoughts" about "sexual life."

CHAPTER 30

WHAT THIS MEANT

FOR ALL OF THEIR SELF-EFFACEMENT and understatement, Richard and Marietta do not minimize the importance of their investigation. They wind things up by pointing out that "Freud's first psychoanalytic publication of a parapraxis and the 'repressed thoughts' connected with it contain already the essence of most of his future ideas and discoveries."

I love their managing to get those "repressed thoughts" in—in quotation marks—one more time. But one can't be sure whether it is what has been "repressed," or the "future ideas and discoveries," that the Karpes have in mind when they immediately follow this sentence with one that begins with the vague antecedent "They." Here Richard and Marietta offer a grand summation: "They deal with death and sexuality, with demons and the psychopathology of Schizophrenia, with the Oediupus Complex and with his conflict in dealing with anti-Semitism. We might assume that his hero-worship of Hannibal later turned towards the study of Moses and his monumental work *Moses and Monotheism.*"

In fact, this is their first mention of schizophrenia. (I like the way they give it a capital *S,* as if it is a religious movement.) Perhaps this is a sequitur to what they have implied about a divided self in Freud; maybe they think it is an element they have already identified in Signorelli's frescoes. In any case, it is a startling and provocative subject to bring up at this late stage of the game and without further discussion.

THE KARPES' FINAL ONE-SENTENCE PARAGRAPH is a bit grand, a bit West Hartford Public Library Lecture Program for me. It is "Thus the trip to Central Italy in September 1897, eleven months after his father's death, was indeed the starting point in Freud's development as the creator of the new science of psychoanalysis." How could these brilliant people have started with that most depressing word "Thus," which, when it begins a sentence, instantly dampens whatever follows it? And, adding insult to injury, inserted that other clunker, "indeed," into the same sentence? These academic tools of detachment dilute the force of the Karpes' finale. But well they should. For even if Richard and Marietta were on solid ground in crediting the parapraxis concerning Signorelli's name with Freud's keen awareness of the importance of memory loss, to call the trip "the starting point . . . of psychoanalysis" is perhaps overdoing it.

OR SO I THOUGHT. I RECENTLY DISCOVERED, from an obituary of Marietta that appeared in 2009, when she died, at age ninety-seven, that, having been born in Pilsen, Czechoslovakia. and having studied law in Prague, she worked directly with Sigmund Freud to translate a lot of his work into Czech. She was clearly fluent in German, since it was the language of the autobiographical novel she published at age sixteen, a book with the enticing title *The Soul of Andre Garaine*. In 1956, she published "The Origins of Peter Pan" in *The Psychoanalytic Review*. Having lost both of her parents and a lot of her other relatives to the Nazi Holocaust, Marietta knew as much about violence as about the insistent youth of Peter Pan; if I have underestimated her insights and expertise, it is my own shortsightedness. Moreover, the obituary, presumably based on information from her three daughters, describes tennis as one of her "passions." The image of her possibly returning a serve of Susie's with a winning cross-court backhand out of reach of my inamorata in her little tennis skirt is my latest imaginary scenario, made all the richer because I remember Susie telling me about playing tennis with Adlai Stevenson on a holiday in Jamaica, which goes to show that the minor things one does easily recall can be just as intriguing as the names one forgets.

WHETHER OR NOT THAT TRIP TO ORVIETO REALLY WAS "the starting point of psychoanalysis"—which I now consider Marietta more qualified to declare than I initially thought, and not only because she was good at tennis—what it shows without question is just how directly and personally Freud reacted to his confrontation with certain artworks. I don't mean the theory of art, or the significance of iconography; I am not talking about all that has been written about Freud as a collector of antiquities (there are numerous volumes on the subject). I mean, rather, his visceral reactions to paintings—the way that art magnified life for him.

That this was so will be all the more evident in those letters Charlotte gave me that preceded the trip to Orvieto by fourteen years. To his fiancée, the future inventor of psychoanalysis felt free to give splendid voice to the intense emotion he experienced when he was face-to-face with certain examples of great art, principally that of the Italian Renaissance. He did not react in clichés; he knew his own taste. The usual canon of greatness—whereby Raphael was on a pedestal—meant nothing to him. What counted above all for Freud were his own reactions to paintings, which, he unabashedly told his future wife, were personal. Forget the "thus" and "indeed" and all the theories; Freud experienced beautiful art in the gonads and in the heart.

CHAPTER 31

SIGNORELLI'S PINUPS

WHY DID THE PEOPLE I WANTED TO CONSIDER as high priests of knowledge not go to Orvieto? Is it just possible that what the Karpes would have seen might have been too much to take?

Had they made the trip, it might have been unfathomable afterward to retreat into their world of library books. Their temperance might have evaporated, the even keel replaced by tumult. For they would have had the uncomfortable experience of understanding all too well what it was about Orvieto that was too much for Freud to remember in its entirety.

Come on, Karpes. Get past the first three letters of Signorelli to the first six. And you have the word *Signor*. Mr., Monsieur, Herr, Señor: Whatever language you translate it into, it's the title for a man.

And then look at Luca Signorelli's *The Elect*. Closest to the viewer, in this fresco on the wall of the altar bay, there are, spaced toward the bottom of the composition, five naked or nearly naked men, the soles of whose feet seem practically in our faces. Each is a more perfect specimen than the previous one of the hefty, muscular type of male built like a gym model. Why they are the elect we do not know—except that they are more fair-skinned and blond than the equally fit fellows who are damned. Perhaps that baby skin on their very mature bodies confers innocence or virginity on them.

The one who catches our eye first is a fellow on his knees. He turns away from us as he extends his left arm to a beatific-looking angel who will lift him into paradise. [plate 31] Perhaps he has gained the right to go

Plate 31. Detail of *The Elect*

Plate 32: Detail of *The Elect*

there because he developed his physique to such perfection; he is enormous, but all muscle and no fat. Signorelli has painted his rear end with
the same intense pleasure that Titian would reproduce women's breasts;
one has the impression that the artist has created his ultimate object of
lust. On each well-rounded buttock, the area nearest to us is bathed in
sunlight, with darkness accentuating the globular slope up toward the

hips. The crack is even darker, a near black that is eye-catching; there is no avoiding looking at it. [plate 32]

This remarkable specimen of masculinity is at the peak of life—that brief moment between youth and age when athletes reach their prime. Everything about him—his legs and arms, his tapered back, even his massive hands—has been developed to perfection. His golden curls, which resemble Signorelli's own, add to his spectacular appearance.

He is only one of Signorelli's dream men. The angel gives its other helping hand to a second idealized male specimen, this one seen from the front. With his long hair and the completely spaced-out look on his face, this guy could best be likened, today, to a gorgeous male hippie. The artist has decorously draped a robe across his middle so that his genitals are concealed—penises and balls are less Signorelli's thing than are asses—but the viewer is invited to admire, besides an impressive naked chest, his entire abdomen, including a thin line of body hair that begins below his navel and extends to his pubic region, of which the top part is on view.

Lest the viewer be deprived of any possibility of male modeling, further strapping specimens in the foreground of the fresco display their bodies from other angles. One of these naked men, standing, has his hands lifted above his head in prayer; beyond its spiritual purpose, the pose enables him to push his backside outward to be admired. His buttocks are formed to perfection; again Signorelli has used light and shadow to accentuate their every nuance. Like all the figures, this one has practically no body hair whatsoever—the better to reveal the forms. [plate 33]

As for the few women in this painting: Andrea and I agreed that, while there is no question as to their gender, their breasts look like add-ons, disproportionately small for their hefty physiques. Their hips are distinctly female, and the curves of their bodies provides a degree of softness, but they are definitely women of the rugby player type, and we get no sense that Signorelli painted them with any real feeling.

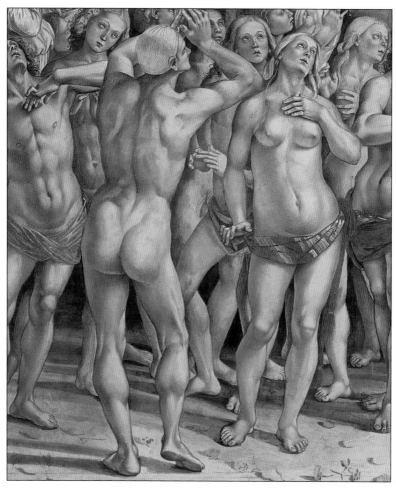

Plate 33: Detail of *The Elect*

Assuming that Freud understood the narrative program in this depiction of earthly paradise and identified the characters in it as the elect, he would have known that these fortunate creatures en route to salvation are presumed to be in a state of innocence. Signorelli's alleged intention was to show all these splendid specimens of male nudity, and the three naked women who are stuck in among the more than a dozen stripped-down men—there are, in addition, some characters in the second tier who may be either men or women, but we cannot be sure which—as devoid of lust, and therefore pure. Dugald McLellan words it nicely: "The perfectly formed, naked, and unadorned body, free from the trappings of worldly existence, best symbolizes the purged will that is at last 'free, upright, and whole,' after having passed through the rigorous but restorative process of purgation."

The angels who are lifting the elect upward, and who function as God's agents, have already achieved this state of grace. Playing their lutes and harps and lira da braccio, with at least one of them visibly singing, they create glorious music for the figures who will enjoy "the final release from the torments of the flesh" and enter "the heavenly realm." The red and white roses with which the angels closer to earth are showering the elect are symbols of chastity.

The message was that to forsake sex is to enter paradise. Those flowers will never die; rather, they will remain perpetually in full blossom. Spring will last forever.

Did Freud understand these layers of meaning? To what extent did he connect this imagery with his own experience? Mourning his father's death—and, as most people whose parents have died understand all too well, imagining his own end in a new way (the natural coefficient of grief as we become the oldest surviving generation of the immediate family)—how did he feel about the idea, fundamental to Catholicism, and to these frescoes, that the original sin is what made humankind mortal to begin with? What did Freud, who attributed so much of the human psyche to the way the sexual drive is or is not realized, make of Signorelli's illustration of the belief that to divest one's self of sexuality is the requisite of achieving paradise on earth?

In Signorelli's hands, that familiar theme has taken new form. For the painter has made the elect his dream men; he has created what he apparently cannot resist. In presenting men liberated from sinfulness, he has invited and demonstrated *his* sinfulness.

And while he has shown idealized male specimens who are

deliberately sexually alluring, he has gone to scant effort—or tried and failed—to include in the group the sort of women who would most attract heterosexual men. I am at a loss to say whether Signorelli's burly and muscular females appeal to lesbians, but they have scant allure to most males who prefer ladies. Nor do I think that Signorelli's men are of the Chippendales, *Playgirl* variety. Heterosexuality is beside the point in the paintings at Orvieto; in these illustrations of sin and punishment and abstinence and reward, the longings are always of men for men. How the viewer reacts depends on the viewer's own inclinations, but there is no question as to the nature of the attraction that pervades these paintings.

Freud certainly hit the nail on the head when he wrote that "the topic of death and sexual life" was "by no means remote" here.

IN AN ESSAY HE WROTE IN 1914, "The Moses of Michelangelo," Freud attempted to define his relationship to paintings: "I may say at once that I am no connoisseur in art, but simply a layman. I have often observed that the subject-matter of works of art has a stronger attraction for me than their formal and technical qualities, though to the artist their value lies first and foremost in these latter."

It's easy enough to apply this to the Signorellis. Aesthetically, they are excelled by many other Renaissance paintings. It is their subject matter that rivets the viewer, and that certainly counted more for Freud than did ideas of design or color orchestration. But if they were not painted as well as they are, the frescoes in the Cappella Nova, however thrilling their imagery, would not have lured the father of psychoanalysis. The vigor and deftness with which Signorelli renders his Herculean men is what makes these characters so powerfully present before our eyes. Had these identical scenes been conceived with less engagement in their visual qualities, and less sheer proficiency, they would not make nearly as strong an impression.

In the 1914 essay, even as he tries to minimize the importance of style and aesthetics—"I am unable rightly to appreciate many of the methods used and the effects obtained in art"—Freud at least recognizes that his own response to art is not entirely straightforward, and eludes full comprehension. When introducing the topic of Michelangelo's large marble sculpture of Moses and his reaction to it, Freud admits that he seeks understanding of the reason art has its impact, and is uncomfortable with leaving it as an enigma. "Some rationalistic, or perhaps analytic, turn of mind in me rebels against being moved by a thing without knowing why I am thus affected and what it is that affects me."

Yet when he cannot explain the mystery of the way great art can penetrate the soul, he accepts the conundrum, almost to the degree of exulting in it. "This has brought me to recognize the apparently paradoxical fact that precisely some of the grandest and most overwhelming creations of art are still unsolved riddles to our understanding. We admire them, we feel overawed by them, but we are unable to say what they represent to us." When he wrote this in the essay on the *Moses* seventeen years after observing his inability to recall Signorelli's name—a prime example of being "overawed"—was he thinking about Orvieto? Was he seeing as an "unsolved riddle" the idea that the Signorellis had made such an impression on him that the intense emotion rendered him unable to remember the artist's name? It seems that this is a rare instance of Freud saying that certain things in life can never be understood.

Yet what Freud subsequently says in the Michelangelo essay could be applied, I believe, to Signorelli's Orvieto frescoes and his own reaction to them. "In my opinion, what grips us so powerfully can only be the artist's *intention,* in so far as he succeeds in expressing it in his work and in getting us to understand it. I realize that this cannot be merely a matter of *intellectual* comprehension; what he aims at is to awaken in us some emotional attitude, the same mental constellation as that which in him produced the impetus to create."

Who among us, who actually looks at the frescoes in the Cappella Nova, can doubt that Signorelli's intention, at least in part, was to create, in as many variations as possible, his male ideals? If these specimens were not to be savored as objects of sexual attraction, at the least they were to be admired for their physical impressiveness. Few more effective examples of power and masculinity, of the effects of testosterone, have found their way to a painted surface. Spectacularly robust, beautifully toned, totally at ease in their nakedness, these athletic men "awaken" in their viewers some of the same "emotional attitude" with which Signorelli painted them. The person who best enables us to understand that process whereby it is the *intention* behind an artist's presentation of his chosen subject matter that has a profound impact on a viewer, and who therefore causes us to grasp some of what lay behind Freud's parapraxis, was Freud himself.

Freud had a brave willingness to admit it when he could not come up with an answer. To the extent that I can comprehend it, in his first published paper, "Observations on the Form and Finer Structures of the Lobular Organs of the Eel, Organs Considered to be the Testes," which appeared in 1876 in the *Mitteilungen der österreichischen Akademie der Wissenschaften,* he allowed that he could not solve the issue of how the unconscious was part of a dynamic system governed by the laws of chemistry and physics—as adumbrated by the recently developed concept of psychodynamics. To try to understand the mating habits of eels, when, as a twenty-year-old medical student, he was at the zoological station the University of Vienna maintained in Trieste, Italy, he dissected some four hundred of these slithery sea creatures but failed to find the organ he'd expected to locate. (He did not know that eels develop genitals only when they need them, and that eels breed about three thousand miles from Trieste.) It strikes me as more than a coincidence that the source of inexplicable mystery had to do with maleness.

I FOUND AND READ A LETTER THE TWENTY-YEAR-OLD FREUD wrote to a friend about the research on eels' testicles in part to determine if I had fallen for a spoof, as the title of his essay and the name of the publication seem more parodic than real. But Freud really and truly studied eels' testicles in Trieste, and wrote about them to Edouard Silberstein. What bowls me over about the letter is the lightheartedness with which young Freud conducts his investigation and the way his drawings resemble Paul Klee's. To be as free-spirited and aligned with the larger cosmos as Klee was has always been one of my ideals in life. One of the greatest of the many strokes of good luck I have ever had was in coming to know Anni and Josef Albers, and while Josef was a teaching colleague of Klee's at the Bauhaus and made, for the rest of his life, art that bears the lasting influence Klee's vision had on him, it was Anni who admitted quite simply that Klee was her "god," and who smiled broadly whenever she said his name. Klee was brilliant, undaunted by any sense of shibboleths, as childlike as he was intellectually sophisticated, and magnificently alive to the beauty of life in infinite ways. The Alberses, through Josef's photos of Klee frolicking on holidays and Anni's stories of his playing music, made him personally alive to me, but it is Klee's art, from the puppets he made for his son to the simplest drawings to the luminous watercolors to the magical large oils, that makes me feel that his achievement is in many ways like human life in its entirety: the cruelty as well as the wonder, but mainly, in spite of the horrors he honestly presents, the magnificence.

Here are two pages of Freud's letters translated into English:

Every day I get sharks, rays, eels, and other beasts, which I subject to a general anatomical investigation and then examine in respect of one particular point. That point is the following. You know the eel [fig. 12]. For a long time, only the females of this beast were known; even Aristotle did not know where they obtained their males and hence argued that eels sprang from the mud. Throughout the Middle Ages and in modern times, too, there was a veritable hunt for male eels. In zoology, where there are no birth certificates and where creatures "according to Paneth's ideals" act without having studied first, we cannot tell which is male and which female, if the animals have no external sex distinctions. That certain of their characteristics are in fact sex distinctions is something that has first to be proved, and this only the anatomist can do (seeing that eels keep no diaries from whose orthography one can make inferences as to their sex); he dissects them and discovers either testicles or ovaries [figs. 13 and 14]. The difference between the two organs is this: the testicles can be seen under the microscope to contain spermatozoa, the ovaries reveal their ova even to the naked eye [figs. 15 and 16].

Recently a Trieste zoologist claimed to have discovered testicles, and hence the male eel, but since he apparently doesn't know what a microscope is, he failed to provide an accurate description of them. I have been tormenting myself and the eels in a vain effort to rediscover his male eels, but all the eels I cut open are of the gentler sex [fig. 17]. That's all I have to tell you for now

Your Cipion

The drawings Freud used to illustrate and then describe his research in Trieste to his friend Eduard Silberstein could easily be by Klee:

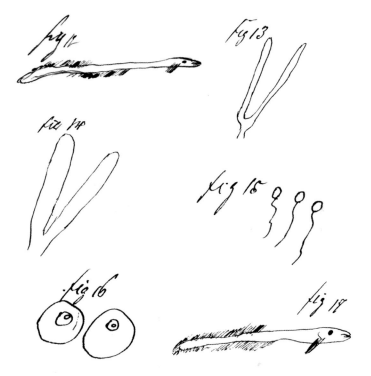

Klee had an aquarium, and kept it stocked with tropical fish. When he invited Bauhaus students to his studio, first in Weimar and then in Dessau, they might have expected to see his latest art, but instead he positioned them in front of the fish tank, periodically using a stick in order, ever so gently, to get the specimens hogging the foreground to move so that hidden ones could be seen. He reveled in that underwater world.

I hope you don't consider it too obvious when I point out that what preoccupied Freud when he was twenty is the same issue that concerned him forever after, and reached an apogee when he saw and later remembered Luca Signorelli's frescoes: the degree to which a guy has balls.

CHAPTER 32

ANDRÉ GIDE BLOCKED, TOO

IN 1934, DOROTHY BUSSY—a sixty-nine-year-old English novelist, openly bisexual, sister of the writer Lytton Strachey and of James Strachey (the first person to translate Freud into English)—sent a manuscript to her longtime friend André Gide. Called "Olivia," it was ostensibly a charged account of lesbianism, but it was also "a disguised love letter to him"—a roman à clef in which the character named Olivia was Bussy herself. The character who represented Gide was a young woman named Mlle. Julie, while another young woman, noticeably withdrawn and detached, Mlle. Cara, was a stand-in for Gide's wife, Madeleine. Laura was Bussy's version of Elisabeth Van Rysselberghe, one of Gide's closest friends.

Bussy accompanied the manuscript with a letter that acknowledged the real subject of the story. Gide did not respond. He had, similarly, failed to react when Proust had sent him a manuscript some two decades earlier—an omission he deeply regretted and for which he sent Proust a letter of repentance.

In 1948, Bussy, having kept "Olivia" to herself for fourteen years, decided to give it to some friends to read. They declared the short novel a masterpiece and persuaded its writer to submit it to Leonard Woolf at the Hogarth Press. Woolf published it in 1949, with Bussy's dedication: "To the beloved memory of V.W." VW was Virginia Woolf, for this was the person who, in 1933, had urged her to write the autobiographic work. (Virginia, who had been married to Leonard, committed suicide in March 1941.)

Bussy sent the book to Gide. She wrote him a cover letter reminding him that he had not responded to the original manuscript, saying that "perhaps you will have the glory of having rejected two bestsellers—Proust and yours truly!" Gide replied promptly that He "had *no* memory" of having read the manuscript. Bussy replied, "The little work that you have so completely repressed, when you come to re-read it, as I hope some day you will, will make only too clear a) the reason you disliked it and b) the reason I wish it to be anonymous."

In 1948, Gide, feeling as if he had not seen the text before, even though he believed Bussy that he had, now read *Olivia* for a second time. He sent a telegram immediately, declaring himself "as repentant and embarrassed as with Proust." Shortly thereafter, he wrote Bussy a letter telling her he had "devoured the whole thing . . . hungrily, delightedly, with anguish, intoxication."

Gide tried to understand the reason he had obliterated from memory his previous reading of such an excellent book. He observed to Bussy, "Freud alone could say and explain what scales covered my eyes the first time I read it." He explains to Bussy that in the case of Proust he had simply read a few pages of *À la recherche du temps perdu* "with a hostile eye" and was clearly jealous. With her book, he had a harder time understanding why he had dismissed it to such an extent that he had no memory of having seen it before. For he realized that on his second reading he recognized everything in the text, and at the same time rediscovered its meaning.

The assumption here, too, is that repression—in the form of memory failure—results from passions so discomfiting to the person who feels them that they must not be allowed to surface. For me, it is comparable to the way that on occasion I inadvertently turn away from a painting. The impact of the beauty is so strong as to be unbearable. It is why we cry out in orgasms: Not only the physical charge but also the fantastic feeling cannot be contained. What Gide calls "intoxication" is, at times, more than a person has capacity for.

But if Gide thought that Freud would explain the nature of *his own* blindness and resistance, he was wrong. At least he would not do so in writing that would make his issues public. As the Karpes point out, in the case of his inability to conjure the name of the artist whom he said had painted the finest artwork in history, he failed to go into any depth as to the real reason for the inability to recall that name, for to have done so would have meant discussing the true nature of the repressed thoughts. Of course, he may have acknowledged them to himself; we will never know.

If Gide thought that Freud could explain why people sometimes kept their eyes closed or covered, he would have been fascinated with how his fellow French intellectual and freethinker, Sartre, depicted Freud on the subject ten years later in *The Freud Scenario*. In the screenplay, Sartre devotes yet another scene to one of the Karpes' main areas of concern—beyond the incident of the cap and the anti-Semite—by, like them, focusing on the elder Freud's funeral and Sigmund's lateness that day, and then the dream in which he was instructed "to close the eyes."

The way Sartre presents the dream accentuates the reasons that the Karpes saw it as a guide to the cause of Freud's forgetting the name Signorelli.

The scene begins with Freud, dressed "in deep mourning," arriving at a barbershop. When Freud expresses dismay that it is so crowded and says it is unusual for so many people to be there at that hour, the owner points out that it is 10:00 A.M. while Freud normally shows up at 9:30. Freud looks at his watch and is surprised.

Freud evinces the sort of disorientation that sets in even when someone with a highly organized mind thinks that he is coping easily with the rituals surrounding death. The action jumps from the barbershop to Freuds' parents' apartment, where the undertaker's assistant, respectful but authoritative, tells those assembled that they cannot continue to delay proceeding to the funeral, even if Sigmund is not yet there. Everyone debates what to do about his now being half an hour late, until Sigmund finally rushes in. The funeral and funeral procession follow—sketchily and rapidly—and then Sartre moves the action into a shop that is "topographically identical to the barber's." There are "huge enamel plaques that have been fastened on all the walls (in place of the advertisements for perfumes or shaving-creams that could be seen there when Freud went in). . . . On all these plaques there is written (printed characters, block capitals or italics or roundhand, etc. as if they were writing-patterns or advertisements for an engraver): YOU ARE REQUESTED TO CLOSE THE EYES." Machines drone noisily until their sound is "drowned by an imperious ringing and, all of a sudden, the dream dissolves."

Oh, Jean-Paul, this is sheer genius! For all that has been written about Freud's lateness and this subsequent dream (even if, as the Karpes pointed out, Freud himself claimed it to have occurred before rather than after the funeral when, four years after the fact, he described it in *The Interpretation of Dreams,* in spite of having written Fliess, shortly following the funeral, that he had had it afterward), there is nothing to equal the way you have recast it. One pictures the Viennese barbershop with its lethal razor blades. In my mind, I jumped to years of having Sal Lavinio (the barber in West Hartford, also on Farmington Avenue, the Karpes' route to the library) do a few strokes of his electric razor to give me my perpetual buzz cut when I was a kid. He did this ritually every couple of weeks, gave me a lollypop, which I didn't want but pretended to like, and said, "Take care, butch." And off I would go. In the summer, at overnight camp, there were barbers who treated us all as if we had the same heads and hair. We would line up outside, where a chair was positioned over some dirt so that there was no need to clean up beyond a bit of raking. It was "Onto the chair!" Buzz, buzz, buzz. "You're done. Next boy!" Shorn to a quarter of an inch, we were at minimal risk for lice and had nothing to fall over our eyes at sports.

Sartre doesn't bother to include further discussion about the castrating aspect of haircuts and shaving and beard trimming. Nor does he analyze the dream and its meaning. He doesn't need to. The lack of amplification is a knowing writer's wise decision, because, rather than divert us with the Karpes' discussion about the ritual of closing the eyes of the dead, or about the concept of closing the eyes to death, he has us consider, in the broadest sense, what it means to be instructed to close our eyes.

Should we close our eyes to the male nudity in Orvieto? Should we be like all the art historians who write about the frescoes, going over image after image in iconographic detail, without ever saying the obvious thing, which is that those devilish men, those Antichrists, those characters who are the antithesis of what is supposed to be right and good, are fantastic specimens of male beauty?

Closing the eyes is like forgetting a name. It's a form of mental block: Whether it is the result of a conscious or unconscious decision, it is a device to prevent information and feelings from getting through.

THERE IS AN IRONY HERE. MY MAIN JOB for over forty years has been to run the arts foundation created by Josef Albers, whose first words in English, when he arrived at Black Mountain College from Germany in 1933, were—or so I was told by Bobbie Dreier, a beautiful and energetic woman who was, for years, in love with him (and of whom he made marvelous photographs in the nude)—"I want the eyes to open." As his mastery of his new language increased, he simplified this to say, frequently, that the goal of his life was "to open eyes." (This is the title of a movie about Albers.)

By declaring his wish to increase vision, Albers was acknowledging the innate human tendency not to see as much as we might. His assumption, I believe, was that the failure to see fully was inadvertent rather than willful, a form of laziness. But Josef's sense of most people's visual alertness was that they might as well have been following that instruction

"You are requested to close the eyes." Albers was fighting against human indifference, more than against the deliberate screening that Sartre presented as stemming from unconscious needs, but it is part of the same phenomena. Most people screen things out; a few take them in fully. Yet to see everything, and accept what we see, is a daunting task—as anyone who has gone through psychoanalysis knows.

I assume that when Sartre wrote about Freud's dream with the sign in the shop and the deafening din of all those machines (blocking the ears from hearing clearly, just as the eyes are kept from seeing), he did not know about the forgetting of Signorelli's name. Had Sartre read about Freud's parapraxis, the great existential writer would have recognized that Freud had to avoid recognizing a side of himself that was too painful to bear when he was surrounded by Luca Signorelli's frescoes. Freud's envy of the mighty males who proliferate in the frescoes in the Cappella Nova; the longing, perhaps, to be more like them; his admiration for their bodies and physical strength; the wish for his father to have had their power; his ambivalence about being Jewish, conjured by the Antichrist; his worries about the connection of Jewishness and maleness—all of it was overwhelming, even to the most probing of minds.

CHAPTER 33

ZILBOORG

OF ALL PEOPLE, THE SVENGALI OF MY WIFE'S FAMILY, the psychoanalyst Gregory Zilboorg, took up the matter of Freud's memory loss relating to his trip to Orvieto. In 1962, Zilly (Great-Aunt Bettina, who was his analytic trainee, liked to say "Zilly was silly") wrote:

> Freud in *The Psychopathology of Everyday Life,* reports how he remembers relating to a fellow train passenger his profound impression of the frescoes in the Duomo of Orvieto. To his amazement, Freud was unable to tell at the moment either the subject matter of the frescoes or the name of the artist. By way of a series of free associations, he finally recalled the name of the master painter, Signorelli. By way of careful self-analysis, he concluded that he had repressed the name because of its first half, *Signor,* to which he arrived via a number of associations, one of them being the German word *Herr.*
>
> It was a remarkable piece of self-analysis on the part of Freud. Yet what appears not less remarkable is that that piece of psychoanalysis done in 1898, . . . lacked the recognition of what now appears so obvious: *Signor* is the Italian equivalent of *Lord* in Church language, as is the German word *Herr.* Freud saw mainly the formal connections in his associations; he failed to see some of the deeper content of the repressed. It is, for instance, of particular interest that

the subject matter of Signorelli's frescoes in the Orvieto Duomo is *The Last Judgment.*

First of all, Zilboorg has his facts wrong. Freud in fact could see the frescoes, clearly, in his mind's eye *until* he remembered the name; the idea that he was "unable" to remember the subject matter is a fallacy that reverses one of Freud's main objects of fascination. As for the rest of Zilboorg's theory: maybe, maybe not, but why didn't he look at the paintings?

It infuriates me to think of Zilboorg—who "treated" both of Katharine's grandparents and her grandmother's lover (George Gershwin)—sitting in an office somewhere, his life funded by his victims, playing with words and texts, and then feeling good about himself for his "Lord" observation. How smug and delighted he must have been!

Having known several wonderful people, relatives through marriage, who told me he did palpable damage to them or people close to them, I detest his sense of his own supreme knowledge and the air of superiority with which he declared "he failed to see some of the deeper content of the repressed."

How did Zilboorg know? Maybe Freud did see that "deeper content" and was just being discreet.

Of course I bear a grudge against Zilboorg. He treated my great friend Eddie Warburg—Katharine's grandfather's first cousin— four days a week for twenty-six years. When I knew Eddie, then in his seventies, the poor guy was obsessed and tormented with the issue of homosexuality. I knew from Philip Johnson that Eddie practically perished out of love for the captain of the soccer team at Middlesex, a private all-boys boarding school, which, like Katharine's grandfather, he attended because it was, back then, one of the few such places where Jews, at least a handful of the right type, were welcome. With me, Eddie talked endlessly about his conquest of a female cousin, and his fondness for certain female dancers when he and Lincoln Kirstein started the future New York City Ballet; he was the original "Thou Dost Protest Too

Much." Yet Eddie knew how he was regarded: Katharine's grandmother quoted him as saying, once while they were watching a parade together, that when he marched into a room everyone sang "Here comes the fag" instead of "Here comes the flag." Couldn't Zilboorg have helped him to accept himself?

Why didn't Zilboorg get off his high horse and go to Orvieto? The paintings make it all perfectly clear. Maleness, homoeroticism: These are the issues. Firm buttocks and washboard abdominal muscles and hard, broad chests. How dare these pompous people who alter other human being's lives sit there and keep their silence and then write their knowing papers? Zilboorg being superior to Freud! What he was represssing may have been evident to him on some level. We do not know the insides of other peoples minds, even if we know what they say. And the issue was in all likelihood nothing unusual at all, just a subtle homoeroticism, the same force Freud acknowledged in his boyhood crushes on swashbuckling warriors, his openness about Hannibal. The world is full of intellectuals who dream of being football players. If Zilboorg had only looked at the paintings instead of sitting in his expensive apartment surrounded by the luxuries his patients had paid for, he might have faced the truth, too.

CHAPTER 34

PICTURING FREUD

I HAVE A MENTAL IMAGE OF FREUD looking at the frescoes in the Cappella Nova that is almost as vivid as my vision of the Karpes standing behind my parents' house as the kettledrums to Susie's violin. More and more, with age, with the yearning for the time in life when the formative events were actually taking place, I see these pivotal moments, the players at a peak of their powers, life ineffably delicious in its sheer richness. Aliveness! How can it ever end? How can the exquisite interactions disappear the way cremated bodies do when the ashes are scattered at sea? Does writing about them at least preserve them in some form for future generations? It is a feeble attempt, perhaps, but as someone intoxicated by the richness of life, I have to hope as much.

My particular image of Freud comes thanks to Stefan Zweig, who for me, as for many people, is one of those extraordinary writers who brings people and places to life so that we feel we have experienced them firsthand. Zweig knew Freud personally. He wrote a long essay on him that was published in his 1931 book *Die Heilung durch den Geist,* translated as *The Mental Healers,* and was dedicated to Albert Einstein, another of his acquaintances. Zweig's narrative is a trenchant and appreciative overview of the impact of the man whose "voice broke the silence" of the "pusillanimous conspiracy of 'moral' silence [that] dominated Europe for a whole century, an interminably long one."

Zweig sprinkles his text with judiciously selected quotations that in effect summarize, brilliantly, Freud's achievement, and at the same time evoke the mental state into which Orvieto put him. They also remind us that, even though Freud invented so much, and gave the world what it never had had before, he was dealing with mental processes that go back to the earliest stages of humankind, and had been addressed by many brilliant thinkers who preceded him.

Zweig opens with a brief quotation from Schiller: "Although by the dim light of everyday emotions the secret working of the forces of desire remains hidden away from sight, it becomes all the more conspicuous and stupendous when passion is strongly aroused." What Zweig uses to elucidate Freud's achievement for others also applies perfectly to Freud's own mental events inspired by the Luca Signorelli frescoes.

And then there is the question posited by Nietzsche with which Zweig opens his first chapter: "How much truth can the mind endure, how much can it dare to entertain?" Does this not help us to understand better why Freud could not summon the name Signorelli for those two days when it eluded him? Another chapter opens with a line from Balzac (in this case, Zweig provides the date, which was 1833) that invokes another kernel of Freud's genius, the reason for which he was the first to acknowledge that his failure to come up with the artist's name on the journey to Herzegovina said volumes more than if he had remembered it easily: "I have myself had evidence that our latent senses are better than our obvious ones."

At the same time that Zweig puts Freudian thought in this universal context, he provides a vivid sketch of the individual himself, at least as the inventor of psychoanalysis presented himself to his friends and colleagues. When Zweig got to know Freud, some thirty years after his visit to Orvieto, the father of psychoanalysis was still the epitome of robust health:

> Freud's intellectual profusion has been the expression of a thoroughly healthy constitution. Until he was approaching seventy, this great physician was never seriously ill; this shrewd observer of nervous workings was entirely free from nervous disorder; this clear-sighted student of mental

abnormalities, this much-vilified pansexualist, remained almost uncannily hale and single-hearted in the manifestations of his personal life. As far as his own experience is concerned, he has known nothing of the everyday lesser maladies which, for most of us, again and again interfere with the smooth source of thought and action, and he has hardly ever suffered from headache or fatigue. Throughout the greater part of his working life, he found no occasion to consult a colleague, and was never compelled by illness to break an appointment. . . . For him, indeed, health is synonymous with breathing, to be awake means the same thing as to work, creation is identical with life. Moreover, just as he tenses every nerve upon his tasks in his working hours, so does his iron frame enjoy the benefit of perfect relaxation during sleep. A brief period of repose suffices him. When he sleeps he sleeps more soundly, when he wakes he wakes more thoroughly, than most of us.

The hardiness makes me think of Dr. Solnit, who never canceled an appointment because of ill health, and was a model of someone who appeared undisturbed by maladies—which was part of his charm for me. We generally had appointments at 6:30 A.M., and I learned from one of his younger colleagues that he regularly worked until midnight. Of course he would never refer to this, since he told me nothing whatsoever about himself, but his physical robustness in his seventies—his age during my treatment—furthered my sense that he was a sort of god. His need for nothing more than brief periods of sleep was part of his mythic image. It became evident to me in a less desirable manifestation on an occasion when I caught him snoring during one of our sessions, but I still admired his fortitude.

I cannot help reading into Zweig's statement that Freud had "a health-record worthy of Polycrates." (Even if we don't know who Polycrates was, we are convinced that this is terrific, and readily picture the most energetic, illness-free of Greeks.) Zweig implies that it is because of the expansiveness of his mind and the acceptance of his own self that Freud had such a terrific physical constitution. Here I go back to the word *pansexualist,* which I just love. Naturally, I think of Signorelli's painting of Pan, beloved to Berenson, even though that mental connection has little to do, at least specifically, with what Zweig had in mind. A pansexualist is someone who is "not limited or inhibited in sexual choice with regard to gender or activity." That idea was a radical breakthrough in 1931, and I like the link that Zweig suggests between such a lack of censorship, of one's self or others, and Freud's remarkable physical well-being.

Having provided this sense of Freud's open-mindedness, Zweig describes the great doctor's external appearance. This sketch, while it comes from a later date than the trip to Orvieto, helps us better to conjure Signorelli's admirer as he walked through the vast space of the cathedral, turned right into the Cappella Nova, and stood transfixed by the remarkable art there:

> His bodily aspect conforms to his mental characteristics. Here, too, all the details are harmoniously proportioned. He is neither too tall nor too short, neither too stout nor too thin. His lineaments are, indeed, so average that his face has long been the despair of caricaturists. In that well-shaped oval they can find no feature that lends itself to the pencil's specious exaggeration. Not even when you compare photographs taken at long intervals, the portraits of the youth with those of the man of middle age, can you detect an outstanding trait, or one of characterological importance. At thirty, at forty, at fifty, he is the same: a good-looking man, virile, one whose aspect is regular to a fault. His dark and searching eyes no doubt suggest the thinker . . . the bearded, strong face of a typical physician . . . somewhat unfathomable, gentle, perhaps over-serious, and nowise bearing witness to powers

that have exerted so far-reaching an influence. . . . We must abandon any attempt to find characterological lights in a countenance so unrevealing in its harmony.

So this was the man who wanted to be Hannibal! Modest-sized and pensive, he exerts, in Zweig's portrait, a quiet force, yet distinctly lacks the bravura little boys want in their warriors. The qualities young Freud put into his toy soldiers, and with which Signorelli endows his fantastic specimens of masculine power, while redolent in Freud's imagination, were absent in his self.

Zweig's Freud had, however, a mental virtuosity equal to the physical prowess of Signorelli's men. Acknowledging his own wish to make Freud appear a bit more easy-going than he was, Zweig later adds:

> We would be afraid of telling a lie to such a man, feeling him to be one whose insight would enable him to detect every prevarication and to flash a revealing glare upon any tricks and turns of evasion. A face that oppresses and frightens rather than one that liberates and charms, but none the less transfigured by the intensity of the profound thinker; the face, not of a merely superficial observer, but of one who sees pitilessly into the depths.
>
> This dash of Old Testament grimness, this unconciliatory spirit that speaks so plainly in the fierce eyes of the veteran, must not be ignored, must not be omitted from the picture under stress of a desire to make it pleasing. Had Freud lacked the ruthlessness and decisiveness that are among his most salient characteristics, his achievement would have been devoid of its best and most decisive features. . . . Courteousness, sympathy, and considerateness would have been wholly incompatible with the revolutionary thought-trend of Freud's creative temperament, his essential mission to make extremes manifest, not to

reconcile them. His combativeness and forthrightness have always made him want a for or an against, a plain yes or a plain no, rather than a betwixt and between, or an admission that there is perhaps about as much to be said on one side as the other. . . . He is thus unfailingly autocratic and intransigent; and it is above all when he is at war, fighting alone against a multitude, that there develops the unqualified pugnacity of a nature ready to face overwhelming odds.

No wonder Freud—ruthless, combative, pugnacious—was drawn to the physical manifestation of the qualities that defined his conduct, if not his physical self. He continued Hamilcar's legacy in the way he fought for his beliefs, even if he was not about to hold Martin over an open fire. He saw the world in Signorelli's Last Judgment terms: where there was a right and a wrong, a blessed and a damned, and nothing whatsoever that was namby pamby. The frescoes in Orvieto put in front of him, in vivid color, though animated brushstrokes, the physical equivalent of his own mental forcefulness. Freud's cerebral strength and will to prevail were, in these frescoes, recast in male muscularity.

CHAPTER 35

THE MAN WHO FELT PAINTINGS
IN HIS HEART AND BONES

THE INTENSITY OF FREUD'S REACTIONS to well-crafted art is palpable in a letter he sent Martha Bernays when she was still his fiancée.

Reading it, I could picture his emotional transport in front of the Signorellis. Maybe only a fellow visual obsessive—I consider myself one—could understand this, but Sigmund Freud was one of those rare people so bowled over by pictures that art alone, as opposed to a lot of peripheral personal baggage, would be sufficient grounds for his having an extreme reaction like the forgetting, for two days at least, of a name that should have been instantly accessible to him.

On December 20, 1883, a Wednesday evening, Freud wrote Martha a letter from Vienna that begins "My precious darling." Several days earlier he had been in Dresden. There he had "spent about an hour" in "the picture gallery" at the Zwinger, the fantastic Baroque palace, now an assemblage of galleries and pavillions, adjacent to the lavish cathedral and grand theater, that make the heart of that city seem like a pastry confection. With its stones and mortar rendered like swirls of whipped cream, and its courtyards full of statuary, the Zwinger feels more like the locale of a dream than an urban experience.

The visit there was a turning point in the life of the twenty-seven year-old Freud. He felt the direct impact of looking at paintings as never before. He wrote Martha, "I believe I acquired there a lasting benefit, for until now I have always suspected it to be a silent understanding among people who don't have much to do, to rave about pictures painted by the famous masters. Here I rid myself of this barbaric notion and myself began to admire." The use of "myself" twice in the same sentence is significant. He was unabashedly discussing the role of art for *him*. It was a rare moment for Freud, the sort of thing he would confess in a letter to an intimate but not in one of his treatises written for publication. Freud would never have addressed this same level of personal engagement in those texts where he announced universal truths.

Discussing the work that most captivated him at the Zwinger, Freud reveals erudition as well as enthusiasm. He begins with the van Dycks, of which he writes that one shows "the children of the unfortunate Charles I, the later Charles II, James II, and a young, plump little princess."

It appears that the installation of this painting at the Zwinger is now pretty much as it was in 1883. When I went to Dresden this past summer to follow in Freud's footsteps there, this enormous canvas by van Dyck was one of the first paintings in view after I walked up the two flights of the grand marble staircase that leads to the museum's spectacular galleries. Thanks to the impeccable restoration that was done after the heavy bombing incurred during World War II, not only can one see the same paintings that captivated Freud but one views them under similar circumstances to those he enjoyed. The Gemälde-galerie—the old masters section of the Zwinger—still embodies the taste of earlier centuries for presenting art with a maximum of natural light, in large galleries that enable the viewer to consider paintings at a distance as well as close-up. The exhibition spaces announce, in the grandeur of their design, the importance of the contents as the treasures of humanity. I might readily have walked by the canvas of Charles I and his children by van Dyck—an artist I admire but whose work is usually something I only glance at while heading to pictures of greater interest—but, knowing that Freud had stood in front of this royal family portrait, I came to a halt and lingered.

Freud was in the museum with two English friends on the day he visited. He told Martha that he "could point out to the two Englishmen" certain paintings, which he characterized as "magnificent things" he knew previously, but only "from photographs and reproductions." The van Dyck fell into that category.

What struck me when looking at the large, brownish, highly varnished composition—painted with bravura and authority, the surface a wonderful testimony to the force produced by vigorous brushwork—was how much Freud's one simple sentence altered my response to it. Freud presumably had in mind Charles I's execution, at age forty-eight, after a quarter century of rule. Charles lost his life largely because he had antagonized his subjects with his faith that kings received their power to rule directly from God; following his marriage to a French Catholic—she would be the mother of these three children—he had tried to bring the Anglican Church closer to Catholic dogma. Freud's use of the adjective "unfortunate" for having been beheaded is just superb, as is his calling the princess "plump": they are funny words from a twenty-seven-year-old, for they sound somehow like the observations of a far older person. It's also intriguing that he saw the boys in their capacity as future kings.

Freud's account of the visit to the Zwinger is a rare glimpse at the reality of how a true art lover goes to a museum. He told Martha that he saw "the Veronese with the most beautiful heads and bodies" but "hardly had time to glance at them all." Following his progress as he penetrated these galleries, I could well understand why. There is a sea of late Venetian art, and good as the Veroneses and Tintorettos are, there are few of us who can deal with their plenitude, somehow so different from Signorelli's, in part because of the Venetians' dark palette, but also because this highly charged work demands a lot of effort if one is to get beyond the blur. It's completely worth doing, but, as Freud suggests, requires time.

Freud, however, found a stopping point.

> In a small room by itself I discovered what, according to the way it is displayed, must be a gem. Looking closer, I saw it was Holbein's "Madonna." Do you know this picture? Kneeling in front of the Madonna are several ugly women and an unattractive little girl, to the left a man with a monk's face, holding a boy. The Madonna holds a boy in her arms and gazes down on the worshipers with such a holy expression. I was annoyed by the ordinary ugly human faces, but learned later they were the family portraits of the Mayor of X, who had commissioned the painting. Even the sick, misshapen child whom the Madonna holds in her arms is not meant to be the Christ child, rather the wretched son of the Mayor, whom the picture was supposed to cure. The Madonna herself is not exactly beautiful—the eyes protrude, the nose is long and narrow—but she is a true queen of heaven such as the pious German mind dreams of.

While this Madonna is the first painting in Dresden about which Freud enthused vociferously to Martha in his letter, by the time I reached it, I had already spent a phenomenal half hour with a Titian he subsequently praised. That reverse order of viewing had a significant impact on my reaction to Freud's feeling for the Holbein. The Titian is a marvel, and Freud's writing about it to his fiancée contains some of the most evocative sentences in the history of the literature about painting. Making my way to the Holbein, I had a new understanding of what Freud wanted out of Christian art: the spirituality, the transcendence over worldly desires (including sexual ones), the utter serenity. I also knew, from his writing on Raphael's *Sistine Madonna* later in the letter, and from having already viewed that painting as well (also out of sequence), that Freud believed that good looks, especially when they attracted him personally, were, in his eyes, antithetical to the subject's being truly holy.

When I saw the Holbein, I was, initially, mainly amused—I reread Freud's description while standing in front of it—by his annoyance over the characters' having "ordinary ugly human faces." I then found it intriguing that this bothered him less once he learned that the Christ Child was "the wretched son of the Mayor" who had commissioned it to cure the boy, as if that medical purpose, however specious it might be from a doctor's point of view, justified the necessity of using an unfortunate looking kid as the model for the young Jesus. But what I found most telling is that the creature he described, all too accurately, with protruding eyes and a "long and narrow" nose was "a true queen of heaven such as the pious German mind dreams of." This was consistent with his view on Raphael's *Sistine Madonna*, about which he wrote Martha in the same letter, that she was too pretty, too attractive to the onlooker, to be holy.

Looks, I discovered, mattered as much to Freud as to my beloved Susie—who has always considered the main criteria of human beings to be whether they were "attractive" or "unattractive," the secondary categories being "MOST attractive" and "MOST unattractive." Given that she was always such a sublime sight herself—beyond that extraordinary face, her figure and posture were flawless, her clothing impeccable—she could afford to make the distinction. But that Freud, the great investigator of what goes on *inside* people, responded so intensely to human appearance came as a surprise. Of course, with Freud the judgments were not simply superficial, but were subject to the analysis of the character traits that accompanied those looks.

At the same time, I was astonished to feel that there was nothing special about the Holbein. On the way to it, I had looked at Dresden's spectacular Vermeers, and its phenomenal jewel of a van Eyck. Perhaps no Holbein would have stood up, but I doubt that that is the case, since the Holbeins in Basel, particularly his portraits of Erasmus, are paintings of unparalleled force, as are the portraits of Oliver Cromwell and Thomas More at the Frick. Holbein at his best can impart the deepest wisdom and humor. His paintings emanate an intensity of mental concentration, which is brought to life by the parallel concentration of the painted surface. Taut drawing works in tandem with an application of oil pigment that, while dense, has the immaculate sheen of a porcelain glaze. But Freud's picture of choice lacked Holbein's normal force.

Of course when Freud saw the painting in 1883, it was, we know from his letter to Martha, in a small room of its own. We would deduce that that setting made seeing it a totally different experience, for today the painting is among the few works at the Zwinger to be presented disadvantageously. It is in the corner of a crowded gallery, awkwardly installed, so that an altarpiece in the middle of the room makes it impossible to have a good view of it from afar. It took me a few minutes and two inquiries even to find it. Freud would have had a dramatically dissimilar encounter.

But he failed to notice a very significant fact. Imagine my surprise when I read the details on the label for this painting Freud had admired and discovered that the work Freud thought was an original Holbein was a copy!

CHAPTER 36

SARBURGH

WHILE ART SCHOLARS AND OTHERS versed in connoisseurship would have questioned the authenticity of the "Holbein," Freud can hardly have been expected to realize that the painting was a copy. Yet, still, one wants him to have been more perceptive than most people, and also to have been more alert to the facts. For in 1848, the original of this Madonna had been discovered in the city of Darmstadt. Once that painting came to light, specialists realized that the version that had entered the Dresden royal collection in 1743 was made by someone other than Holbein. The original, which hangs today in the Schlossmuseum Darmstadt, was painted in 1528 for Jacob Meyer zum Hazen, the former burgermeister of Basel (he had held the post from 1516 to 1521); the copy in Dresden was painted in around 1635 by an artist named Bartholomäus Sarburgh, who was born in 1590.

There had been a Holbein exhibition in Dresden in 1871 where the real Holbein from Darmstadt and the Dresden copy were shown next to one another, with the Sarburgh identified as such. Nonetheless, in 1883, when Freud was there, the museum in the Zwinger still identified it as a Holbein; it was only in 1905 that the label was changed to reflect the truth. While Sarburgh's name was not given, the work was from then on called "a copy." This remains the case today—still with no mention of Sarburgh or the date of the copy.

My reactions to Freud's error were the same as on the rare occasions when I had doubts about something Dr. Solnit had said. Initially, I could not accept the idea that the fount of wisdom could ever be wrong. Even when I disagreed with his opinion about a given subject, I justified his position in my mind. Similarly, on those occasions when I thought that the Karpes had either gone down the wrong path or not taken one they should have taken, I gave them the benefit of the doubt. In the same vein, I concluded that Freud's mistake about a painting he treated as an original, but that was a copy, was insignificant. "Pious German minds" had been what interested him, not the art of Hans Holbein. He had a right to react to a painting whatever its authorship was; what counted was the artwork, not who had made it. His lack of knowledge of the correct authorship was, I assured myself, a detail of little significance.

Nonetheless, I wonder what Freud himself would have thought if he knew about his own mistake with the Holbein. In "The Moses of Michelangelo," he addresses the issue of artistic copies.

> Long before I had any opportunity of hearing about psychoanalysis, I learned that a Russian art-connoisseur, Ivan Lermolieff [whose writing was translated into German in 1874] had caused a revolution in the art galleries of Europe by questioning the authorship of many pictures, showing how to distinguish copies from originals with certainty, and constructing hypothetical artists for those works whose former supposed authorship had been discredited. He achieved this by insisting that attention should be diverted from the general impression and main features of a picture, and by laying stress on the significance of minor details, of things like the drawing of the fingernails, or the lobe of an ear, of halos and such unconsidered trifles which the copyist neglects to imitate and yet which every artist executes in his own characteristic way. I was then greatly interested to learn that the Russian pseudonym concealed the identity of an Italian physician called Morelli, who died in 1891 with the rank of Senator of the Kingdom of Italy. It seems to me that

his method of inquiry is closely related to the technique of psycho-analysis. It, too, is accustomed to divine secret and concealed things from despised or unnoticed features, from the rubbish-heap, as it were, of our observations.

Of course, Freud never claimed to look at art psychoanalytically. He considered himself an amateur when it came to paintings. As a simple art lover and observer, he cannot have been expected to uncover secrets as he did with his patients.

It's interesting, nonetheless, that he offered such strong ideas on the matter of the difference between an original and a copy in this text he wrote in 1914 without having any idea that thirty-one years earlier he had scrutinized a painting in depth, considering also the audience to which it appealed, without recognizing that the attribution next to it was incorrect. When he was making his pronouncements about the Holbein that was not a Holbein, and when he was comparing Morelli's craft to his own, how would he have felt about his failure to have done enough research to know that this particular Madonna had already been determined to have been painted a century later, and by a different artist, than was stated on the label that identified it?

CHAPTER 37

RAPHAEL

ONE OF THE REASONS I WAS SO INCLINED to dismiss Freud's mistake as unimportant is that by the time I had reached the Holbein copy, I had, because of the order of the installation of the paintings in Dresden, already concluded that the father of psycho-analysis was unparalleled in his sensitivity to the true nature of art-work. He had written Martha:

> Now, I happened to know that there was also a Madonna by Raphael there and I found her at last in an equally chapel-like room and a crowd of people in silent devotion in front of her. You are sure to know her, the Sistina. My thoughts as I sat there were: Oh, if only you were with me! The Madonna stands there surrounded by clouds made up of innumerable little angel heads, a spirited-looking child on her arm, St. Six-tus (or is it the Pope Sixtus?) looking up on one side, St. Bar-bara on the other gazing down on the two lovely little angels who are sitting low down on the edge of the picture. The picture emanates magic beauty that is inescapable, and yet I have a serious objection to raise against the Madonna herself. Holbein's Madonna is neither a woman nor a girl, her exalta-tion and sacred humility silence any question concerning her specific designation. Raphael's Madonna, on the other hand, is a girl, say sixteen years old; she gazes out on the world with such a fresh and innocent expression, half against my will she suggested to me a charming sympathetic nursemaid, not

from the celestial world but from ours. My Viennese friends reject this opinion of mine as heresy and refer to a superb feature round the eyes making her a Madonna; this I must have missed during my brief inspection.

When I looked at the *Sistine Madonna,* I realized that Freud GOT it. She is a girl, a teenager! Raphael's Madonna is more the pretty young lady who modeled for the Virgin than she is the Virgin. [plate 34]

I love the way that Freud paid no attention to the usual cant. Astonishingly few people respond to art with such originality, and allow it to be so personal. For forty years, in public lectures to audiences ranging from kindergarteners to elite groups associated with museums, this is what I have implored everyone to do: not to say what is correct, not to reel off facts, but to look at paintings in the most personal of ways, to allow themselves to react. I never suspected that Sigmund Freud would end up being the ultimate exemplar of someone who did just that.

WHILE FREUD SAW THE *Sistine Madonna* in a small chapel-like room of its own, with its viewers in "silent devotion," when I visited Dresden, it was at the end of a large gallery. It has been placed there to encourage traffic flow through the space, the way that the *Mona Lisa* does at the Louvre, assuring that, as they approach the leading attraction, the flocking tourists will at least glance at the lesser-known work in the rest of the room.

As for the idea of silent devotion: It belongs to another era. I would love to know what Freud would have made of the swarm of Japanese tourists who descended on the painting as I stood there contemplating it. Not a single of the thirty or so people looked at the actual artwork for more than fifteen seconds. Most of the viewers concentrated only on framing shots with his or her digital camera, often with a friend

Plate 34. Raphael, *The Sistine Madonna*, 1512, oil on canvas,
Gemäldegalerie Alte Meister, Zwinger Palace, Dresden

posing for a photo in front of the painting. They were focused more on their camera adjustments than on the Raphael.

Would Freud have been disgruntled by this? Or, rather, would he mainly have evinced a keen understanding of the human needs that were manifest in this way of looking at artworks, this mind-set that required preserving the experience of having been in the proximity of a masterpiece more than relishing the actual viewing of it? Would his fascination with human behavior have superseded his reverence for the richness of feasting one's eyes on paintings?

SUDDENLY, I HAD A MOMENT OF SOLITUDE and silence with the Raphael. The shutterbugs had all run off as quickly as they had arrived, leaving me to study the painting undisturbed.

I became aware that the tourists could not possibly have noticed that the clouds are heads. I am not even sure that I would have, had I not read Freud's description to Martha and looked accordingly. But then I began to have a somewhat different take on the Madonna than Freud did. First of all, I had misread his letter. My initial take on his having written "My thoughts as I sat there were: Oh, if only you were with me!" had been that he was mentally addressing the Madonna, not Martha. I also knew that he had a crucial connection to his own nursemaid, so his comparing Raphael's young woman to "a nursemaid" invested her with immense force. I imagined Freud coveting the woman in the painting, and I quickly began to feel that way myself.

Like Freud, I found Raphael's robust young lady to be very much of our own world—rather than a spiritual presence. But to me she was a hoyden, not someone possessed of innocence. Beyond her unquestionable physical vigor, the girl Freud guessed to be sixteen years old has an insolence. This healthy Madonna is nothing so much as a brash teenager, possibly a naughty one.

The angels, while precious, are also slightly mischievous, which is part of what makes them adorable. They are ruffians, and Saint Barbara looks at them as if they are naughty schoolchildren.

As for the Christ Child: In Raphael's painting, he is an energetic toddler more than an infant. His body is well on its way to being formed, and we feel as if he is ready to walk off on his little muscled legs. This makes good sense. His earthy mother has alighted as if from a run—she could be a counselor at a New England summer camp—and he is made of the same material in his sportiness.

DID FREUD, THEN OR LATER, KNOW THAT FYODOR DOSTOEVSKY, about whom he would write in the essay "Dostoevsky and Parricide" in 1928, and whose *Crime and Punishment* he considered "the most magnificent novel ever written," "placed Raphael above all painters and considered the *Sistine Madonna* the summit of his art?" I only know this bit of information, provided in the memoirs of Dostoevsky's wife, Anna Grigorievna, because it is in a note to the text of Richard Pevear and Larissa Volokhonsky's splendid translation of *Demons* (formerly known as *The Possessed*), in reference to an encomium by the character Stepan Trofimovitch when he writes his wife from Germany to say "it is all quite noble: there is a lot of music, Spanish airs, dreams of universal renewal, the idea of eternal beauty, the Sistine Madonna." Stepan Trofimovitch's wife concludes that her husband is not "sitting twelve hours over books" every day as he says; . . ."Oh, well let him have a good time."

Freud's main thesis in his essay is that Dostoevsky's supposed epilepsy was, in fact, a physical symptom of repressed guilt over his father's death, which is why he only began having the fits at age eighteen, his age when his father died. (The theory would in part be disproved when it was discovered that Dostoevsky's children were also epileptic, suggesting the biological nature of the illness. A friend of mine who is a psycho-therapist, Patrick Dewavrin, has pointed out, however, that this does not mitigate the connection between seizures and their psychological origins.) Whether or not Freud was aware, as he faced the painting Raphael had made between 1512 and 1514 for the high altar of the Church of St. Sixtus in Piacenza, that he was in the space where one of his favorite writers, whose work and life Freud connected directly to his theories of the Oedipus complex, had stood in similar rapture, it makes sense that both were greatly affected by the painting. The *Sistine Madonna* has the charge of life, the sexual energy, the intensity of emotion Dostoevsky experienced at age eighteen when his father died—all with the fire particular to adolescence. The fetching beauty in the painting—whom Freud imagined as being sixteen—exudes the unrivaled aliveness, the Hannibal-style intensity, of the interlude in one's existence that follows the onset of puberty and that subsides considerably, at least for most people, when maturity kicks in. This is the same delicious fury I knew as a sixteen-year-old once Susie had entered my bedroom and made me feel I had a romantic power I had never felt before.

THE *Sistine Madonna* GENERATES A FORCE rare in the history of man-made objects. Nearly a century after Dostoevsky feasted on it, and sixty years after Freud experienced what he called its "magic beauty," Adolf Hitler deemed the painting so splendid that he had it locked in the museum vault. This is why it survived the bombing of Dresden. Then Stalin, just after the war, put it in a vault in Moscow. (It was returned to Dresden following Stalin's death.)

Few men could resist this gamin "with such a fresh and innocent expression" who is "not from the celestial world but ours."

CHAPTER 38

FREUD ON DOSTOEVSKY

Freud's "Dostoevsky and Parricide" was first published in 1928 in a book about *The Brothers Karamazov*. Freud says Dostoevsky's "place is not far behind Shakespeare," and that his "episode of the Grand Inquisitor, one of the peaks in the literature of the world, can hardly be valued too highly." In his essay on the Russian novelist he admired so deeply, Freud manages, I think, to hit the nail on the head about himself and Signorelli. In so doing, he also homes in on what it is in my own life experience that I identify with aspects of his. For one thing, Freud discusses Dostoevsky's intense fear of death as a child, and the melancholic states into which he would fall: "We know the meaning and intention of such deathlike attacks. They signify an identification with a dead person, either with someone who is really dead or with someone who is still alive and whom the subject wishes dead. The latter case is the more significant. The attack then has the value of a punishment. One has wished another person dead, and now one is this other person and is dead oneself. At this point psycho-analytical theory brings in the assertion that for a boy this other person is usually his father."

In the period of mourning when Freud himself was in Orvieto, looking at those images of punishment after life, he would have been subject to many of the same feelings himself.

Freud, discussing Dostoevsky, amplifies; "The two attitudes of mind combine to produce identification with the father; the boy wants to be in his father's place because he admires him and wants to be like him, and also because he wants to put him out of the way. This whole development now comes up against a powerful obstacle. At a certain moment the child comes to understand that an attempt to remove his father as a rival would be punished by him with castration. So, from fear of castration—that is, in the interests of preserving his masculinity—he gives up his wish to possess his mother and get rid of his father."

In my own case, I found the perfect substitute for possessing my mother: I would fall in love with her archrival/closest friend, and convince myself it was okay. It was easy, since, to quote a crusty woman who knew Susie, she was "the prettiest thing that ever walked."

What draws me to Freud, to Signorelli's frescoes, and to my memories of Susie are the ways that all these people make thoughts that on the one hand seem extreme appear to be very normal. Freud, after saying that a boy "gives up his wish to possess his mother and get rid of his father"—"from fear of castration"—writes "We believe that what we have here been describing are normal processes, the normal fate of the so-called 'Oedipus complex.'"

On the other hand, I think there was something in Freud himself that was not so rational, and that did not buy the "normal" idea for himself. It caused him to forget the name Signorelli—which on some level was like forgetting his own, Sigmund. This destabilizing element was the homosexual element so blatant in the Orvieto frescoes.

Again, Freud, writing on Dostoevsky, provides crucial insight: "A further complication arises when the constitutional factor we call bisexuality is comparatively strongly developed in a child. For then, under the threat to the boy's masculinity by castration, his inclination becomes strengthened to diverge in the direction of femininity, to put himself instead in his mother's place and take over her role as object of his father's love. But the fear of castration makes this solution impossible as well. The boy understands that he must also submit to castration if he wants to be loved by his father as a woman. Thus both impulses, hatred of the father and being in love with the father, undergo repression."

There, of course, is the key term: "repression." It's the word he always used about the Signorelli parapraxis. The sources for that repression would have been particularly alive to him as he confronted all that male nudity in the period following his father's death.

In my own spontaneous musing, brought on by my investigation of Freud's dealing with his father's death, I reveled in my own father's admiring my arrogance, like my mother's, in front of Mr. Weinstein; his encouraging my love of art, which made me like my mother, who was a painter; his being the dark-haired brown-eyed one, while I have my mother's coloring and blue eyes. The instinct to have your father love you as your mother—yet also as himself (how I am my father's son! I feel it a hundred times a day, in the voice, the posture, and so many attitudes)—may be hard to accept, but it is also undeniable. And all that complexity of the father-son relationship would have come alive to Freud in front of Signorelli's art, and again when he was thinking of Turks and their sexuality, and death and of the news he received in Trafoi of his patient's suicide, and must have been overwhelming to him, as it is to all of us, thus forcing his mental processes to come to a halt, a necessary stop. Even if the result—the forgetting of a name—tortured him, it may have helped calm him down.

Freud did not expect most people to accept these ideas easily. In the Dostoevsky essay, he goes on to say:

> I am sorry, though I cannot alter the facts, if this exposition of the attitudes of hatred and love towards the father and their transformations under the influence of the threat of castration seems to readers unfamiliar with psycho-analysis unsavoury and incredible. I should myself expect that it is precisely the castration complex that would be bound to arouse the most general repudiation. But I can only insist that psycho-analytic experience has put these matters in

particular beyond the reach of doubt and has taught us to recognize in them the key to every neurosis. This key, then, we must apply to our author's so-called epilepsy. So alien to our consciousness are the things by which our unconscious mental life is governed!

And of course it was his own "unconscious mental life" that forced him to forget a name.

CHAPTER 39

THE TITIAN

Iᴇᴛᴜʀɴᴇᴅ ᴛᴏ ᴛʜᴇ *Sistine Madonna* several times that afternoon in Dresden. Each time, I was struck anew by how astute Freud was. Raphael's Mary is, indeed, someone we could know in our everyday lives—and absent any dimension of holiness. On each occasion, I imagined myself a teenager again, and knew I would have wanted to go out with her. I reconsidered my error in thinking that Freud was summoning this robust young woman, not Martha, to be with him. It was all part of my own nostalgia for youth, for longing without guilt, for the time of one's physical prime.

Then, on my third viewing of the Raphael, I became uncomfortable about my idea that she is mischievous, while Freud thought that her subsuming quality is her innocence. How could I perceive the young woman differently from the way the master of human psychology did? On the other hand, I then thought, He didn't know a real Holbein from a copy.

Yet—there is always a "yet"—the essence of Raphael's Madonna is her humanness and vitality. That she is alive in a very human way, and seems neither immortal nor incorporeal, is what counts—more than the issue of her attitude. This is an earthy, sexy picture, not a spiritual one. One understands the deep significance of that fact to Freud only by looking at the third picture he described to Martha, the Titian.

THIS ACCOUNT OF HIS REACTIONS TO THE HOLBEIN and the Raphael
are a preamble to the descriptions of Freud's first true rapture in front
of a work of art. He next wrote his fiancée:

> But the picture that really captivated me was the *Maundy
> Money* [*The Tribute Money*], by Titian, which of course I
> knew already but to which I have never paid any special
> attention. This head of Christ, my darling, is the only one
> that enables even people like ourselves to imagine that such
> a person did exist. Indeed, it seemed that I was compelled
> to believe in the eminence of this man because the figure
> is so convincingly presented. And nothing divine about it,
> just a noble human countenance, far from beautiful yet full
> of seriousness, intensity, profound thought, and deep inner
> passion; if these qualities do not exist in this picture, then
> there is no such thing as physiognomy. I would love to have
> gone away with it, but there were too many people about,
> English ladies making copies, English ladies sitting about
> and whispering, English ladies wandering about and gazing.
> So I went away with a full heart.

Rarely have truer words, or greater depth of feeling, been expressed
about a painting. In my own profession, among the well-reputed scholars, only Meyer Schapiro, Erwin Panofsky, and Kenneth Clark come
close to being as appreciative of the radiance of an artwork, as capable of emotional transport, and as articulate in describing the impact
human achievement can have.

If you want to understand Freud's sensitivity—not his ideas, but the
yearnings of his soul—you need to see this Titian. The state of enchant-
ment in which it put him as a young man and which he described to
the woman with whom he knew he would spend the rest of his life,
is a side of Freud's persona that is rarely seen. Feeling art in all its
humanity, devoid of the canon of art history, miraculously free of the

burden of too much information, he became flooded with pure emotion. In Orvieto we have seen the source of his tortured excitement; in Dresden, we can observe the picture that satisfied his serious wish to appreciate Christianity. [plate 35]

Plate 35. Titian, *The Tribute Money*, c. 1516, oil on panel,
Gemäldegalerie Alte Meister, Zwinger Palace, Dresden

Freud's conscientiousness in trying to understand holiness through art was remarkable, given both his agnosticism and his investigations into the psychological reasons for believing in deities.

Freud, after all, considered most religion to be an invention stemming from human need; in his theoretical writing, he never hints that it might be based on facts. It is as if he sees the Bible as pure fiction, however fascinating the myths may be. Reading the letter to Martha, I was astounded to find that one of his criteria for evaluating paintings was whether or not they successfully conveyed the existence of Jesus and Mary consistently with their portrayal in the New Testament, as if the biblical doctrine was an irrefutable truth. For Freud, the Titian inspired a degree of faith surprisingly at odds with his theoretical opposition to what he officially characterized as superstition.

Of course what excited Freud about Titian's Jesus was more His "eminence" than His being the Son of God. In some ways, it is comparable to Freud's reverence for Hannibal. Freud worshipped what is noble. The Titian afforded him the chance, the way the heroes of his childhood had, to behold a peak of human excellence.

Beyond that, the painting in Dresden induced communion with a state of grace Freud prized. Fascinated by the human face in general, thrilled by his new discovery of the particular power of visual art, he was delighted when in tandem these epitomized excellence. That a man-made object had the force to make the actual existence of Jesus Christ plausible, His virtues palpable, inspired him to make exactly the sort of joke—that if all those English people had not been there, he would have stolen the painting—that on other occasions he would have disparaged. Even as he and Martha would remain "people like ourselves," through portrait art they could succumb to unexpected delights.

Do what I did; have the letter to Martha in your hand, and look at the Titian! You will readily understand the way Freud was moved, and will in all likelihood have many of the same feelings yourself.

RETRACING FREUD IN DRESDEN, YOU ENTER HIS WORLD. It is not Vienna, but it is a place where his mother tongue is spoken. The pastries that he adored, and considered his weakness, are available there; you can be primed by what you eat in a way that makes you open to the great man's experience. The café-restaurant at the Gemäldegalerie has the best poppy seed cake I have ever tasted, and the perfect strong coffee to go with it; I was fortified by them on my fourth visit to the Titian in the course of three hours. I kept going back to this wonderful painting in part to imagine all the better Freud's revelations in front of it, but also because I, too, was drawn to the purity of spirit of its Jesus, and was also enchanted by its regal colors and bold, compact forms. This is one of those small paintings of few forms and limited palette that, in its concision, is monumental.

The Zwinger epitomizes the Baroque style Freud liked so much, with its many staircases inside and out, variegated surfaces, and endless chambers and wings; it is also like a parable for the human mind. When you find the Titian, you will have the joy of arrival at a holy site after a pilgrimage. On each visit, I enjoyed the journey and then the feeling of reaching a haven. You can behold his treasure in perfect silence, with daylight pouring in through a window that opens on a lush garden.

No wonder, but how remarkable, that Freud fastened upon this relatively small object, a mere seventy-five by fifty-six centimeters, in a sea of pictures! When we stand in front of the Titian, where he stood, and look at the faces of Jesus and the man who is presenting Him with tribute money, they are living beings. This is one of those rare paintings from which physical force and thoughtfulness and feeling radiate. You are in the presence, more than you believe yourself to be when walking elsewhere in the city and passing Dresden's galumphing tourists, of real flesh and intense reflection.

The modern world being what it is, I was—unlike Freud—totally alone with this masterpiece. Dresden's malls and beer gardens were full of people on the warm July day I was there; in the picture gallery where the Titian hangs, there was, for the initial half hour I spent with it, and on my return visits, not another soul. When I was not facing the painting head-on, I sat on a well-worn sofa of quilted leather, placed against a wall at a right angle to the painting. I was able to concentrate totally, and bask in the pleasure to my heart's content.

Freud's Titian, painted in oil and wood, is perfectly composed. Jesus' brick red robe, His blue cloak, and the yellow of the other man's robe are a spectacular sequence of hues: the colors are not only rich to look at; they are the means by which the artist succeeds in placing the two bodies in space with such plausibility that we feel we could measure the distance between the other man and Jesus with calipers. The palette and its tonality work perfectly with the drawing and modeling of the figures to locate the other man, who stands at an angle, nearer to the picture plane, with the frontal Jesus positioned a foot or so behind him. The physical reality is entirely convincing.

That verisimilitude enhances the palpable thoughtfulness of the two men. And more powerful still is the spiritual aura of Jesus, the calm He emanates, the qualities Freud describes to Martha but which, as he would have been the first to admit, are beyond words.

CHAPTER 40

THE JEW AGAIN

THERE IS, HOWEVER, AN ELEMENT of the Titian painting that Freud failed to mention to Martha, and that was, I believe, central to his experience. The extent to which Jesus appears "noble"—Freud's adjective—is accentuated by the contrast between Him and the other man. And the other man is the quintessential Jew.

What is being illustrated here would have been readily recognizable to a man of Freud's generation. It is the moment in the New Testament when the Pharisees ask Christ whether they should adhere to the law requiring that they pay taxes to the Romans. The Pharisees were a Jewish sect, the name of which comes from the Hebrew *perushim,* meaning people who were "set apart." Christ asks whose name and portrait are on the coin. As recounted in Matthew 22, Mark 12, and Luke 20, one of the Pharisees replies that it is Caesar's. Christ then instructs him, "Render therefore unto Caesar the things that are Caesar's; and unto God the things that are God's."

The only character in the painting about whom Freud wrote Martha is Jesus, but there can be no doubt that the portrayal of Jesus' counterpoint made a big impression on him. The Pharisee is the epitome of a Jew for whom money has disproportionate meaning. With his hooked nose, dark and oily skin, and sly, eager look, as well as the earring with which he flaunts his wealth, this particular Pharisee is pretty much how I picture the Jewish man whom the sixteen-year-old Freud could not stand on the train journey, and about whom he wrote his friend Fluss.

The way that Titian has painted the scene, it suggests that the

Pharisee is attempting to trap Jesus. While pretending to ask if he should make payment to the Romans, he tries to hand the coin to Jesus. His dark hand, the shiny coin, and Jesus' pale fingers tell the story. Jesus' hand gesture makes clear that He is not accepting the payment, and also points to Caesar. Unlike Ceasar's minions, He is above giving or taking bribes. The otherworldly look on His face confirms His lack of any trace of the materialism and greed that are redolent in the Jew.

WHEN I WAS IN DRESDEN, I HAD NO IDEA who the second man was; I only learned this in subsequent research. I swooned to the magisterial forms and saturated colors of Titian's small masterpiece, and felt a rapport with Freud in his profound joy over Jesus' tranquil grace and quiet strength. The contrast of the two personalities surely affected me, but I did not know why. Then, six months after the pilgrimage to Dresden, I decided to try to identify the man holding the coin, so that I could stop saying "the other man" when writing this text and could replace those vague words with a name when referring to the unpleasant character next to Jesus. Upon learning that he was "a Pharisee," and finding out what the biblical moment was, I decided I had achieved my goal, and stopped my investigation. But then I realized that I did not know who the Pharisees were. When, after further research, I found out that they were Jews, I was surprised.

My education—good enough by American standards, given that I received a B.A. and an M.A. from two Ivy League universities, and attended a traditional preparatory school as well as Sunday school at the local Reform Jewish temple—had taught me none of this. But I assume that Freud's had.

Once I had that knowledge that the fellow alongside Jesus was as Pharisee and hence a Jew, when I looked at the Titian in reproduction,

I began to see the man next to Jesus practically as a Jewish caricature—of the type one sees, for example, in anti-Semitic cartoons about the Dreyfus affair. Was this because of my own way of seeing things more than because of objective reality? I sought to verify the matter.

I discovered that, even if recent books steer clear of the delicate subject of the Pharisee's appearance, in older texts on Titian, the scholars saw him as I did (and, more important, the way we imagine Freud would have seen him). One distinguished art historian writing sixty years ago refers to "the sly attitude and the perverse expression of the Pharisee, this merchant of Venice, this tempting and vindictive Shylock." A French professor who wrote an excellent book on Titian's early years, published in 1919, calls the Pharisee Titian's "Jew with a hooked nose . . . a sly and groveling beast." For that man writing almost a century ago, the painting is all about contrasts, with the two figures' hands even more telling than the difference between Christ's beautiful visage in full sunlight and the Pharisee's largely in shadow:

> Titian has not only opposed two heads; the contrast of the hand is of as gripping an eloquence as that of the faces. The heavy paw of the Pharisee, modeled out of coarse material, is formed to amass and hold on to gold; it advances, twisted and hypocritical, and presents its gold crown like a trap offering its bait. The long and pale hand of Jesus drops with indolence an infinity of sweetness and disdain.

Just as the faces "contrast a vile profile against a divine face," so do these limbs position evil against good. How marvelous to observe a hypocritical hand!

I remain fascinated that Freud wrote only about Jesus, while never acknowledging to his fiancée, a far more observant Jew than he was, that one of the main reasons we feel the magnificence of Jesus' character is because of His contrast to the hideous Pharisee, and His resistance to the Pharisee's connivery. In 1935, in a fine text on Titian that was published by the French sculptor Henri Laurens in a series enchantingly called Les Grands Artistes, Collection d'Enseignement et de Vulgarisation (Great Artists, Collection of Instruction and Popularization), Maurice Hamel writes:

> Christ's face, seen head-on, radiates a spiritual beauty. His fine and noble face, the frame and simple gesture of his hand that points out the effigy of Caesar, is opposed with a gripping clarity to the muddy color, to the sly and wily expression, to the insidious allure of the Pharisee. One could have found no better way to give this scene its moral meaning than by the antithesis of two natures.

Someone as alert as Freud was to what it meant to be Jewish was certainly aware of the function of the hook-nosed, loathsome, and crafty character trying to trap Jesus, and of the way that Jesus' resistance to all that the Jew represents enhances his spiritual beauty.

It is no wonder, in fact, that Freud did not mention in the letter to Martha that the guy dangling money before Jesus was a Jew.

He was too embarrassed, and too tactful, to say as much. I understand this because of my own issues. Here goes, although this is uncomfortable to admit, and I feel ashamed of myself.

Even though Jesus, of course, was also a Jew, the Pharisee was "the wrong type" of Jew, the type described in the remarkable book *Poor Cousins*—an answer to Stephen Birmingham's *Our Crowd*—in which Andrea Manners describes how the Our Crowd set (meaning, among others, my wife's Warburg and Lewisohn relatives) tried to enact legislation to keep poor Yiddish-speaking Jews (like Katharine's relatives on her father's side) from getting into the United States. The Pharisee could have been one the people on the beach in New London,

Connecticut, to which my fair blue-eyed maternal grandmother (brought up Jewish, but who, so the story goes, was born to a Catholic farmgirl and brought home to his wife by my randy great-grandfather who had conceived her with the creature I always picture as a pretty wench, like the *Sistine Madonna*) refused to go because the people had "too much black body hair."

He could equally have been the loud guy from Long Island from whom I was so determined to disassociate myself when he and I were the only two guys to miss classes because of Yom Kippur on the third day of freshman year at Loomis, when I was still okay about it all but didn't want to be likened to someone leaving the campus with his mother, who was driving a Cadillac to temple.

I came by this unattractive—you might say loathsome—snobbery honestly.

I remember a conversation in the car following a ski outing when I was about twelve years old that sums up what I mean by that. My mother and I had gone to Mount Tom, about an hour's drive north of Hartford. The year was 1959, before there was man-made snow, and one had to take advantage of decent conditions as they occurred. There had been an ample snowfall a couple of days earlier, and so Mom had volunteered to take Ricky and me on the first day of our February vacation from the public junior high school.

Now that I think of it, I realize what a sport she was. The temperature was about fifteen degrees that day, and once we got to the ski area, Ricky and I went off to the steepest slopes, leaving her on her own. We met at midday for lunch in the cafeteria, but we didn't see Mom again until it was time for her to drive us home.

What most fascinates me in retrospect is that on that car ride she chose to tell the following story in front of Ricky. Mom was a great raconteur, and described in vivid detail a long line to get on the T-bar lift. On the line, there was one area that required the skiers to negotiate a mound of snow. A woman about twenty people ahead of Mom had, in effect, created a traffic jam. She simply could not get up the mound. My mother amplified: "She had shiny new skis, expensive boots, and a ski outfit that must have cost a fortune, with a fur-trimmed hood, but she had obviously never skied before. She would try to work her way up the mound—with a sort of herringbone, the way other people did, or sideways—but she kept not making it. Yet she would not step aside. She was holding everyone up, and she acted as if she were the only person there, with her perfect clothes and equipment, and refused to let other skiers get around her. Finally, an instructor gave her a hand, and she waddled the rest of the way to the lift."

Ricky, who adored my mother, thought the story was hilarious. And then Mom continued:

"My problem was that I could not stop thinking the woman was Jewish. I was furious at myself. For the rest of the afternoon—this occurred just after lunch—I kept asking myself, Why do you think she is Jewish? I was desperate to be proven wrong."

Ricky and I waited to hear what had happened next.

"Then, as I was waiting for the two of you in the parking lot, I saw the woman again. You couldn't mistake the white fur trim. And she was with a group of other similar ladies, all with their perfect skis, sitting on a bus. And I saw a sign on the bus that said 'B'nai B'rith Ski Trip.'"

The three of us just laughed and said nothing more.

WHEN I WAS A SENIOR AT PREP SCHOOL, and applying to colleges, I had good reason to think I would get into Columbia, my second choice, if not Harvard, my first. But the college adviser recommended that I pick a safety school. He told me about Brandeis, of which I had never heard, characterizing it as having the qualities of the schools I wanted, with a strong emphasis on the arts, but not mentioning that there was anything Jewish about it.

That night, I told my mother I had heard about this great-sounding school I wanted to visit and apply to. She looked interested until I told her it was Brandeis. Then Mom made about the same face she had made when she saw Elia Kazan.

"What's the problem?" I asked.

Mom cleared her throat. "It's hard to explain, Nicky, but you just would not be happy there. It's not for you. How about Amherst or Williams, dear?"

Years later, she denied it all, but laughed unconvincingly. No wonder that when I gave my mother's eulogy, and looked out at the four hundred or so well-turned-out people who packed the large sanctuary at Temple Beth Israel, I had to fight hard to resist telling them all my mother's definition of a nymphomaniac: "A Jewish woman who goes to bed with her husband the same day she's had her hair done."

Freud certainly wasn't stupid enough to tell his observantly Jewish fiancée the role of the Pharisee when describing his reaction to the Titian double portrait. But I'm convinced I understand. It was the same issue.

The Tribute Money WAS PAINTED BETWEEN 1510 AND 1516. The authorities differ on its date but concur that Titian finished it before he was thirty—although the artist's birth date is also uncertain. What everyone agrees on is that it is among the artist's earliest known works, yet is one of his masterpieces.

Vasari writes that Titian painted this wooden panel to go inside the door of an armoire or a clothes closet. Whatever its purpose, it has a fantastic quality of finish. Jesus' skin is as smooth as glazed porcelain, while both men's hair and beard are coarse and thick. The silkiness of Jesus' clothes—the regal blue cloak draped over His broad shoulders has a luminous sheen—gives Him a sense of majesty. The edgy lines and mottled surfaces of the Pharisee make him as discomfiting as Jesus is reassuring.

But what this painting evokes above all else cannot be verbalized. Looking at it, our breathing is altered by its indescribable religiosity, by the beatific qualities that emanate from it. The drama between the Pharisee's emphasis on money and Jesus' eschewal of it not only makes this holiness all the more impressive but creates a thrilling scenario that engages the viewer the way that great theater does. The dark void between the two figures assumes the representation of mental intensity; Jesus' and the Pharisee's contrasting thoughts seem to penetrate it. This field of black is all the more powerful in contrast to the bright shimmer on the copper coin—an electric spark in the scenario.

Jesus seems to know everything. He recognizes that people will lie and betray Him. His face makes clear that, alive as He is, He will die.

There is no escaping that brutal fact. The mixture of otherworldly spirituality and earthly realism is what gives this painting its élan.

Jesus resembles His own mother—to an unusual degree. If you take away the facial hair, He is the same person as in many images of the Madonna; the cast of His eyes is both tender and full of foreboding. There is, nearby in the same gallery at the Zwinger, a *Mother and Child* by Titian where the Virgin Mary has the identical tilt to her head, as well as the same features. Jesus' combination of male and female qualities in Freud's chosen Titian makes Him all the more impressive.

Even regardless of the Jewish theme, which can only have added to the allure of the work, it is no surprise that Freud—the ultimate connoisseur, possessed of a keen eye and the rare gift to single out what mattered—was moved above all by this exquisite image of Christ resembling his mother. After I had toured the entire incredible museum, and returned to this Titian, I realized that, even more than the Vermeers, it is *the* masterpiece. Nothing else is quite as human and intimate, or provides such a close-up focus on the soul. No other painting evokes the way a man is often remarkably like his female parent.

I CANNOT BE CERTAIN THAT THE PAINTING STILL HANGS exactly where it did in 1883. But Freud was there—with Titian, in Titian's aura—as I was. In front of the painting, I felt closer to the great doctor than I did at either Bergasse 19 or 38 Marsfield Gardens, both of which I have diligently visited. In the glow of this Renaissance masterpiece, I had the sensation that I, too, was confronting humanness, death, beauty, intelligence, maleness, light (physical and spiritual), and the supreme mastery of the technique of painting. Beyond that, as Paul Klee said, great art looks at us—as much as we look at it.

The spell Susie cast when she stood with the Karpes was because she belongs in the same category as Jesus and as Freud: people who respond in every fiber of their being. She engaged; 100 percent alert, she was one of the rare ones who do not go through life in a daze. The same, of course, can be said for her great frienemy, my mother.

Freud's last words about the Titian to Martha slay me. "So I went away with a full heart."

CHAPTER 41

THE LETTER TO FLIESS

I AM PUZZLED THAT THE KARPES DID NOT QUOTE MORE directly from the letter Freud wrote Fliess on September 22, 1898, in which he discusses his inability to recall the name of the artist of the Orvieto frescoes. It was only at the very end of my explorations that I had (again thanks to Charlotte) the actual letter in front of me; it changes my slant, if only slightly, on what Luca Signorelli's work was all about for Freud.

For one thing, he begins that letter by saying that, while he has "been back barely three days" after the trip during which he incurred the memory loss, "all the bad humor of Vienna has already descended upon me. It is sheer misery to live here."

I think it adds to our understanding of Freud's issues concerning Signorelli's chapel if we consider the full context in which Freud presents the incident that occurred "during a short trip to Herzegovina, which I made from Ragusa." (That description leaves open the issue of whether the carriage was one on a train or one drawn by horses.) By reliving the memory loss, he was returning, mentally, to thoughts of travel to a fascinating part of the world, a lot that he preferred to Vienna: the thrill of Italian Renaissance painting, Turkish sexuality, and the behavior of the human mind—in this case his own, with all its puzzles. All this excitement was in marked contrast to his current gloom. Additionally, Freud brings up his memory loss just after telling Wilhelm Fliess his thoughts about their relationship.

Fliess, a Berlin otorhinolaryngologist, was two years older than

Freud. Although he was a couple of inches taller, in photos of these two men with their full but neatly trimmed beards and mustaches and correct dark suits, they look almost like twins. They met in 1887, after Fliess heard Freud speak in Vienna. Their exchange was a rich one; they were mutually supportive friends as well as intellectual colleagues who batted ideas back and forth with profound attentiveness to each other's views.

Fliess had developed a theory of "reflex nasal neuroses" that included a consideration of bisexuality and proposed that pathological processes develop in a cyclical way, over a period of twenty-eight days in women and twenty-three in men. While he did not agree with everything posited by his colleague and friend, Freud was particularly interested in Fliess's concept of bisexuality, which would figure in his own writing on sexuality as he formulated his theories on the subject after the turn of the century. He also credited Fliess with having called his attention to the importance both of jokes and all popular fantasies.

In that letter written just after his unhappy return to Vienna, once he has described his miserable mood, Freud declares his terrific respect for Fliess, and his longing to have his friend challenge his own views: "I wish you thought less of my masterly skills and I had you close by so that I could hear your criticisms more often. I am not at all in disagreement with you, not at all inclined to leave the psychology hanging in the air without an organic basis." In light of all the current thinking about wiring and chemistry as central sources of the variables of human mental health, this statement from the young Freud is crucial. It also may further illuminate the reason he could not conjure the name.

Just before explaining what happened on the journey into Herzegovina, Freud allows, his despair evident, that the reason he has been unable to connect the organic and the psychological "I have not even begun to fathom." It is then that we get to the moment that prompted him to examine the components of Signorelli's name.

Freud begins, "I could not find the name of the renowned painter who did the *Last Judgment* in Orvieto, the greatest I have seen so far."

Freud continues by saying that he briefly considered Botticelli, and then Boltraffio, as the name of the painter, but that he quickly knew these were not correct; here the Karpes represent Freud's experience exactly as he did.

But then Freud says something to Fliess that I find extremely provocative and demanding of a bit of exegesis, yet which the Karpes leave out. He writes, "At last I found out the name, Signorelli, and immediately knew, on my own, the first name, Luca—as proof that it had been only a repression and not a genuine forgetting."

The way that instant knowledge of the name Luca established the distinction between repression and forgetting is a superb example of Freud's brilliance and originality. So is Freud's continued amplification to Fliess on components of the name in question:

> It is clear why Botti-*celli* had moved into the foreground; only Signor was repressed; the Bo in both substitute names is explained by the memory responsible for the repression; it concerned something that happened in Bosnia and began with the word, Herr [Signor, Sir], what can be done about it? I lost the name Signorelli during a short trip to *Herze*-govina, which I made from Ragusa with a lawyer from Berlin (Freyhau) with whom I got to talking about pictures. In the conversation, which aroused memories that evidently caused the repression, we talked about death and sexuality. The word *Trafio* is no doubt an echo of Trafoi, which I saw on the first trip! How can I make this credible to anyone?

Wow! First of all, this is contrary to what the Karpes write about the person Freud encountered on the train having been a stranger. It changes things to learn that he had not struck up this unusually profound conversation with someone whose name he did not know, but that he was with this acquaintance he identifies to Fliess as a lawyer with the name of Freyhau.

Chastising Richard and Marietta for this omission, I imagine them just smiling at me knowingly, as they smiled at Susie, and making me wonder about why I felt impelled to correct them, and why I insist on being a detective. I can picture them asking what *my* issue is. In a similar vein, I well remember that day I heard Dr. Solnit snoring. I broke the rules of psychoanalysis by turning around to look at him, and then politely woke him from his sleep. Quickly, the issue switched from the problem that my psychoanalyst was sleeping on the job to how I felt about it. Did I think that my parents slept through anything they did not want to hear from me? Why did I consider Dr. Solnit so godlike that I became convinced he could hear me even while he snored? Then, a moment later, why did I believe that my own thoughts were so significant that it mattered if he slept?

And *now* some six months after writing the paragraph above, I note that I have used the word *omission*. It should have been *error*. But I was initially unable to question the Karpes' authority to that degree.

What would Susie have thought if she knew that the Karpes made mistakes? I started this exploration of Freud's trip to Orvieto with the notion that their article about it was flawless. Now I am wondering if they read only excerpts from Freud's letter to Fliess, and whether they did not in fact see the entire text. Here, too, were the limitations of the West Hartford Library decisive?

The detailed analysis of the names, which Richard and Marietta also leave out, is instructive. Trafoi is a mountain resort in northern Italy, known mainly as a holiday destination for noble families from the Austro-Hungarian Empire at the end of the nineteenth century. I cannot help wondering if Freud was in his way trying to avoid the main point with his buddy Fliess by just associating from name to name. Why would Freud's memory of a trip to the mountains have affected his choice of an artist's name? To go from Botticelli and

Boltraffio to Bosnia because they start with the same two letters also seems like a way of avoiding the point. On the other hand, when Dr. Solnit once pointed out to me that I said the three syllables of my closest male friend's name, Nick Ohly, in such a way that they had the same rhythm as my grandmother's name, Rosalie—which my doctor pronounced, as if echoing me, as *Rose-ah-lee*—and practically rhymed with it, I considered it a complete breakthrough, a valuable observation in my attempt at self-understanding. The dissection of words can prove far more fruitful than the dissection of eels.

My own view on the reason that Freud came up with two names that start with *Bo* rather than the correct one, which begins with *Sig,* is that *Bo* sounds like *beau*—the masculine form of the French adjective for "beauty." The names of the two incorrect artists thus conjure the quality of the males in those frescoes that Freud felt was lacking when the *Sig* of Sigmund was involved.

This fits with Freud's admission in *The Psychopathology of Everyday Life* that what prompted the name confabulation when he envisioned the Orvieto frescoes were his "repressed thoughts." In the conclusion of his letter to Fliess, he complains of his solitude at home and the possibility that he might go to Berlin because another colleague wants him to consult on a difficult case; such a trip would allow him to visit Fliess. To me, that loneliness and the yearning for the company of a male friend he admired is central to the impact of those fantastic frescoes of naked men in central Italy.

In that same letter, Freud himself admits, "I must not provoke gods and men by further travels, but instead wait here patiently for the little sheep to gather." Maybe this is tongue and cheek, but he was saying it to the colleague who believed that every joke and quip had its rich meaning. The idea of gods, of men who could be provoked, of people as docile as sheep, and the implicit notion of others as wolves—all this was what came to mind just after he had recounted the experience of being unable to recall the name of the painter of those strapping brutes in the Cappella Nova.

I ALSO WISH THE KARPES HAD INCLUDED THE FOLLOWING from that pivotal letter Freud wrote Fliess on November 2, 1896. After saying he feels "uprooted" following "the old man's death," Freud reports:

> Otherwise, I am writing about infantile paralyses (Pegasus yoked) 2 and am enjoying my four cases and especially look forward to the prospect of talking to you for several hours. Lonely, that is understood. Perhaps I shall tell you a few small wild things in return for your marvelous ideas and findings. Less enjoyable is the state of my practice this year, on which my mood always remains dependent. With heart and nose I am satisfied again.
>
> Recently I heard the first reaction to my incursion into psychiatry. From it I quote: "Gruesome, horrible, old wives' psychiatry." That was Rieger in Würzburg. I was highly amused. And, of all things, about paranoia, which has become so transparent!
>
> Your book is still keeping us waiting. Wernicke recently referred a patient to me, a lieutenant who is in the officers' hospital.

Then, after describing his dream the night after his father's funeral, and the sign he imagined seeing in the barbershop, he tells Fliess:

> I see little of the betrothed couple and the affair, unfortunately, gives me little pleasure. He is more sober and calmer, but his (and your) parents-in-law seem to show little adroitness in handling the relationship. It is not a pleasant topic

between us; if you prefer, we shall not talk about it. It's all rubbish, in any event.

My most cordial greetings to I.F. and R.W.; my wife probably is already with you.

Your
Sigm.

P.S. If Martha needs some money for purchases, you will no doubt lend it to her.

We don't know who the betrothed couple was, or what the unhappy affair consisted of, except that it apparently involved a man married to Fliess's wife's sister. But what we do know is that Freud, in private matters, voiced his views strongly, and was determined to maintain the upper hand. We also see in this letter, written in the shadow of the assured character most people now make him out to be, that Freud was highly volatile, with pronounced mood swings and an honest awareness of them. Beyond being the great observer of humankind, he engaged deeply.

Maybe Dr. Solnit did, too—not that he would ever have shown it to me. Maybe Richard Karpe got an erection looking at Susie, and was not just the wise old man standing there. As Freud himself acknowledged about the memory loss, it all comes back to *feelings*.

CHAPTER 42

The Psychopathology of Everyday Life

RICHARD AND MARIETTA KARPE CLAIM in their article that Freud minimalized "the importance of names" in *The Psychopathology of Everyday Life.*

I suppose that their reason for saying this was Freud's statement in that book, written in 1901, which opens with the incident of his forgetting the painter of the Orvieto frescoes: "The reason for the escape of the name *Signorelli* is neither to be sought in the strangeness in itself of this name nor in the psychological character of the connection in which it was inserted." But in fact Freud places great significance on the substitutive names he used when he could not remember the correct one when looking for the "the name of the master who made the imposing frescoes of the 'Last Judgment' in the dome of *Orvieto.* Instead of the lost name—*Signorelli*—two other names of artists—*Botticelli* and *Boltraffio*—obtruded themselves . . ." This we know from his letter to Fliess, of course. But in the text from 1901, he goes further in examining the reasons for the Botticelli and Boltraffio—even though he had rejected them "immediately . . . as being incorrect."

Here Freud says that he was traveling with a stranger from Ragusa, Dalmatia, to a station in Herzegovinia. He says that he asked his unnamed "companion whether he had been in Orvieto and had seen there the famous frescoes of—" Here I have to wonder why Freud says this person was a stranger—which, of course, is why the Karpes identify the Berlin lawyer Freyhau as such. When he wrote Fliess, closer to the actual event, the man was clearly identified. Why was Freud now pretending, three years after the fact, to have no connection with someone he had previously said was a person he knew, a lawyer from Berlin? Tell me, please, was Freud again forgetting a name? Or was he purposefully restating the facts? If he was forgetting, was he doing so on purpose or by accident?

For all these vagaries, he acts, in the 1901 text, as if his approach to his own mind is meticulous and scientific. He puts the results into five categories, according each a letter, ranging from (a) to (e). The (b) category is devoted to explaining that the reason for forgetting was because of "the theme discussed immediately before this conversation" in which they discussed traveling in Italy. Freud is excited by the discovery he puts into italics: "*a disturbance of the newly emerging theme caused by the theme preceding it.*" Here he explains that he and his companion had been talking about the customs of Turks living in the places toward which they were traveling. This was when he went, as the Karpes tell us, from discussing both the Turkish faith in physicians and their "complete submission to fate" to thinking about, but not discussing, "a second anecdote which was next to the first in my memory. These Turks value the sexual pleasure above all else, and at sexual disturbances merge into an utter despair which strangely contrasts with their resignation at the peril of losing their lives." But, Freud writes, "I refrained from imparting this characteristic feature because I did not wish to touch upon such a delicate theme in conversation with a stranger." Of course that statement has added significance when we consider that his companion was, in fact, someone he knew.

Now Freud brings up the news he had received in Trafoi, which he explains in far more elaborate detail than he had to Fliess, thereby making its importance easier to understand. He says that his deliberate avoidance of any mention of the Turkish belief that without sexual activity "life no longer has any charm" caused him to take another step in stopping his own chain of thoughts. "I went still further; I also deflected my attention from the continuation of the thought which might have associated itself in me with the theme 'Death and Sexuality.'" Freud characterizes himself as being "under the after-effects" of something he learned a few weeks earlier when he was in Trafoi. "A patient on whom I had spent much effort had ended his life on account of an incurable sexual disturbance." Freud was fascinated to recall that "this sad event, and everything connected with it, did not come to my conscious recollection on that trip to Herzegovina."

He then maintains that the way that the name Boltraffio virtually incorporates the name Trafoi convinced him that "despite all the intentional deviation of my attention" he was actively thinking of what he had learned in Trafoi.

Freud concludes that, rather than being accidental, the forgetting of the name Signorelli was the result of "the influence of a motive." He had deliberately put aside his thoughts about Turkish customs. That, in turn, "influenced me to exclude from my consciousness the thought connected with them:" the receipt of that news in Trafoi. "That is, I wanted to forget something, I *repressed* something."

Freud was certain that he "wished to forget something other than the name of the master of Orvieto."

He explains what he thinks happened. I have to admit that here I had to read Freud's own words, at least as Brill translated them, four times to understand what he is saying—or trying to say. Then I saw Freud's obtuse language to mean that there was something about what he was repressing—those two examples of how sexual problems could in one instance cause the sufferer to desire death and in the other to go so far as to kill himself—that was associated with the name Signorelli. Because of this, "my act of volition missed the aim, and I *forgot the one against my will,* while I *intentionally* wished to forget the other."

Freud goes on to show a diagram he made as a graphic representation of his associations. Again, we see the *elli* of Botticelli as coming from the *elli* of Signorelli, while the *Bo* of both Botticelli and Boltraffio come from the *Bo* of Bosnia. The *traffio* of the second name comes from Trafoi. *Signor* had to be repressed because, when translated into German, it is *Herr,* and Freud felt an unconscious need to repress the name Herzegovina and the *Herr* of "Sir, What can I say"—when the subject that followed those words was death and sexuality. That is to say that for Freud everything revolved around the way that the names Herzegovina and Bosnia and Trafoi were all associated with death and sexuality for him.

At this point, I have to quote what Freud himself writes, as translated by Brill, in the hopes that other readers can understand it better than I do.

> Its substitution was formed in a way to suggest that a displacement took place along the same associations— "Herzegovina and Bosnia"—regardless of the sense and acoustic demarcation. The names were therefore treated in this process like the written pictures of a sentence which is to be transformed into a picture-puzzle (rebus). No information was given to consciousness concerning the whole process, which, instead of the name Signorelli, was thus changed to the substitutive names. At first sight no relation is apparent between the theme that contained the name Signorelli and the repressed one which immediately preceded it.

> Perhaps it is not superfluous to remark that the given explanation does not contradict the conditions of memory reproduction and forgetting assumed by other psychologists, which they seek in certain relations or dispositions. Only in certain cases have we added another *motive* to the factors long recognized as causative in forgetting names, and have thus laid bare the mechanism of faulty memory. The assumed dispositions are indispensable also in our case, in order to make it possible for the repressed element to associatively gain control over the desired name and take it along into the repression. Perhaps this would not have occurred in another

name having more favourable conditions of reproduction. For it is quite probable that a suppressed element continually strives to assert itself in some other way, but attains this success only where it meets with suitable conditions. At other times the suppression succeeds without disturbance of function or, as we may justly say, without symptoms.

I could not help but feel as I read this, more than once, that someone was trying to run circles around me. This narrative gives the feeling of a very clever attempt to avoid something essential.

What was missing? Was the incurable illness that caused a patient to commit suicide, as Freud learned at Trafoi, homosexuality? Could this have been the issue, ignited by Signorelli's frescoes, that forced the repression? Or was there a different element entirely? Something more precise than what the Karpes allow, or that Freud himself, for all his writing in circles, tells us?

CHAPTER 43

JACQUES LACAN'S TAKE ON IT

THERE IS NO EXPLAINING WHY INFORMATION COMES when it does, but it was only late in the game that I discovered that Jacques Lacan had written about Freud and Signorelli. He did so in 1973, six years before the Karpes wrote their paper. Surprisingly, the Karpes make no mention of it.

Lacan first addressed the subject near the end of a seminar on "The Freudian Unconscious and Ours." In 2004, a scholar named Margaret Owens wrote on the subject:

> Here Lacan comments on the "denuded metonymy," the linguistic pathway, that cryptically inscribes *Freud's* repressed desire. Lacan notices that in forgetting "Signorelli," Freud has forgotten himself; he has engineered his own efface-ment. *Sig*norelli, after all, shares the first syllable of *Sig*mund. Indeed Freud has a double claim to *Signor,* as an approxima-tion of his first name and as an honorific, the equivalent of *Herr.* In Lacan's reading of the incident, forgetting "Signo-relli" is a defensive gesture against the Absolute Master, or Death. Ironically, in striving to ward off this threat, Freud has effaced himself, unconsciously rehearsed his own castra-tion and his own death.

Owens's summation is helpful for the clarity with which it articulates Lacan's idea that in trying to ward off death by forgetting Signorelli's name, Freud "effaced"—symbolically killed off and castrated—himself.

285

Lacan's own words are harder to grasp, but they are worth reading as an indication of how far one can go with the notion of what the forgetting of Signorelli's name could be seen to mean:

> The term Signor, Herr, passes underneath—the absolute master, I once said, which is in fact death, has disappeared there. Furthermore, do we not see, behind this, the emergence of that which forced Freud to find in the myths of the death of the father the regulation of his desire? After all, it is to be found in Nietzsche, who declares, in his own myth, that God is dead. And it is perhaps against the background of the same reasons. For the myth of the God is dead—which, personally, I feel much less sure about, as a myth of course, than most contemporary intellectuals, which is in no sense a declaration of theism, nor of faith in the resurrection—perhaps this myth is simply a shelter against the threat of castration.
>
> If you know how to read them, you will see this threat in the apocalyptic frescoes of Orvieto cathedral.

Is this psychobabble, or is it wisdom? Should I accept the complexity of a lot that I find difficult to understand, or was there still some very simple explanation I had overlooked?

CHAPTER 44

MINNA BERNAYS

IN 1896, MARTHA FREUD'S YOUNGER SISTER, Minna Bernays, had moved into the Freuds' apartment at 19 Berggasse. She was unmarried; her fiancé had died in 1886, the same year that Sigmund and Martha were married.

It has long been thought that Freud and Minna had an affair; Carl Gustav Jung said that Minna confessed this to him. The Karpes may have been among the Freudian stalwarts who acted as if to believe that Freud and his sister-in-law were lovers is heresy, but it remains surprising that they did not even mention that possibility and Freud's guilt over it as part of the reason for the parapraxis.

After all, at the time of the memory loss, Freud had just been discussing sexual potency. His thoughts had then progressed to paintings that depict the Last Judgment, suggesting that sins of the flesh merit eternity in hell. The paintings he was picturing vividly portray naked men, powerful young males presumably with great sexual force. Then Freud was unable to remember the artist's name, which began with the same first letters as his own. It all makes sense that guilt over some aspect of his own sexuality was seminal to Freud's parapraxis. Was it possibly his malaise because he was regularly screwing his wife's sister?

Later in the same summer when I saw Susie and the Karpes talking at my parents' house, she and I came off the tennis courts at about the same time. She had come up from Fairfield County to play with some friends. On the prime viewing court at the country club—the club that had been created in the 1920s by a small band of snobby German

Jews who, although fair-skinned and refined in manner, knew better than to try for admission at the all-Protestant Hartford Golf Club—there was an important doubles tournament match being played by some very good players. The tennis was first-rate, and on the grassy hill where some forty spectators were watching it, I positioned myself directly behind Susie. She wore a short white tennis skirt; I was in regulation white shorts. I pressed myself against her and developed what I remember as the firmest erection possible, of longer duration than any other I have ever had.

In my memory, it lasted at least an hour, never flagging in the slightest. She did not move an inch. She just kept that sweet little ass of hers, absent an ounce of fat but wonderfully soft, the skirt taut, pressed against my throbbing cock. Even though Susie completely obsessed me, and even though, on the night she appeared in my bedroom, I had been focused totally on the little black bow between the cups of her bra, this was the only form of sexual encounter, if you can even call it that, she and I ever had. And how do I feel when writing this? I feel a mix of excitement and embarrassment, of thrill and taboo; I think joyfully of blatantly phallic African sculpture celebrating virility and male potency in general, but anticipate the shock of some of my readers at my indiscretion, and am sorry if the revelation is offensive. An adolescent boy and his mother's friend, standing on the grassy bank that overlooked the red clay courts, glued to each other, with every deuce and tying of the game score being a joy for me because it meant the match was not yet over. I am amused; I am appalled. I remember it vividly; I want to suppress it.

In recent years, I thought that if I had been French rather than American, we would have had marvelous trysts—the whole caboodle—on afternoons in verdant parks, the way Tony Perkins and Ingrid Bergman did in the movie *Goodby, Again,* based on Françoise Sagan's *Aimez-vous Brahms?* But I am lying to myself and fantasizing. The difference was not cultural; it was constitutional.

On a summer afternoon, a friend of mine, at age eighteen, our parents in the social set, returned a serving tray to a friend of his mother's who had lent it for a large party. The pretty friend, twenty-five years his senior, invited him in, led him upstairs, and they "did it." I was never that casual or confident.

But how provocative Susie was. My senior year at college, I had a fabulous girlfriend, Kippy Dewey, who could best be described as a hippie debutante. (She had been "presented" to society in a white ball gown at a cotillion; she also had large peace signs painted in purple on her beaten up VW Beetle, and directed a theater program in a poor neighborhood in inner city Boston.) We were together for over a year. When our romance was in full heat, and we were well-known to one another's families, although our parents had never met, Kippy's mother and father, both from old Boston Protestant families, went to a party at a Protestant country club in Connecticut. Susie was there. She made a point of meeting Talbot Dewey, Kippy's father. The next day, she telephoned my mother to report that they had danced together all evening. He was "a divine dancer, and most attractive." She knew full well that his daughter and I were lovers. As Dr. Solnit would ask, "What was all that about?"

When Susie was about eighty-five to my sixty, Katharine and I invited her for lunch. I know how ridiculous this sounds, but I was like a teenager getting ready for a date, and wore the jeans that made me feel the most stud-like. That was it—a frisson, a charge, an animal flirtation. But there are few forces as awakening, or as exciting, as physical magnetism. The following day I was still so keyed up that I wrote that the obsession of over forty years was both clearer and less clear to me. Susie was still among the most alive people I had ever known. My journal entry was hypomanic: "She is now as warm as she was once haughty. She is rich and worldly, but earthy. She is regal yet primitive."

I was on fire, as animated as Signorelli's frescoes, as obsessed as

Freud with male youthfulness. "She *notices* everything. Yesterday, I felt young, virile, and eighteen years old in her company. Did she remember the feeling of my prolonged teenage hard-on pressed against her when we stood there over forty-two years ago?"

I had prepared a great lunch, and she caught everything—about what she ate, about whatever we discussed. I was struck by "her total recall and wicked sense of humor. She is, as she has always been, so unbelievably *alive*. She excites me so."

A lot was different, though. She now identified herself, much more than back then, as being Jewish. Lots of references to it. She was wildly enthusiastic about the house, the Albers Foundation, and me. We went through a shared cast of characters, some alive, some dead, and she kept coming back to the subject of how people flirted "back then." I felt like someone on speed, not knowing what to do with all the emotions: much as did the great sage of the human mind, Sigmund Freud, when aliveness and power were so vivid to him in Orvieto.

Five years after that lunch—Susie was ninety!—she invited Katharine and me and our daughter Lucy and our son-in-law to dinner. She suddenly turned to me, in the middle of a conversation about politics, and said, "Nicky! Your eyes are *so* blue." I was a total idiot in my delight.

And if you ask what this last detail has to do about Freud and his block about Luca Signorelli's name, it is because the issues are the same. Blue eyes—one of the telltale markers of "ein gute Arian." The incredible force of attraction: whether it is the attraction to someone else, or the feeling that someone else is attracted to you or doing a damn good job of pretending to be. You can write about the id and penis envy and the Oedipus Complex until the cows come home, you can pontificate about human development all you want, you can even try to analyze your feelings about being Jewish and their connection to your father and what it means to have blue eyes when his were Galician green, but there is nothing that replaces the charge of irrational feelings.

It is easy enough to see why the sight of the reprint in my parents' library, in the year following my mother's death, beckoned me, for what better foil is there to death than sexual power? The mind never stops making leaps, with splendid sentiments coming to the rescue when sadness has dominated. But the mind is also forever stopping itself. Excitement becomes confusion; we have to shut down. I can readily understand how Freud could have jumped from discussing Turks and their views on sex to thinking of those paintings of male power to blocking on the name of the man who had made them.

This is something I had to come to grips with, painfully, in psycho-analysis. For the first year or so, I had no problem talking, and doing what I thought was a good job of plunging into the depths of my own inner life as I spewed anecdotes about my childhood as well as my present life. It was clear, however, that my doctor thought I had barely put my feet into the water.

Eventually, I learned to free-associate. It was, I believe, the hardest thing I have ever done. In some ways, it was comparable to the moments in rock climbing, a sport I adore, when you reach upward absolutely as far as possible with your arms, grab with your fingertips the bumps that are nothing more than infinitesimal protrusions, and jump upward, stretching one leg as never before, to find the slightest foothold, a minuscule inclination or crack, on which to balance the toe of your impossibly tight climbing shoe and then jump up with the other leg to another similar perch.

When I climb cliffs, however, I am harnessed and supported by carefully tied ropes. It is not a risk. It requires confidence and hope, but it never feels entirely dangerous. Free-associating is more difficult.

If I really reveal the bizarre sequence of thoughts and images that jump into my mind, I sound like the visual equivalent of a Jackson Pollock—with everything connected but with no single element readily discernible. It took at least a year before I was convinced that Dr. Solnit would not throw me out of the room like an idiot if I just spat out all that was flooding my mind, if I did not control my thoughts and impose order. I in no way allowed the apparent randomness of free association to occur, nor did I grasp that what might seem haphazard was in fact connected.

I imagined that if I let myself go, my doctor would laugh at me the way a master at Loomis once did when I fell on some sleek crust on a snowbank I was trying to walk up, in plain view of where he was seated at morning chapel. This teacher, who taught math, told me in front of the whole class that morning that he had seen me trying to perform this impossible feat and then fail, my books sliding this way and that as I sank into the snow. "I laughed"—pronounced *loffed*— "and I laughed and I laughed," he said with his sadistic grin in front of all the other boys.

To leap into the realm in which one lets one's mind explore all the possibilities, rather than to impose a series of halts, requires breaking the habits that are reinforced day and night both by the rules of civilized behavior and by the fear of derision. It is indeed like walking on thin ice.

I am not sure of my unconscious reasons, but with the investigation of what happened to Freud when he could not remember the name of the painter of the Orvieto frescoes, I convinced myself I had gone as far as I could. Yet this was a form of self-deceit. Something had me stop when there was a vital link I had not yet made. I was like a climber on the face of a cliff who thinks he is doing well by ascending on pronounced protrusions that are like shelves but who is unwilling to try the areas that are more challenging.

Then I showed everything I had written to date about the Karpes' text and Freud's parapraxis and my theories on Jewishness and maleness and my associations with Susie to Victoria Wilson, the editor of the books I have been writing about artists and architects and art patrons for the publisher Alfred A. Knopf for over twenty-five years. Vicky has always been as insightful and savvy and tough a reader of my writing as I have ever known. I felt that I had researched my subject to its maximum, that I had expanded my horizons and ventured into a new area of writing, and that I had gone to the summit.

Vicky responded enthusiastically but also said that I needed to make the links clearer. She wanted everything to be "crystalline"; the way things were connected needed more precise explanations.

I realized that the detail I needed to consider more fully was the real importance of this information Freud had acquired in Trafoi a few weeks before he was unable to recall Signorelli's name. I have to admit that, about a year ago, my main response to learning about Trafoi was simply to find out where it was. I then did research to determine if it would be a good place for a ski trip, combining my favorite sport with the knowledge that I might do it at a place where Freud liked to spend holidays. Given the tools of research now available via the Internet, I should have done better. It's as if I were trying to divert myself by imagining whooshing down the snow-covered slopes, rather than addressing an important matter head-on.

I now realize that, suppressing something in myself, I had completely failed to go down a road that would provide a vital linkage of facts. I am not sure if I had been timid or just sloppy, but what is clear is that I had closed *both* eyes to a vital detail.

When the Karpes were writing, of course, the affair with Minna was only a rumor. It's understandable that they did not consider it as a factor.

I have no such excuse. In 2007, a German researcher discovered that on August 13, 1898, the forty-two-year-old Freud and the thirty-three-year-old Minna Bernays registered as a married couple at the Schweizerhaus, an inn in Maloja—a village high in the Swiss Alps, near St. Moritz. They stayed in room 11—one of the largest in the inn—for three nights, and while Freud wrote postcards to Martha, who was in Vienna, and described the glaciers and the mountain scenery, the documentation at the inn names the woman staying with him as his wife.

It was not so hard to access, online, the newspaper article and other sources that make this information definitive. And, oddly, they all leave out what I consider a very important fact, which is that Freud's eldest sister, Anna, was married to Martha and Minna's older brother, El. So the connections between the Bernays and Freud families already exceeded normal boundaries.

Trafoi and Maloja are near each other in the Tyrol. But what I now grasp, and had failed to discern at a point when I thought my research was essentially done—until Vicky Wilson, like a psychoanalyst, encouraged me to go further, to seek clarity, really to understand what led to what—is that only a month before Freud vividly remembered those images of virile men brandishing the effects of testosterone, yet could not remember the name that had the same first three letters as his own, those letters being associated with words in various languages for "man," he had spent three nights in a hotel room with his young sister-in-law, having checked them in with false names. I now think that Freud's efforts to blame the misfired memory loss on what happened in Trafoi were a subterfuge; it was what occurred in another mountain village, a few days later, that he was trying to forget—or cover up.

Talk about guilt!

If we follow Freud's methodology, as he describes it in the *Parapsychology of Everyday Life*, then his efforts to keep one thing secret caused him to miss the target and keep another thing secret. The thing he kept secret concerned names. He had lied about the identity of Mrs. Sigmund Freud. In Italian, and we are speaking of the Italian part of the Alps, the word for "she" is *élla*. Signor is Mr.; *élla* is "she." The combination is mighty close to the name Signorelli. Freud had, in fact, concealed the truth about who the *élla* was with the signor. He had also lied about signorina (also lied by concealing the truth that his companion was a *signorina*—as indeed Miss Bernays was—and making her a *signora*). Now his mind concealed the name Signorelli.

On the other hand, Minna and Sigmund often traveled together, apart from the rest of the family, with everyone's knowledge.

We also know from a letter Freud wrote Fliess two years later, when he and Martha were yet again going to Trafoi, that he scheduled *that* trip so it would not coincide with his wife's menstrual period, during which time she was "not capable of enjoyment." So he still had sex with his wife, and planned his mountain holidays accordingly! The "affair with Minna" obsessives—and there are many—are unjust in claiming that Martha, the mother of six small children, no longer made love, which is what forced Sigmund to turn elsewhere.

Maybe he and Minna were being frugal, and so stayed in one room, yet had to register as husband and wife because it was the law. As my maternal grandmother used to say, "Unless you're under the bed, you don't know, and even then you can't be sure."

CHAPTER 45

SOBRIETY

IN SPITE OF MY REASONS FOR DOUBT, I convinced myself I had struck gold. Now that I knew about the hotel registry and Freud's falsification of Minna's identity, I understood the memory loss.

The finding of the German scholar in Maloja was no secret. It was the subject of a major article in the *International Herald Tribune,* and was known to have persuaded certain skeptics about the affair with Minna. Peter Gay, it was reported, was now among the scholars to have altered his view and decided that the in-laws had really screwed. Articles sprang up all over the place, reiterating what was considered conclusive evidence. But the deceit in the hotel registry was still not so well known that it had ever been connected with the forgetting of Signorelli's name some three weeks later. I felt like Perry Mason at the moment of triumph, when he leaves no question as to the verdict. I managed to dispel my own scepticism; the explanation was too tidy to resist.

THEN I STARTED TO READ A BOOK OF FREUD'S TRAVEL LETTERS given to me by Sophie de Closets, my editor at the French publishing house Fayard, a sage and enthusiastic reader who understands my idiosyncratic obsessions and is a true ally in supporting my pursuits. Here is what I found:

On August 12, 1898, Freud wrote Martha from Pontresina. "My dear treasure," he begins. He explains his plan for the upcoming days.

"We" would be going to Maloja, and would stay in a hotel. Minna added three paragraphs to the same letter, addressing her sister as "My dearheart!" She, too, told Martha their plans, adding that it was raining hard and then suddenly had begun to snow.

The following day, Freud wrote his wife from Maloja. He extolled the wonders of the glacier, lake, and mountains, and told Martha she would be pleasantly surprised "when you hear us" describe them. He explained that "we are staying in a modest Swiss hotel . . . and will stay here tomorrow."

If a man were cheating on his wife, would he have written this? Why did all the people who flipped out in 2007 about the hotel registry in Maloja not read these letters.

How had I been duped? Why do I get so excited by things that evaporate? Was everything with Susie a case of my self-deception? Does longing makes us blind?

WE LOOK INTO SOMEONE ELSE'S LIFE; we look into our own. We think we have answers and understanding, and then it all goes up in smoke.

The reasoning that seemed crystalline ends up being specious. It is all a game of cat and mouse, with the mouse always winning.

When Lucy was about three months old, Katharine and I, at 3:00 A.M., heard a mouse running around in the bathroom between her room and ours. I tried to catch the lively rodent, but it was too fast for me. I was irrational. I kept shouting at the little creature that it could not get near my daughter, while every time I tried to grab it, it scrambled out of reach up the tiled bathroom wall, along the tub, behind the sink. For half an hour, I swung and missed, Katharine laughed, and our baby slept soundly.

At last I managed to grab the small brown animal by the body, with its nasty tail hanging out. Victorious, I marched downstairs and out the front door of our house, then across the country road where we live. Stark naked, facing the woods, I shouted, "Don't you get near my baby! No one can ever intrude into her life!" and I heaved it. The next day, when our furnace broke down, the repairman found a rat's nest inside it; I had been holding a young rat.

Is there a moral here? Did the ridiculous scenario mean that if you do truly grasp what eludes you, it will be a rat?

Do I understand any of it? The reason Freud forgot a name of such importance? Why the image of Susie in my mind could be like a drug that made me a happy lunatic?

One thing I know for certain, though. What we take in through our eyes transforms us. The visual has inestimable force.

CHAPTER 46

THE SEARCH CONTINUES

IN 2010, I MADE A QUICK TRIP TO A WONDERFUL untouched bit of paradise in the south of France, overlooking the Mediterranean about half an hour from Saint-Tropez. I had been invited there to visit the eighty-four-year-old Jean-Jacques Pauvert. Pauvert is best known for having published the complete work of the Marquis de Sade and for having written Sade's biography. The first publisher of *The Story of O,* he has devoted much of his life to fighting censorship. He was living with about ten thousand books, all of which he had read at least once, and was one of the most erudite, literate, and astute people I have ever encountered.

The meeting was arranged by Brigitte Lozorec'h, a woman some fifteen years Pauvert's junior. Having been his mistress for many years, she was at the time still a dear friend, and had become his regular companion in his bucolic paradise of decrepit buildings—his old house was falling apart, its foundation stones propped by wooden supports—and overgrown trees and shrubbery. Wonderfully, he would ask her to marry him a couple of years after my visit, and by the time he died in Toulon in 2014, they were husband and wife, with her bringing remarkable grace to the end of his days.

Jean-Jacques had written me a nice letter about my book on Balthus, which Brigitte had given him, and had told her he wanted to meet me. Although I had had no plan to discuss Freud and Signorelli with this distinguished writer and editor, when, following lunch, he showed me his incredible library in a former garage and pointed to his hundred of volumes of erotica, I decided to show him two Signorelli reproductions—both of details of *The Damned.*

Jean-Jacques Pauvert studied the fresco scenes carefully. For him, there was no question: This was a homosexual vision. He pointed out the lust with which one man, clothed, eyes another who is naked. He also observed Signorelli's inability to make women really female, for all of the artist's impeccable rendering of male nudity. The great authority on Sade said it was indisputable that in Signorelli's art violent strength is used to endow men with an eroticism particularly appealing to other men. The allure of these extraordinary paintings was as a revelation of male attraction to other men, and their success was in their ability to excite those feelings openly.

The day after my meeting with Jean-Jacques Pauvert, I visited Cézanne's studio in Aix-en-Provence. Katharine and I had been there together thirty years earlier, and I thought it would be nice to go back, although I feared it would have lost its authenticity and become a tourist trap. To my delight, it was as I remembered it: a real working space with the actual objects one knows from so many masterful, mysterious paintings. I could still feel the earthiness and solid truthfulness central to Cézanne's art, much as I had on the previous visit. In little time, I had tears in my eyes.

This, I thought, is what it means to be a serious painter and to love seeing. I looked at the table used for *The Card Players,* the bowls that reappear in the still lifes, the apples and oranges, the skulls, the statue of Cupid, the side chairs—all old friends to a fan of Cézanne's work. Then, through my tears, I saw something I had certainly not noticed when Katharine and I were there three decades before.

In the middle of the wall to the west of the wall of glass that floods the space with daylight and faces toward Mount Sainte-Victoire, there is a faded print of a study of two naked men that Luca Signorelli made in preparation for the Orvieto frescoes. One of these men, seen from behind, is straddled by the other. It looks as if the standing one is carrying the second man on his shoulders, but, to those of us who know Orvieto, the man on top is, in fact, about to pull the guy beneath him up toward the fires of hell. What mattered to Cézanne, however, was, I imagine, not so much the event being illustrated as the power of the form and the splendid rendering of the male body. It became apparent to me that Cézanne used Signorelli as a model for his own male bathers.

In this, I think, there is *no* sexuality. For Cézanne, Signorelli had made the perfect prototype of the male body; there was no better example of the rear view of a naked man. This was about reality: the same truthfulness that exists in apples, rocks, and in simple wooden furniture. Eroticism is absent. The issues are weight, mass, musculature: the fundamentals of human physicality, the marvels of standing and holding.

Is this, then, what overwhelmed Freud: the miracle of life, which Luca Signorelli captured with such fidelity and bravura? Was Jean-Jacques Pauvert overreading in his certitude about the homoeroticism? Maybe the reason for Freud's memory loss was entirely his conflict at having checked into a mountain inn, registering his wife's younger sister as if she were his wife. Perhaps it was the impossibility of understanding the amorphous territory where male narcissism and homoeroticism interact, where the maleness one admires in other men is the maleness one enjoys and cultivates in one's self, and where, if you throw in the added issues of one's sense of one's father, and whether Jewish men can be tough enough, one is way beyond the possibility of being able to parcel out what has come in through the eyes, especially when the visual impetus is a knockout. How does one ascertain the truth? And isn't the only truth the reality that there are no precise explanations for anything? To know that, and accept it, and exalt in the beauty in life, and know that "the heart has no reasons," and maybe the mind does not, either, strikes me as the only possibility. The journey toward comprehension is wonderful, as long as somewhere along the way one realizes that one never reaches the destination, because it does not exist.

CHAPTER 47

Wanting an Answer, and Yearning for the Authority That Will Provide One

I REALIZED LONG AGO THAT A SINGLE SOLUTION or an absolutely correct explanation rarely apply to human situations, yet I seem unable to rid myself of the idea that I will find an answer to impossible questions.

At first, the Karpes seemed beyond reproach in every word they uttered about the impact of the trip to Orvieto on Freud—just as they appeared to be the incarnation of wisdom when smiling at Susie in that sea of chitchat at my parents' house. Then I discovered that they had made minor mistakes, like the misspelling of both the first and last names of Maud Cruttwell, their sole art historical source. For me, that was an amusing, insignificant error—nothing more. But then, after months of intense consideration of my subject, discovering vital information that the Karpes had left out, and details they had gotten wrong, I came to feel as if my seers had—here I must use my wife's grandmother's pronunciation of the word, for it reflects the word's meaning—mizzled me. ("Mizzled" is how the wonderful Kay Swift always said the word *misled*—with a laugh.)

Richard and Marietta plumbed their subject in depth—both providing profound insight and opening one's mind to fascinating speculation—but the people whom I wanted to be infallible were not.

It's strange, this need to assume that someone has godlike powers. For many people, that person has been Sigmund Freud. I know that when I embarked on my own psychoanalysis, at age forty, I assumed that the white-haired, bearded colleague of Freud's daughter Anna who was going to "treat" me would have the attributes of a deity. He would lead me to see everything I needed to know about my mother, my father, my grandmother, and my sister; he would enable me to come to grips with the feelings that still overwhelmed me about Susie. Not only that but he would guide me in the present—on how to conduct my marriage, bring up my children, deal with a million issues I considered unresolved. It would all be tidy now, and he would accept me and berate me as necessary to make me the person I wanted to be.

For seven years of treatment, I had an image that kept coming to mind. It was of an event that occurred when I was four years old, in February of 1952. The family was at Lake Placid for a winter holiday. My grandmother had given us skis (wooden, with spring bindings) and boots (leather lace-ups). I worked hard on my snowplow, day after day, and then, on the last day of the weeklong vacation in paradise, a young instructor took me to the top of the mountain. He had me face downhill, positioned himself directly behind me, put his skis to the left and right of mine, and held me firmly by the shoulders. I was not using poles, and all I had to do was relax and stand upright, with my knees slightly bent. This beautiful athlete skied me down the mountain at high speed, in perfect control.

More than sixty years later, I still feel the thrill. We whooshed down, as I looked out at white Adirondack peaks under a perfect winter blue sky. We made graceful turns, my weight instinctively shifting in tandem with his. The instructor was handsome; he was strong; he was capable. He was the older brother of my dreams, and at that moment—I say this with guilt—the father of my dreams, too. (Dad, while very gifted at many sports, was never a good skier.)

My idea was that Dr. Solnit would be just like the ski instructor: a god who would take me by the shoulders and guide me through every turn, while I felt nothing but unequivocal joy and the simple pleasure of having complete confidence in someone who was in charge.

Dr. Solnit, of course, did not even laugh whenever I relived those ten minutes of paradise at Lake Placid. He met the frequent retelling invariably in silence. But about halfway through my second year of treatment, he asked me a question that was, I now see, related. Why had I, in several checks I had written him and verbal references, called him Albert L. Solnit rather than Albert J. Solnit, his actual name? Wasn't it odd that I kept getting his middle initial wrong?

I instantly replied, "That's because A.L. is Al, which is how people refer to you."

"Uh-huh," he said. Then we both fell silent.

It was not long before I saw, in my mind's eye, the face of a man who resembled the head at the top of a paper mobile of the characters in *My Fair Lady*, which Ricky had in his room when he was little. This cardboard person was clearly the master manipulator, with everyone else—Eliza Doolittle and the others—dangling from him.

"A.J. is A. J. Feldman."

I explained. Abraham J. Feldman, often referred to just as "A.J.," was the rabbi at Temple Beth Israel in West Hartford when I was a kid. He was ponderous, grandiose, and pompous; and I thought, starting at age six, that he was God. Not just God for me personally—but the character God, historically, as he appear in movies and children's stories and Ricky's mobile. The rabbi had just the right full white mustache and the white hair; he wore the robes; he spoke as if he were the Creator. I made fun of him, of course, but in some way I really thought he was immortal and all-powerful. When we did the responsive reading, one side of me questioned and even mocked it all, but I often thought that A. J. Feldman could see and hear everything, and would rule heaven once he had left the earth.

When I was fourteen, I had a pivotal moment with A.J. I had to have a private meeting with him, because I was starting at Loomis, which had classes on Saturday morning, and therefore I would miss Saturday school at the temple in the year before confirmation. Confirmation mattered, because I had chosen not to have a bar mitzvah. (My parents gave me the option, but they were clearly relieved when I said no.)

When we met, he said I could do some reading on my own, and he then asked my summer plans. I said I was going to spend two months in a program to learn Spanish in Quito, Ecuador. "And I will be in Mexico with Mrs. Feldman," he said, conjuring for me an image of the woman whose chartreuse Nash Rambler amused me beyond words. "With you and me out of town," he said with a smile, "there will be no one of importance left in West Hartford." I still love the remark.

Then, about a month before confirmation, we had a rehearsal of the upcoming ceremony. It was on a Sunday afternoon, and although I hated giving up time on my one free day to be in the building I had once heard Susie call "that Byzantine monstrosity on Farmington Avenue"—the thoroughfare which keeps reappearing in this narrative—I had no choice but to attend. Following the rehearsal, Rabbi Feldman assembled the 110 confirmands—the largest class to date, since we were "the postwar baby boom."

"My students," he began, addressing us in his most pontifical voice. "On this momentous occasion of your graduation from our religious school, I am going to do unto each and every one of you a great honor. I am going to bestow upon each and every one of you a photograph of me, Rabbi Feldman. It will be an eight-by-ten-inch glossy image, taken by our renowned local photographer, Defert Dechert. I will sign each photo, individually, to each and every one of you.

"But you may accept it only under one condition. You must promise neither to hide nor to conceal it. You must assure me that you will frame it, and hang it on the walls of your room, or position it upon your desk. There is no point in taking the image of your rabbi, inscribed, and then not seeing it."

A. J. Feldman then explained that he would go through the class list alphabetically, so we could say whether we accepted or declined his offer. By the time he had reached the *W*'s, after a hundred names, every student had said yes. Jane Karpe, Richard and Marietta's second of three daughters, had not hesitated. After my friend Ellie Waxman gave her consent, the rabbi said, "Nicholas Fox Weber."

"No thank you, sir," Everyone stared, and he glared at me. Then the rabbi continued, with a final chorus of yeses.

When I got home, I told my mother about it. She beamed. "Wonderful, Nicky! I'm proud of you. But write him a letter."

I did. I explained that I did not even have pictures of my parents or anyone else I knew in my room, and I could not in all honesty tell him that I would put his photo up, since I could not imagine him alongside the Brigitte Bardot pictures I had cut from magazines, or my Cézanne and Gauguin reproductions.

He wrote me back a surprisingly thoughtful and understanding letter.

I had still not gotten over him twenty-eight years later. There was something about God, and authority figures, and male power still so vital to me that I kept resisting that my analyst was an A.J., just the way God the rabbi was.

The tricks of the mind—the names we cannot get quite right—tell us a lot.

CHAPTER 48

THE YOUNG BLADE

O N THE ENTRANCE WALL OF THE CAPPELLA NOVA at Orvieto,
there is a portrait that fits into the rare category of art objects
from which I inadvertently turn away, so powerful are the emotions
they induce. This painting is a tour de force. This is one of those occasions when Luca Signorelli painted an architectural setting so that it
is completely plausible, and then brought people to life as fully three-
dimensional characters occupying the illusory space. This is a wonderful feat, rarely accomplished by any artist in spite of all who have tried
to achieve it in myriad styles during different epochs.

The setting Signorelli created is a deep-set circular window cut into
a richly decorated wall and framed by an ornate wooden molding that
captures the light in ribbonlike scrollwork that, we are convinced, was
carved with a chisel. A young man stands inside the room on to which
this window opens, propped against the interior wall. His legs and feet
are blocked from view by it, but his torso is visible, for he leans back
through the opening, with the top of his turbaned head practically outside and his face inside the chapel, which he surveys with total concentration. He is presented from the only angle that could have succeeded
in making this conceit succeed: three-quarters from behind, so that the
left profile of his face is brought into precise focus. [plate 36]

I don't know if I can do justice to the excellence of this tondo. We
are completely convinced of the weight of the young man's left arm
on the wide windowsill; we apprehend exactly the extent to which
he is leaning backward and has arched his rib cage. This sculptural

Plate 36. Empedocles

feat has been achieved with marvelous colors. His tunic is a golden yellow, his turban a tomato red. A white scarf is wrapped around the turban; it is a further example of Signorelli's mastery of the art of painting. This remarkable floating scarf is offset beautifully by the matte black of the background of the scene.

The young man's face is even more extraordinary than his clothing and his golden ringlets, which catch the light as they fall over his shoulders. His skin is illuminated so as to seem real, and his expression is one of fascination and hope.

Dugald McLellan has a theory about who the man is. "Although usually identified as Empedocles, he has none of the conventional characteristics of an ancient philosopher and sage, and seems more like any number of *vitelloni* or young blades Signorelli would have seen in the streets and piazzas of Orvieto." Whoever he was based on, there is no question about what he represents to us. He is the essence of youth.

He has a capable body. He is full of expectation and optimism; he is eager and engaged. Everything else in the chapel he is surveying is about the end of life, about death and pain, but the young man embodies the marvelous beginning of adulthood. He evokes the immense pleasure of being human on this earth.

Oh my God, what an incredible joy: to be in one's late teens, healthy, nimble, comfortable with one's self. To have the luxury of leaning backward and contemplating life. To arch one's back with no muscle aches and have the simple pleasure of taking it all. To stand there in my parents' garden and be with Richard and Marietta and their big minds. To feel obsessed—exhilarated, guilty, edgy, amorous, secretive, cocky, crazed—and to relish it. To exult in the complexity of Freud and repression and human longing. To have all those years in front of me again. To be able to explore and celebrate forever.

AFTERWORD

AFTER RETURNING THE LATEST VERSION OF THIS TEXT to the copyeditor, I became plagued by my use of the term "throbbing cock." It would not be too late to delete it, I realized, and my doing so might spare some people their possible discomfort.

Yet, while I greatly value decorum in life, and cherish what Edmund Burke called "the decent drapery" of existence, something made me want to retain these more-than-direct words. My motive was neither shock value nor braggadocio. It is because I want to get past the euphemisms, masking, veiling, and the retreat from reality to the escape mechanism of convoluted language that is a lot of what this book is about. (My apologies to whoever actually said "Prepositions at the end of sentences are something up with which I will not put." I still remember the fellow student at Loomis from whom I first heard this and who attributed it to Winston Churchill, an error I accepted as fact for over fifty years until it was corrected in an earlier version of this afterword.)

Why the unflinching, even coarse, language? Why the memory from the all-boys school I attended as an adolescent? And why the need to tell you that what I assumed, for over half a century, to have been a certainty—the attribution of that witticism to Churchill—was false information? Because I long for truthfulness, for simplicity, for authentic responses, for accepting the way things are, for calling a spade a spade, not just for accuracy but for a correction of myths.

You could fill a large library with the literature on Freud and homosexuality. You could find scholars to say he considered it an illness to be treated, a mark of arrested development in the so-called "normal" progress of healthy human beings. Not exactly to the contrary, but with different emphasis, other knowledgeable people will focus on the innate human bisexuality Freud discussed with Fliess. Regardless, in adolescence, sexuality, whatever its form, becomes a preoccupation for most of us, and the thinking and imagining and desiring and wondering tend to outdo the action. Moreover, little is certain; there are few cut-and-dried facts. Feelings and wishes elude easy identification.

All the theories! All the verbiage! All those elaborate analyses, devoid of clear vision, about why Freud forgot a name! Little boys—at least most of them—admire bold men. We want to be one of them. Our dads are rarely the he-men the hero Hamilcar was to Hannibal. Narcissism, pansexuality, the Oedipus complex: all these, and many more, psychological conditions and processes occur as we grow up and, even before puberty, life stops being based purely on instinct— that absolute marvel of babyhood—and becomes inextricably complicated. None of the lingo and terminology and theorizing is adequate to pinpoint the feelings, because intuition and emotion elude language and explanation.

My grandson at twenty-one months likes holding his penis and smiling and calling it his "bee bee." Wilder Fox Smith is as great an enjoyer of life as I know, and he is proud to stand with his nappy off and hold the goods. Maleness is terrific for most men, but the whole thing becomes so much trickier after Wilder's age and the questions begin. Whose maleness is it that appeals to us? Our own, someone else's, our father's, that of the alternatives with whom we have replaced our fathers, of the older brothers we have or the ideal ones we wish we had, the mixture of any of these people? Why did Freud, so perceptive about paintings, so on to the earthiness of Raphael's Virgin, simply not realize that those frescoes in Orvieto are testosterone itself? Not just the male hormone, but also its realization in visible beauty.

Why could he not see—or, if he did see it, then acknowledge—that this display of forceful, naked manhood was understandably overwhelming for him with all the ramifications of his father's death and his reflection on the Turkish idea that once you become unable to have an erection, then life is not worth living. All the issues of what it means to be a man and the feelings he did or did not have for other men, linked with the surprising but real relationship that being male and being Jewish has for many of us, were cloudy and unfathomable in this period when his father had recently died. The issue of the little "*signor*," "*Signorelli*," and "*Sig*mund" was just too much for him to cope with. (Sorry again, person-who-is-not Sir Winston, even if I suspect that I will never succeed in disassociating this stipulation about prepositions from the man who led Britain so nobly in wartime. How do we ever train ourselves to unlearn something, especially as delightful an idea as the notion that the courageous spokesman who invoked "blood, sweat, and tears" prized the rules of grammar and was as playful as he was powerful?) Those bare buttocks at Orvieto give you no choice but to see what naked maleness, in fine and muscular form, is. It also unequivocally depicts physical battle and sheer brute force, and makes raw strength, at least in these illustrations of it, a vital element of masculinity. Freud could not accept, or face—or, in any event, discuss—his own reactions and issues.

Another brilliant authority on human development, Charles Darwin, for all his exceptional intellectual awareness of the natural world, was even more uptight about innate instincts, or at least their expression. He was horrified by his grandfather's championing of group sex in his poetry—the wonderfully named Erasmus Darwin also flaunted the existence of his illegitimate children, much to his grandson's embarrassment—and was so traumatized by the death of his mother when he was eight that, while suffering from extreme anxiety and depression in assorted manifestations for his entire life, in adulthood he wrote a condolence letter to a cousin in which he said he had never had a close relative die. When playing a game similar to Scrabble, in which another player put an "m" in front of "other," Darwin immediately said that the new creation was not a real word.

It took a while before Charles Darwin could be convinced that "mother" is an actual word. Sometimes what is represented by language is too painful, because it touches us so profoundly, that we cannot let verbal language penetrate our consciousness. The inability to see or remember a word or name becomes a protective barricade to the truth.

My own use of words and images that may be too colloquial or frank for some people's taste is simply because I think that there is no reason for the guises, any more than I think there is anything wrong when Wilder holds his penis and smiles. What's the big deal? Why not celebrate visceral feelings, the way kids do? Why the anguish? Why the need to create an elaborate explanation that obfuscates what is intuitive? Why was Freud, the great master of the human mind, so uptight about the pleasure of it all?

Ever since I was a university student and began to read texts by Freud that at times were tough sledding for me, I have been fascinated that, lifelong, Freud retained his sweet tooth, manifest in his weakness for Viennese pastries. Sheer physical enjoyment! Sensuous satisfaction! Aren't they better than death, whatever form earthly delights take, as long as they do no one else any harm? What counted for the Turks was potency: the source that inspires it was a secondary matter. I want to say to all of you: enjoy it! Forget the guilt and repression. Let the power of those frescoes, the memories of other time periods in your life, delight you, and fire you up.

The marvel is that Signorelli's paintings had such an effect on Freud. Why could the warrior worshipper not just enjoy the colors and the forms and the painting and the naked maleness and give himself a break from the subsequent convolutions of his mind?

MUCH OF MY WORK THESE DAYS IS DEVOTED TO WRITING the biography of Piet Mondrian. And one of the most striking aspects of Mondrian's approach to art was his constant repainting and refining.

Toward the end of his life, just after he moved to New York at age sixty-eight, one of Mondrian's recent compositions was exhibited in a major show of abstract art. His inclusion in this important event was a nice welcome to America. But the moment the painting was returned to his studio in a brownstone walkup at the corner of First Avenue and Fifty-Sixth Street, he changed it, adding colors and recalibrating lines. This is how some of us always feel about our books. Why had we not added or taken out some element? Could we not shine more light on our subject? Have we done the best possible service to you, the reader?

I realized only this morning that I had never considered Berenson's judgment of Signorelli's aesthetic qualities. What Freud is to psychiatry, Berenson is to art history. I won't even attempt to analyze what prevented my previously delving further into the views of the famous B.B. (please don't tell me it has something to do with Wilder's calling his penis his bee bee), but I decided to reconsider what Berenson really thought. I, too, am sixty-eight years old, and more determined to go the extra step to get something right than I used to be. And, like Mondrian, I relish the process.

Berenson was iffy about Signorelli, and begins his discussion of him by amplifying the painter's weaknesses. The ultimate authority on Italian Renaissance painting, Berenson allows that "the painting of the Nude is the supreme endeavor of the very greatest artists; and, when successfully treated, the most life communicating and life-enhancing theme in existence," and that the master bar none was Signorelli's follower, Michelangelo, but that the student was markedly superior to the mentor. Signorelli's "entire treatment is drier, his feeling for texture and tissue of surface much weaker, and the female form revealed itself to him but reluctantly. Signorelli's Nude, therefore, does not attain to [sic] the soaring beauty of Michelangelo's."

Then, however, Berenson gives Signorelli a break. What he says is so insightful that I am requiting some of his statements in the main text of the book, now with the gaps filled in. "But a truce to his faults! What though his nudes are not perfect; what though as in candour must be said his colour is not always as it should be, a glamour upon things, and his composition is at times crowded and confused? Luca Signorelli nevertheless remains one of the grandest—mark you, I do not say pleasantest—Illustrators of modern times. It is as a great Illustrator first, and then as a great artist that we must appreciate Signorelli."

Berenson allows that Signorelli's work has "virtues of its own a certain gigantic robustness and suggestions of primeval energy. . . . It would not have been possible to communicate such feelings but for the Nude, which possesses to the highest degree the power to make us feel, all over our own bodies, its own state."

I have come back to the great authority on Italian Renaissance art because I now see that here he homed in on what I believe was pivotal to Freud: the way that Signorelli, more successful showing naked men than naked women, makes men feel about our own bodies.

Berenson was another Jew who was uncomfortable about being Jewish—although his case was more extreme in both directions than Freud's, since he was brought up Orthodox, and when he made anti-Semitic statements did not prevaricate. The comment that is most striking in relationship to Freud and the Orvieto frescoes, meanwhile, is one Iris Origo quotes in her introduction to the art historian's late-life diaries. Berenson was in his eighties when he had switched from being vehemently anti-Zionist to supporting the idea of a Jewish homeland. Relatedly, he said of "his people": "The fact that contempt is felt for them by the majority of non-Jews makes them not only resentfully unhappy or cringingly eager to be good bourgeois, toeing the mediocre line in every land, but also to feel this contempt for themselves. . . . The remedy may be found in statehood plus . . . military glory."

"Military glory": isn't that exactly the remedy onto which Freud latched so enthusiastically, the antidote to his father's cowardice in the face of anti-Semitism?

And why some of us are drawn to any thought associated with Winston Churchill, his unabashed self-confidence as well as his will to better the lives of others?

BERENSON LED ME TO WILLIAM BUTLER YEATS via Iris Origo. In her introduction to those late diaries—another timely gift from Charlotte, the day after she called my attention to Darwin's inability to recognize "mother" as a word—Origo credits what Berenson wrote at the end of his life as opening the way to "the rediscovery, always lucid and sometimes merciless, of the true figure, as a tree sheds its leaves, leaving the tracery of its branches bare against the winter sky." In that vein, she quotes Yeats on what I consider to be the nuts and bolts issue of this book. My attempt has been, quite simply, to demonstrate that a forgotten name, and an elaborate series of conjectures and linguistic complexity, may have, at their core, nothing more, or less, than raw feeling and the forces of human attraction. Origo on Berenson's late-life comfort with his real self quotes Yeat's exquisite:

> I made my song a coat
> Covered with embroideries
> Out of old mythologies
> From heel to throat;
> But the fools caught it,
> Wore it in the world's eyes
> As though they'd wrought it
> Song, let them take it,
> For there's more enterprise
> In walking naked.

I think that Freud, and the people I would call the genuine Freud-
ians—the Karpes, my own Dr. Solnit, the remarkable Stefan Stein,
and, oddly, regardless of his dispute with certain Freudian ideas, Sartre—as well as artists like Cézanne and Mondrian and Anni Albers and
Josef Albers exemplify the pursuit that Yeats describes in a letter he
wrote Ezra Pound on July 15, 1918: "After all one's art is not the chief
end of life but an accident in one's search for reality or rather perhaps
one's method of search."

Yeats's perpetual quest, which he put into some of the most exquisite
poetry ever written in the English language, was for the truth within:

> But I, whose virtues are the definitions
> Of the analytic mind, can neither close
> The eye of the mind nor keep my tongue from speech.

This poet who wrote as beautifully of heterosexual love as anyone ever has, who could capture women's pleasure as unabashedly as
men's, who was a connoisseur of female beauty and a wonderful pro-
ponent of lust between men and women, was as relaxed, and brave,
about homosexuality as one would hope. This was a vital issue because of the trial and execution of Roger Casement, the extraordinary
humanitarian who had battled for the rights of victims of oppression
in the Congo and in South America, and who had an unequaled
impact in fighting colonialism when Ireland was still part of the Empire. The key evidence that sent Casement to the gallows was the
publication of his *Black Diaries,* a frank account of one after another
homosexual encounter, thought by some to be real and by others to
be falsified, in the middle of his trial. Yeats wrote, quite simply, "If
Casement were homo-sexual, what matter!"

Yeats was always battling for the same sort of blatant power evident
in Signorelli's frescoes. His candor and artistic boldness, his unabashed-
ness, give his words a quality akin to the Orvieto paintings with their
unparalleled presentation of male nudity and strength, of the attrac-

tion of violence, and of muscular force. Yeats knew the temptation of anecdote and sideways thinking, but prized, beyond them, reality in all its harshness, and recognized the "beauty"—there is no other word for it—of that reality:

> I have passed with a nod of the head
> Or polite meaningless words,
> Or have lingered awhile and said
> Polite meaningless words,
> And thought before I had done
> Of a mocking take or a gibe
> To please a companion
> Around the fire at the club
> Being certain that they and I
> But lived where motley is worn:
> All changed, changed utterly:
> A terrible beauty is born.

In 1937, Yeats said his thesis for an upcoming radio debate was "[t]hat the exclusion of sex appeal from painting, poetry, and sculpture is nonsense (are the films alone to impose their ideal upon the sexual instinct?). That, on the contrary, all arts are the expression of desire—exciting desirable life, exulting desirable death." Luca Signorelli's *Last Judgment* is a case in point.

Source Notes

My primary source for this book is a reprint of the article "The Significance of Freud's Trip to Orvieto," by Richard Karpe and Marietta Karpe. Their essay originally appeared in *The Israel Annals of Psychiatry and Related Disciplines* 17, no.1 (March 1979). *The Israel Annals* was published by the Jerusalem Academic Press for the Israel Psychiatric Association, but I do not know any precise details concerning the reprint. For all I know, my father, who owned Fox Press, a printing company, produced it for Richard and Marietta. My parents often played bridge with them, and I can just imagine a copy of *The Israel Annals* lying on this Viennese couple's coffee table, my mother picking it up and seeing the article and becoming fascinated, my father suggesting that Fox Press could make copies for the Karpes' family and friends (at no cost; my father would not have dreamed of letting them pay for this), and its being in my parents' library, where I found it by chance, as a result of that sequence of events. But maybe the Karpes had the reprint made on their own (difficult though that would have been in those days before photocopying was as easy as it is today), or the magazine's publisher provided tear sheets.

Throughout this book, I often quote from the Karpes' article. Richard and Marietta presented this as a joint publication, with no distinction between them as co-authors, an idea that I find utterly charming, reflecting a rapport and ease at working together that few married couples could imagine, but, that said, I cannot help feeling that, in the more scholarly moments, Richard's is the dominant voice, while, in the announcements of certain conclusions, it is Marietta whom we are hearing. After all, he was a psychoanalyst, used to saying little in his daily practice, habituated to probing for information and delving into his rich knowledge of other people's views of the human mind, while she was a psychiatric social worker, more inclined to express her observations in order to help people take precise action. But all of this is hypothesis on my part.

When I quote the Karpes quoting other people—for example, from Freud's letters to Fliess—I have done so, unfortunately, without knowing *their* sources, because Richard and Marietta's endnotes do not name the publisher or the translator for the material they have used. In the following references, however, I have indicated my own sources, the literature beyond the Karpes' article to which I gratefully turned in exploring the subject that Richard and Marietta make so provocative.

I cite herein each of my sources in connection with the first occasion I used it. Many of these sources, such the Karpes' article, Freud's letters to Fliess (published by Harvard University Press), etc., are subsequently used throughout the book.

Freud's Memory Loss

Here my first source is *The Complete Letters of Sigmund Freud to Wilhelm Fliess 1887–1904*, translated and edited by Jeffrey Moussaieff Masson (Cambridge: Harvard University Press, 1985). I do not know who translated the material from Freud's letters to Fliess that the Karpes quote, but Jeffrey Masson's rendition of these letters is lively and, I assume, exceedingly true to what it was that Freud wanted to communicate to his colleague.

When quoting from Freud's essay "The Psychical Mechanism of Forgetfulness," I have used the version in the *Standard Edition of the Complete Psychological Works of Sigmund Freud, vol. III* (1893–1898). This essay was initially published in the series Early Psycho-Analytic Publications (London: Hogarth Press and the Institute of Psycho-Analysis, 1898). In the case of Freud's own writing on forgetfulness, I have a strong preference for this translation of 1898, the same year that Freud wrote the essay in German—with the title "Zum psychischen Mechanismus der Vergesslichkeit." Not only was this its first translation into English, with that timing making it seem so much more directly connected to the German original, but it has the added appeal that its translator was James Strachey, brother of Lytton Strachey, who is one of my favorite biographers and literary figures. James Strachey was a friend of many in the Bloomsbury group, which I consider to be an impeccable credential.

Throughout this book, I have used the Strachey translation.

The other source I have gratefully used is Gerald Corey, *Theory and Practice of Counseling and Psychotherapy*, 6th ed. (Belmont, California: Brooks/Cole, 2005).

Chapter 5

I have to admit to personal reasons for my choice of translation for Freud's magisterial *The Psychopathology of Everyday Life*. Freud wrote the text in 1901; I have used the psychoanalyst A. A. Brill's translation (New York: Macmillan, 1914). I have probably done so more out of snobbery than scholarship.

If you wish, you can read a lot about which translations into English of Freud's writing are closest to the original; it is a favorite subject of experts in the field. My choice of Brill is what I would have to call entirely impure, and one I might not even recognize had I not been psychoanalyzed myself.

My wife's great-aunt, a psychoanalyst named Bettina Warburg, made me executor of her estate, and, since in that capacity I had the choice of certain books, I kept her copy of Brill's translation of Freud. Moreover, I always thought it was a mark of class when a Warburg cousin, a member of the Lewisohn family, said that she and her sisters and their father and mother were all analyzed by Brill. She said this as if it were the equivalent of their owning paintings by Cézanne and Seurat (as they did) and getting their bibelots at Cartier's. Most of you will deplore these credentials, and consider them foolish, but if you have read this book to this point, you already know a thing or two about its writer.

Chapter 7

I was overjoyed one day, while waiting for a meeting in the offices of Fayard, my French publisher, to see that, in 2005, they had published Sigmund Freud's *Notre cœur tend vers le sud: Correspondance de voyage, 1895–1923*. One never knows when a book will appear, by chance, that provides enlightening material on a subject, but this haphazard occurrence led to my finding great riches concerning my subject; the translation from French into English is my own.

Chapter 9

Here I have drawn on Dugald McLellan's *Signorelli's Orvieto Frescoes* (Perugia: Quattroemme Srl, 1998). Again, I had great luck in finding a first-rate source. This slim volume was for sale at the souvenir shop operated by the ticket seller for the cathedral in Orvieto. It is an exceptionally intelligent guide to Signorelli's series, of far greater use than the usual art history texts.

Chapter 13

In this chapter, I have drawn on some new sources. One is Peter Gay's *A Godless Jew* (New Haven: Yale University Press, 1987). I had the good fortune to have Peter Gay as my professor for a course on the Enlightenment at Columbia College, and I have great respect for the adroitness this distinguished professor had with regard to a range of subjects. Freud's letter to Isaac Landman, from August 1, 1929, is quoted in that book.

I also quote from Lou Andreas-Salomé, *Correspondance avec Sigmund Freud, 1912–1936* (Paris: Gallimard, 1970). And now, as if I have taken a drug called "free-associate," I must admit that I have always had a bit of a crush on Lou Andreas-Salomé, the name suggesting a certain Susie-like quality, as if she were sexy and brilliant. When writing the biography of Balthus, I encountered Lou because of her connection with Rainer Maria Rilke, who was Balthus's mother's lover and an indelible influence on both Balthus and his older brother, Pierre Klossowski. Pierre's "Psychoanalytic Study of the Marquis de Sade," which he wrote and published in a French medical journal in 1933, the year before Balthus painted his scandalous *The Guitar Lesson,* has a candor and honesty and insightfulness quite different from Balthus's form of manipulation. *The Guitar Lesson,* with its violent and sexually charged imagery—the gender issues no simpler than they are in Signorelli's art, and the rage and energy comparable—appeared as a full-page color reproduction to illustrate an excerpt from my biography of Balthus in *The New Yorker,* causing some people to cancel their subscriptions. Back to Lou: I knew about her mainly from Marie Bonaparte's biographer, a wonderful woman named Celia Bertin. Marie Bonaparte was another intellectual hoyden who, in my lurid imagination, had an effect on Freud similar to Susie's on Richard Karpe. Diagnosed with a "marked virility complex," she was, at the end of Freud's life, his pet analysand, to whom he famously gave daily two-hour sessions and talked about himself a lot; she served as a replacement in his affection for Lou. Celia proposed that I write a biography of Henri Cartier-Bresson, and suggested it to both the head of Fayard and to Cartier-Bresson's wife, the photographer Martine Franck. Franck did her best to steer me away from the project, with Bertrand telling me that there was a fear I would uncover some violence in the photographer. It is not just that he was said, at times, to shoot with a camera as if shooting with a gun; there were other secrets. I have always suspected they were connected with almost all the same issues, except for Jewishness, that come up in connection with Freud and his reactions to Signorelli's frescoes. This ramble is to say that maybe a lot that is awakened, or repressed, in connection with the art in Orvieto is inherent in many more people than would ever acknowledge it.

In this chapter, I also quote from the excellent writing of Paul C. Vitz, who wrote "Sigmund Freud's Attraction to Christianity: Biographical Evidence" published in *Psychoanalysis and Contemporary Thought 6, no. 1* (January 1, 1983). I am grateful beyond words to my younger daughter, Charlotte Fox Weber, a psychotherapist in London, for providing me with this, as well as with most of the material I have from psychoanalytic journals, which she uncovered at the library of the Tavistock Institute and other places where she studied.

The letter to Emil Fluss that Freud wrote on September 18, 1872, was published in Ernst Freud, "Some Early Unpublished Letters of Freud," *The International Journal of Psychoanalysis,* 50 (1969).

CHAPTER 15

The article by Silas L. Warner, "Freud and the Mighty Warrior," was published in the *Journal of the American Academy of Psychoanalysis* 19 (1991).

CHAPTER 16

Maud Cruttwell's *Luca Signorelli* was first published in London by George Bell & Sons in 1899; I used a reprint.

CHAPTER 20

Again, I have depended on a Strachey translation: Sigmund Freud, *An Autobiographical Study* (1935), translated by James Strachey (New York: W. W. Norton, 1963).

CHAPTER 21

Here I have depended on a couple of the staples of any art historian's library: *Vasari's Lives of the Artists,* in this case the version translated by Betty Burroughs (New York: Simon & Schuster, 1946), and Bernhard Berenson's *The Central Italian Painters of the Renaissance* (New York: G. P. Putnam's Sons, 1899). Both books are full of malarkey, but at least Vasari and Berenson were enthusiastic, and really liked looking at painting as well as living well; they beat the more academic types of today.

CHAPTER 22

Here I add to my sources a fine book on Hannibal: Theodore Ayrault Dodge, *Hannibal: A History of the Art of War Among the Carthaginians and Romans Down to the Battle of Pydna, 168 B.C.,* (New York: Da Capo Press, 1995). I also researched Hannibal in Livy's *The History of Rome,* published in so many forms and so many languages and in so many ways on the Internet that, accurate or not—which I am ill-equipped to say—it is the gospel.

CHAPTER 27

Here two great new sources enter the mix: John Gerassi, *Talking with Sartre* (New Haven: Yale University Press, 2009), and Jean-Paul Sartre, *The Freud Scenario,* translated by Quentin Hoare (Chicago: University of Chicago Press, 1985). Sartre's screenplay, with Freud as the leading character, must be one of the least well known aspects about Sartre's life, its obscurity making it all the more fascinating.

Chapter 31

The text I used for "The Moses of Michelangelo" is from Sigmund Freud, *Writings on Art and Literature* (Stanford: Stanford University Press, 1997).

The gem of a letter on eels' testicles, with those amazing drawings, comes from *The Letters of Sigmund Freud to Eduard Silberstein 1871–1881*, edited by Walter Boehlich, and translated by Arnold J. Pomerans (Cambridge: Harvard University Press, 1990). The specific letter quoted is the one Freud wrote to Silberstein on April 5, 1876. If it is the sort of thing that interests you, you can find out lots more about eels' testicles, a fertile subject, about which many people have written.

Chapter 32

Here I have used the very good book by Alan Sheridan, *André Gide: A Life in the Present* (Cambridge: Harvard University Press, 1999).

Chapter 34

Like many people, I am an ardent devotee of Stefan Zweig. That said, his book *The Mental Healers,* translated by Eden and Cedar Paul, (New York: Viking Press, 1932) is, in spite of the qualities I mention in my text, a real disappointment. It just doesn't sing the way Zweig's writing usually does. I much prefer my other source in this chapter: *The Concise Oxford Dictionary, Tenth Edition* (Oxford: Oxford University Press, 1999). Like all good dictionaries, it offers surprises and rich material on every page.

Chapter 35

The superbly revealing letter from Sigmund Freud to Martha Bernays, which Freud wrote his fiancée on December 20, 1883, and from which I quote again in chapter 38, is from *Letters of Sigmund Freud 1873–1939* edited by Ernst l. Freud and translated by I. and J. Stern (London: Hogarth Press, 1961).

Chapter 38

I am among the people who think that the translators Richard Pevear and Larissa Volokhonsky have made a life-altering difference to the felicity with which we can read all sorts of fantastic Russian novels, which even in their earlier translations are superb. In this chapter, I have quoted from Pevear and Volokhonsky's notes to Fyodor Dostoevsky's *Demons* (New York: Vintage Books, 1984).

CHAPTER 39

My source for Sigmund Freud, "Dostoevsky and Parricide," is, again, Sigmund Freud, *Writings on Art and Literature* (Stanford: Stanford University Press, 1997).

CHAPTER 41

Here I add three new sources: Jean Babelon, *Titien* (Paris: Librairie Plon, 1950); Louis Hourticq, *La Jeunesse de Titien* (Paris: Librairie Hachette, 1919); Maurice Hamel, *Titien* (Paris: Librairie Renouard, 1935). I could claim some scholarly reason for having used obscure French sources on Titian, and you might be especially impressed that the sculptor Henri Laurens was the publisher of the series in which the latter appeared. The real reason, however, is that, following a squash game in Paris, I decided to spend some time in the excellent small library of the club where I played. The Parisian pundits I read that happy day had such a great feeling for the Titian paintings of interest to me that, yet again, chance brought me insight.

CHAPTER 44

Here I draw upon a new source on Luca Signorelli, from the marvelous magazine *American Imago* of wich Freud was a cofounder. The article by Margaret E. Owens, "Forgetting Signorelli: Monstrous Visions of the Resurrection of the Dead," appeared in *American Imago* 61, no. 1 (2004).

Like most people, I really struggle to understand Jacques Lacan, but for his views on the Orvieto incident, he was relatively clear, or else I was relatively sharper than usual, and I benefited greatly from Alan Sheridan's translation of Lacan's *The Four Fundamental Concepts of Psychoanalysis* (New York: W. W. Norton,1978). The original French edition was published in Paris in 1973.

AFTERWORD

First, I want to credit Crystal Sikma for the Churchill correction. I feel blessed to have had this text reviewed by someone who catches what most people would let fly, tracks things down, and corrects falsities, even widely accepted ones, graciously.

I find that one of the single greatest pleasures in life is to receive a book from one of my daughters that shows how much she is plugged into my interests in life, especially since, by the standards of the day, my tastes are pretty arcane. Charlotte recently gave me Bernard Berenson's late-life diaries *Sunset and Twilight*—I blame the publisher, Hamish Hamilton, good as they are, for that trite title, which Berenson himself would not have countenanced (the book came out in 1964, five years after his death)—with its superb introduction by Iris Origo. How I wish that there were more writers as articulate and as engaged in the pleasures of life, especially as manifest in the glories of Italian civilization, as those two were. Origo led me to thinking about William Butler Yeats, whose splendid biography by R. F. Foster, published by Oxford University Press in 2003, I have, not surprisingly, in the library of our house in Ireland, and there I found the wonderful poetry I quote in this afterword. Yeats's lines seem both perfectly on target for my subject and are—to use an adjective I, with unabashed sexism, believe should generally be struck from the vocabulary of males, but is, on very rare occasions, the only word that really applies—divine.

ACKNOWLEDGMENTS

BERNARD BERENSON'S FAMOUS CRITERION for great art was that it be "life-enhancing." The marvelous friends and family members who have made this book possible all, blessedly, have that quality.

First, there is the dedicatee, Lucy Swift Weber. Lucy is generous of heart, fabulously energetic, as quick as anyone I know, and a superb connoisseur of human behavior. Lucy has always been a loyal supporter of her father's efforts in every domain, a devoted and attentive reader, one of the joys of my life. She is our older of two daughters, and from the moment she was born, life took on a new meaning and vibrancy and sense of connection of unimaginable power. When I say this book is "for" her, I do so with love and adoration. Lucy has qualities of strength and tenacity, and a flair for living, that are a perpetual marvel.

Charlotte Fox Weber, as you know from these pages, has, with her rapier-sharp mind, brought one key source after another to my attention; this witty and lively woman, gloriously candid, ever insightful, as full of mischief as of kindness, is an unequaled ally. I have no doubt that as a psychotherapist she does the greatest honor to her profession in truly aiding people to greater comfort with themselves and wisdom in their choices. I adore her husband, Robert Foster Smith, for many reasons, among them his strength of character and qualities of warmth and loyalty as well as tough intelligence; you also know from these pages that I consider him truly to be what Hamilcar was for Hannibal, as great and devoted and attentive and manly a father of a son as I have ever seen. I am also grateful to Robbie for adding Irishness to the family blood with our dazzling Wilder Fox Smith, so that, among other things, this wonderful, breathtaking, joy-filled little boy brings the brilliantly truthful and exquisitely artful Yeats that much nearer to the culture of the family. Wilder, a year-and-three-quarters old as I write this, is the most inspiring person I know, in his pleasure and vivacity and humor and tenderness. I hope that when he is old enough to read a narrative of this sort, should he choose to do so, his grandfather has brought him some pleasure.

My wife, Katharine, has always accepted and been devoted to the strange fellow who wrote this book—and I think you know exactly what I mean.

Nothing in this text about the woman with the pseudonym of Susie surprises her, and since, as a writer, Kathy is bold and original, and possessed of a skill with language and an imagination both of which are unequaled, I hope the beautiful woman to whom I have been married for forty years will forgive me any excesses in these pages.

My sister, Nancy Weber, has, as a writer, always been the exemplar of independent thinking, true freedom, and a unique sense of the astonishing connections that exist between seemingly disparate subjects. Her novels and journalism are, to use our mother's favorite word, panache itself. From earliest memory, I have considered Nancy a magician, and musician, with words, and a terrific honor to our parents, for whom books were the stuff of life. But, beyond that, Nancy is as loyal, as bright, as devoted, and as astute a sibling as there has ever been. And her feelings for this particular book have been an unequaled boon. A lesser person would not have been as generous, as unpossessive, as Nancy has been about whatever I have shown of our childhood. When I write, I so often picture Nancy being the first reader, alert to every word and to the feelings behind it, her standards impeccable and her passion omnipresent, and if I call her my "partner in crime," it is with love, admiration, and sheer delight.

I am grateful beyond words to the energetic, perceptive, and kind William Clark. We have not known each other for very long, but from the moment he became my literary agent, he made me feel the support and sense of professional guidance that make all the difference in a writer's life.

And what a publisher he found for this book! Erika Goldman is among the few people I have ever met who understands passionately what it means to be obsessed with art, and to have one's reactions to paintings be an utterly personal and marvelous experience. With Bellevue Literary Press she has created an extraordinary organization, one devoted above all else to the scope of human thinking, remaining not-for-profit and therefore true to the greatest values of life. Erika is quick, energetic, and on the ball in a thousand different ways; her brilliant mind and warm spirit enhance the lives of others immeasurably.

I am profoundly thankful also to Matthias Persson, not just for the countless ways in which he has helped with the production of this book, but for his wisdom and originality and kindness as a human being and his knowing input as an exceptional artist. Philippe Corfa has, as often before, shown a tenacity and capability in dealing with my particular way of writing—text written higgledy-piggledy in a way no one else could read, barely legible passages going from here to there with arrows—that staggers me, and for which I am grateful beyond my ability to express it. Crystal Sikma has been amazing in the efficiency and grace with which she has seen to so many details of the publication, her Churchill research being just one of many examples of her erudition. Anne Sisco, Nick Murphy, Nicole Marino, Molly Mikolowski, Carol Edwards, and Joe Gannon have been superb participants in this undertaking. Lou Rose has provided generous and helpful council. Sophie de Closets, as always, has been—with her passion for knowledge, her humor, and her enthusiasm—an invaluable presence in this endeavor. Oscar Humphries has offered encouragement and wisdom and a worldly perspective that belie his young age.

Dick (RWB) and Nancy Lewis, receiving me on the Piazza Santa Croce after my first trip to Orvieto, were the friends they have always been, as Nancy is in spades to this day (Dick, a true mentor, having died in 2002): fun, enthusiastic, bright, graceful, knowledgeable, and utterly joyous. Charlie Kingsley has a wisdom and kindness that provide a center, and boundless pleasure, to my existence. George Gibson—endlessly insightful, as astute as he is generous—exemplifies all that friendship should be. Stefan Stein, in his wisdom about the human mind and his openness to the feelings as well as the vicissitudes of life, has been an unequaled support. Fiona Kearney, understanding and enthusiastic, adds pleasure in more ways than she can imagine. And Laura Mattioli, so generous of heart, so incredibly knowing about art, so open to the way the visual touches us in every way, has been, as ever, one of the most glorious people I know, and particularly understanding of my search.

Mickey Cartin is a terrific friend who "gets" so much, and whose knowledge of art and life, humor, and warmth, never fail to enhance my life. Sanford Schwartz, Julie Agoos, Kathy Agoos, Brenda Danilowitz, Brigitte Lozerec'h, Mike Adler, Margaret Jay, Roland Walters, Tom Doyle, Conor Doyle, Mareta Doyle, Danjoe O'Sullivan, Veronique Wallace, Brigitte Degois, and Gilles Degois have been superb as they always are. Patrick Dewavrin, with his insights into the art of psychiatry and his generous support, has helped me tremendously. Seamus O'Reilly, so quick and erudite and one hundred percent present, has offered invaluable help. Annette Langseth and Charlie English and Louis Valentin and Jacqueline Ortega have no idea how much their kindness and verve for life mean to me in everything I do. The splendid poet John Riordain has, as always, offered sage advice and his keen understanding of the wonder of life. Alan Riding, as great a friend as he is a writer—which is saying a lot—has been supportive and generous in spades.

Victoria Wilson's engagement with this text, her superb suggestions and intelligent responses to it, and her perpetual generosity of soul, continue to be a vital component of my life. And I am grateful to certain people who are angels in the background except when they are angels in the foreground:

Azeb Rufin, Ed Victor, John Gordon, Shawn O'Sullivan, Fiona McCarthy, Benjamin Morse, Richard Mason, Allegra Itsoga, Romain Langlois, Edouard Détaille, Toshiko Mori, Richard Phelan, Nick Murphy, Samuel Gaube, Sophie Dumas, Pierre-Alexis Dumas, Andrew Seguin, John Doyle, Fritz Horstman, Sam McCune, Karis Medina, Jeannette Redensek, Gloria Loomis, Thomas Nash, Sergio Schwartzman, Matthais Dahm, Fiona O'Reilly, Catherine Heggarty, Ross Ferrara, Anne Heggarty, Hugh O'Donnell, Jodie Eastman, and John Eastman.

Regina Tierney is as energetic, supportive, vibrant, and engaged a professional, in what for me is the new world of social media, as anyone I know, and has all the same qualities in the ancient art of friendship.

The generosity and kindness of Jeremy Holmes in his response to this book has brought me extraordinary joy. To Colm Tóibín—astute, supportive, concentrated in his unique way—I owe profuse thanks as well. And John Banville, with his exceptional feeling for visual art as part of the fabric of life, and his magnificent mind and feeling for literature, has demonstrated, yet again, a rare gift of encouragement that I appreciate deeply.

As always, I am grateful beyond words to my cotrustees of the Josef and Anni Albers Foundation. I have described Charlie Kingsley earlier, and the glorious Emma Lewis, with her spirit and intellect and enthusiasm, is a boon to my life. Here I thank them both in their professional capacities in sharing our fabulous mission of what Josef and Anni determined as the goals of the foundation: "the revelation and evocation of vision through art."

NFW, Glandore, Cork, Ireland

One Last Gem

October, 2016.

CHARLOTTE JUST TOLD ME THAT, IN AN EXCITED MOMENT, Freud had said that we do not desire the people we love, but desire the people we cannot love. I was jumping up and down with thoughts about how this pertains to his response to those frescoes. I asked her to send me the precise quotation. It comes from "On the Universal Tendency to Debasement in the Sphere of Love," an essay Freud wrote in 1912. The title alone makes me think of a prissy schoolteacher picking up a possibly contaminated handkerchief with tongs.

I mean, really! He makes it about "they"—as if he does not have any such conflict himself. My daughter, whose mind never stops, loved having it pointed out that Freud ascribed the dichotomy to "the other" but not to himself, while she remembered it as inclusive.

In this text, Freud sums up what he deems a tremendous conflict for *his patients*: "Where they love, they have no desire, and where they desire, they cannot love."

Yet might this compact, brilliant observation about the conflict between our animal instincts and the emotions of our hearts not have been a personal revelation on the part of the doctor so alert to the minds and urges of humanity at large? What did and did not exist in Freud's feelings for his wife, as opposed to her sister? How charged was he by the sight of all those naked musclemen, the powerful warriors so unlike the father he loved unsatisfactorily?

Beholding paintings, Freud reacted in the gut. He could love, in all ways, the woman who is Raphael's Sistine Madonna. He could swoon to Titian's beauty. Is it not quite likely that, standing in the football locker room of the Cappella Nova, Freud experienced a feeling that he could better analyze in others than in himself: desire? And that it put him in such a state of conflict that, a year later, grieving for the father who was not the Hamilcar to the Hannibal Freud idolized and longed to be, this is why he was, although at the prime of his mental powers, totally blocked on the name that had the same first three letters as his own, and the same first six letters that, in the language used by this artist whose identity eluded him, identifies a person as a MAN?

332

INDEX

BELLEVUE LITERARY PRESS is devoted to publishing
literary fiction and nonfiction at the intersection of
the arts and sciences because we believe that science and the
humanities are natural companions for understanding the human
experience. With each book we publish, our goal is to foster
a rich, interdisciplinary dialogue that will forge new tools for
thinking and engaging with the world.

To support our press and its mission, and for our full catalogue of
published titles, please visit us at blpress.org.

BELLEVUE LITERARY PRESS
New York